# Japanese Prisoners of War

Edited by

Philip Towle, Margaret Kosuge
and Yoichi Kibata

Hambledon and London
London and New York

Hambledon and London

102 Gloucester Avenue
London NW1 8HX (USA)

838 Broadway
New York
NY 10003-4812

First Published 2000

ISBN 1 85285 192 9

A description of this book is available from the
British Library and from the Library of Congress.

Typeset by Carnegie Publishing,
Lancaster, LA1 4SL

Printed on acid-free paper and bound in
Great Britain by Cambridge University Press

JAPANESE PRISONERS OF WAR

# Contents

# Acknowledgements

The editors would like to thank the Daiwa Anglo-Japanese Foundation and its Director-General, Christopher Everett CBE, for their consistent support. They would also like to thank Martin Sheppard of Hambledon and London, without whose editorial skills, diligence and encouragement it would have been completely impossible to bring this project to a successful conclusion.

# Contributors

Kent Fedorowich is Senior Lecturer in British Imperial History at the University of the West of England in Bristol. His publications include *Unfit for Heroes: Reconstruction and Soldier Settlement in the Empire between the Wars* (1995) and *Prisoners of War and their Captors in World War II* (1996).

Hisakazu Fujita is Professor of International Law in the Faculty of Law, Kobe University. His publications include *International Humanitarian Law* (1993), *On War Crimes* (1995) and *Wars and Individual Rights* (1999).

Harumi Furuya is currently a research student at Harvard University. She previously took an M.Phil. in European Studies at Cambridge University. She has published articles on Nazi racism towards the Japanese and on toleration.

Robert Havers has just completed his Ph.D. from Cambridge University and teaches in Cambridge and London. He has published articles on the treatment of POWs in Singapore in the Second World War.

Yoichi Kibata is Professor in the College of Arts and Sciences at the University of Tokyo. He is the author of *Price of Imperial Rule: Imperial Mentality and the Break-Up of the British Empire* (1987), *The Twilight of the British Empire: British Policy towards Japan and Malaya, 1947–1955* (1996), *and Historical Development of the International System* (1997).

Clifford Kinvig is a retired Major-General in the British Army and a former Director of Army Education. His publications include *River Kwai Railway* (1992) and *Scapegoat: Percival of Singapore* (1996).

Hideo Kobayashi is Professor at the Asian-Pacific Research Centre in Waseda University. He is the author of *The Great East Asian Co-Prosperity Sphere* (1988), *Asia under the Japanese Military Administrations* (1993) and *Hong Kong under the Japanese Military Administration* (1996).

Margaret Kosuge is Assistant Professor in the College of Liberal Arts and Sciences at Yamanashi Gakuin University. Her publications include *Tokyo Trial Handbook* (1989) and *The Mistreatment of Allied POWs and Japan's Post-War Responsibility* (1993).

Kazuaki Saito is Vice President of Academic Affairs and Professor of the College of Liberal Arts in the International Christian University in Tokyo. His publications include *English Poems Pure and Simple* (1972) and *Ars Poetica: An Approach to English and American Poetry* (1993).

Philip Towle was Director of the Centre of International Studies at Cambridge University from 1993 to 1998. His publications include *Arms Control and East-West Relations* (1983), *Pilots and Rebels: The Use of Aircraft in Unconventional Warfare* (1989) and *Enforced Disarmament from the Napoleonic Campaigns to the Gulf War* (1997).

Susan Townsend is Lecturer in Modern History at Nottingham University. She was previously a member of the Faculty of Oriental Studies at Cambridge and of New Hall College. She specialises in Oriental History.

# Introduction

## Philip Towle

The treatment of prisoners of war constantly arouses interest and concern in the west. More has been written in the English-speaking world by former POWs about their experiences in the Second World War than by almost any other group of veterans. In part this is because POWs find writing a form of therapy. Their experiences are both dramatic and easily understandable, and so books about them are readily marketable. Prisoners and their guards are face to face, they have a personal relationship, whereas most modern warfare is fought at long range with the combatants barely within sight of each other. Thus the psychological relationship between guard and prisoner is generally more interesting than the relationship between other wartime enemies. Furthermore, the reader of accounts by former prisoners does not need to be familiar with military formations or modern weaponry to understand and relate to the situation. Everyone fears being totally at the mercy of malevolent strangers, some fantasise about what they would do if they were given total power over their enemies.

All soldiers have to be trained to do things which are totally impermissible to civilians. Enemies have to be depersonalised. This may not be too difficult with warfare at a distance, but one would expect that guards, who see their prisoners day after day, would find depersonalisation much harder. The influence of the captors' government and military hierarchy, and the selection and training of the guards, largely determine how far this depersonalisation continues and how the relationship between POWs and guards will develop. The development of Japanese society in the twentieth century and its interaction with the international community thus shaped Tokyo's treatment of Allied POWs in the Second World War.

Japanese ruling circles were particularly sensitive to foreign slights after they were forced by Commodore Perry to open their ports to outsiders in the mid nineteenth century. The refusal by Germany, Russia and France to allow Tokyo to keep the spoils of its war against China in 1895, the unwillingness of the Australian delegation in Paris in 1919 to accept a racial equality clause in the League Covenant, and the ending of the Anglo-Japanese alliance in 1921 all rankled. As a consequence of this sensitivity and insecurity, the Japanese often acted a part, treating Russians POWs well in 1905 to show that they were part of the civilised world, maltreating Asians and European POWs after 1941 to demonstrate their superiority.[1] The Japanese attitude to race was profoundly split.[2] They resented the growth of European racism but did not want to overthrow the hierarchy of races which became a central part of the Nazi creed in the 1930s. They accepted their status as 'honorary Aryans' offered by Nazi Germany and they wanted to be at the top of the hierarchy, even if many Japanese disliked and despised some of its worst aspects – including antisemitism.[3]

Some Japanese intellectuals responded to their country's slights by finding ways to justify Japan's expansion into China and the rest of Asia.[4] The study groups founded as a consequence aspired to the regeneration of China under Japanese guidance and saw this as a way of reasserting Asian culture against western influence. Tokyo's divine mission was propagated in Japan and the rest of Asia by films and other media; and, even if the ferocity of Japanese domination alienated and terrified many, there were Asian nationalists who responded favourably to anti-western propaganda. Some also appreciated the extent to which Japanese colonialism helped to develop the Asian economies, assistance exemplified by the tens of thousands of Japanese working in Asian industrial enterprises by the end of the Second World War.[5]

There were, of course, very different sides of Japanese life. There was the Japanese Red Cross initiated in the nineteenth century with the blessings of the imperial household to try to reduce the suffering brought by war.[6] There was a powerful tide of anti-militarism in the 1920s and there was the determination of individual Japanese to honour their Jewish teachers in the 1930s and 1940s, whatever Japan's German allies thought about such a procedure.[7] On the other hand, there were those who were afraid of foreign influences, who opposed the establishment of the Japanese Red Cross, who believed that Japanese soldiers should die in battle rather than surrender, and who argued that Japan won its victories against China in 1895 and Russia a decade later because of the superiority of its spirit.

---

[1] Margaret Kosuge, 'Religion, the Red Cross and the Japanese Treatment of POWs', below, pp. 149–61.

[2] Harumi Furuya, 'Japan's Racial Identity in the Second World War', below, pp. 117–34.

[3] Ibid.

[4] Susan C. Townsend, 'Culture, Race and Power in Japan's Wartime Empire', below, pp. 103–15.

[5] Hideo Kobayashi, 'The Post War Treatment of Japanese Overseas Nationals: A Comparison of Chinese and Soviet Policies', below, pp. 163–72.

[6] Kosuge, 'Religion, the Red Cross and the Japanese Treatment of POWs', below, pp. 151–53.

[7] Furuya, 'Japan's Racial Identity in the Second World War', below pp. 132–33.

The interaction between Japanese and western culture justified the empire's expansion in the eyes of Japanese ministers, many members of the armed forces and of the intelligentsia. Once the series of wars had begun, the bravery of Japanese soldiers, and the emphasis on conquering at all costs, ensured that they would be fought with great ferocity. In so far as they continued to follow European military example, they emulated the German pattern, which had always been brutal but became much more so under the Nazis. Using German tactics, the Japanese armed forces crushed Korean opposition after the Russo-Japanese War and tried to employ the same methods to dominate China in the 1930s.[8] Here the size of the Chinese population and the determination of Mao's Communists frustrated their efforts, despite all that ingenuity, courage and brutality could achieve. When the international community brought increasing pressure on the Japanese government to abandon its expansion into Asia, the Japanese turned southwards towards the resource-rich and ill-protected European colonial empires. So it was that British, American, Australian, Indian and other troops found themselves prisoners of war in Japanese hands from December 1941 onwards.[9]

The western democracies saw themselves as the defenders of international law as it stood before the Second World War. Because Europe had dominated the world throughout the nineteenth century, its legal tradition had spread across the globe. But European international law was regarded by many anti-colonialists in Japan and elsewhere as part of the colonial tradition, to be rejected along with the other trappings of European power and prestige. Even in Europe it was threatened by the growth of totalitarianism, which treated the individual as of no consequence in comparison with the Nazi state or with the Communist parties, and saw international law as a bourgeois device to entrench their own power.

Under international law POWs were supposed to be well treated and returned to their native countries at the end of the war. Maltreatment was regarded as a serious war crime.[10] The United States had executed the commandant of a Confederate camp for his behaviour towards Federal soldiers during the Civil War. The Americans and the British had also prosecuted their own soldiers for maltreatment of prisoners during the colonial wars at the beginning of the twentieth century.[11] In the First World War allegations of enemy maltreatment of prisoners caused immense

[8] Philip Towle, 'The Japanese Army and Prisoners of War', below, pp. 4–7.

[9] Robert Havers, 'The Changi POW Camp, February 1942-May 1944: Myth, Reality and the Burma-Thailand Railway', below, pp. 17–36.

[10] Howard S. Levie, ed. *Documents on Prisoners of War*, 60 (Newport, Rhode Island, 1979).

[11] Ibid., p. 46. See also the debates on the trial and execution of Australians for killing prisoners during the Boer War, *Parliamentary Debates, House of Commons 1902*, 8, columns 487–90.

bitterness on both sides. Afterwards the protection given to POWs under international law was enhanced in the Geneva Convention of 27 July 1929.[12] None of this meant that soldiers fighting for democracies would always take prisoners or treat them well. Military concerns, hatred for the enemy during the fighting and belief that other states were ignoring international law could only too easily lead soldiers to ignore restraints. These have been particularly fragile during anti-guerrilla operations: most armies are infuriated by partisan actions and the applicability of international law to such conflicts has always been disputed in Germany and elsewhere.[13]

In Europe Nazi racism caused considerable difficulties within the Japanese-German alliance, but the two allies were not likely to fall out over their treatment of POWs.[14] In Germany this depended entirely on their nationality and on strategic and economic convenience. Poles, Russians and others scheduled for extermination or enslavement would only be kept alive if to do so suited the Nazi state. Hundreds of thousands of east European POWs died in German hands. The worst period for the Soviet POWs was around October 1941, when maltreatment and reductions in their diet led to many thousands of deaths.[15] Later the advantages of using POW labour saved them from complete extermination. 1,600,000 Soviet soldiers and civilians were working for the Germans on 20 November 1942, together with 1,300,000 Poles and 931,000 French POWs.[16] If the Poles or Russians were unable to work, they were sent to extermination camps. Western prisoners, including French and Belgians, were by contrast treated more or less according to international law and in roughly the same way as they had been treated by the Germans between 1914 and 1918. Occasionally Hitler threatened to change this policy and to maltreat British and American POWs, particularly when he was unable to halt, or retaliate against, the bomber offensive. By and large, he either failed to follow up his threats or was frustrated by his subordinates.[17]

---

[12] James W. Gerard, *My Four Years in Germany* (London, 1917), chapter 10; Daniel J. McCarthy, *The Prisoner of War in Germany* (London, 1918).

[13] Towle, 'The Japanese Army and Prisoners of War', below, p. 1.

[14] Furuya, 'Japan's Racial Identity in the Second World War', below, pp. 117–34.

[15] Martin Bormann, *Hitler's Table-Talk* (Oxford, 1988) gives the flavour of Hitler's views on race, POWs and other issues. Ulrich Herbert, *Hitler's Foreign Workers* (Cambridge, 1998), p. 155 and passim. See also Alexander Dallin, *German Rule in Russia, 1941–1945: A Study of Occupation Policies* (London, 1957), chapter 19 and particularly p. 427 for mortality rates for Soviet POWs.

[16] Herbert, *Hitler's Foreign Workers*, p. 194.

[17] David A. Foy, *For You the War is Over: American Prisoners of War in Nazi Germany* (New York, 1984), chapter one. David Rolf, *Prisoners of the Reich: Germany's Captives, 1939–45* (London, 1988), pp. 142–43, 149.

The Japanese did not want to exterminate other races, as the Nazis did, though they did accept the notion of a racial hierarchy and their racial views deeply influenced their approach towards POWs. On the one hand, they deliberately humiliated their western prisoners in front of the various Asian nations to prove that the period of European superiority had ended. On the other hand, they treated Chinese and other Asians far more brutally than Europeans. Although it is Europeans who have subsequently publicised what happened, it was the Asian labourers, *romusha*, who suffered most during the construction of the Thailand-Burma railway.[18] Many Japanese intellectuals wanted to spread Japanese culture but not to dominate the continent militarily. Yet their views hardly counted in the middle of so ferocious a conflict. If Japan was to win, then its forces in Burma had to be supplied via a railway hacked out of the jungle, its coal mines in Formosa and Japan had to be operated, and its ships repaired. POWs and Asians had to be made to work until they were either incapable of working any more or their tasks were achieved.[19]

Japanese military leaders made clear to their associates (though not to western governments) that they did not accept international conventions governing POWs. The Japanese army was determined that the fate of POWs would be decided by strategic and economic convenience, a determination which had dire effects on the POWs used to build the Burma-Thai railway.[20] Japanese military doctrine suggested that POWs were both despicable and responsible for their own fate. They should not have surrendered and, if they survived subsequently, this was due to the generosity of their captors. They expected the POWs in their hands to appreciate this generosity.

Allied soldiers had a very different idea of the status of prisoners and of the way they should behave. For example, the western view was that the prisoner had not only a right but even a duty to attempt to escape and the law laid down that, if recaptured, such escapers could be punished only with disciplinary or minor punishment. The Anglo-German agreement in 1917 stated that this should not exceed fourteen days' imprisonment.[21] To the Japanese any attempted escape was a capital offence, a punishment widely inflicted during the Second World War. This had a particularly

---

[18] Clifford Kinvig, 'Allied POWs and the Burma-Thailand Railway', below, pp. 37–57.

[19] Ibid. See also Russell Braddon, *The Naked Island* (London, 1951); Stanley S. Pavillard, *Bamboo Doctor* (London, 1960); Sir John Fletcher-Cooke *The Emperor's Guest* (London, 1971); Thomas Pounder, *Death Camps of the River Kwai* (St Ives, Cornwall, 1977); Aidan MacCarthy, *A Doctor's War* (London, 1979); R. Keith Mitchell, *Forty-Two Months in Durance Vile: Prisoner of the Japanese* (London, 1997).

[20] Kinvig, 'Allied POWs and the Burma-Thailand Railway', below, pp. 46–47.

[21] Levie, *Documents on Prisoners of War*, p. 90.

deleterious effect on POW morale as the chances of escaping would have
offered many POWs an objective during their years of captivity.[22] Morale
was also vitally important if the POWs were to survive malaria, typhoid,
beri beri and the other diseases which afflicted them.

The confrontation between Japanese and western points of view over the
treatment of POWs and other legal and ethical issues was bound to intensify
the conflict. It should be viewed as a further spiral in the racial interaction
analysed in this book. Inside the Japanese POW camps western prisoners
regarded Japanese behaviour as barbaric and said so. Racism was deep,
pervasive and largely unconscious in western societies at the time and Allied
POWs assumed that the brutality of Japanese and Korean guards was typical
of the behaviour of inferior races. The prisoners generally knew nothing of
Japanese higher culture. Only a handful had ever had contact with Japanese,
let alone had read any of their literature.[23] They knew nothing of the dignity
and etiquette of Japanese life, or of the earlier efforts by the Japanese Red
Cross and imperial family to humanise warfare. The prisoners' belief in
their own superiority helped them to live with their daily sufferings and
humiliations. The guards' knowledge that this was how the prisoners felt
naturally increased their anger, as their aim was to impose their own view
of the prisoners' position on the POWs. They understood a good deal of
the English expressions used by the prisoners towards them. They knew
that, far from accepting the Japanese view of the relationship between the
two groups with Japanese victors superior to their vanquished enemies, the
experience was only hardening Allied prejudices and that the prisoners'
vituperation and scorn for them was increasing. This explains, for example,
the scene described by Sir John Fletcher-Cooke when his camp commander
yelled at the assembled POWs, 'You think that the British are superior to
the peoples of Asia. I tell you, you are wrong. You are soft. You are decadent.
You believe in material things. We believe in the things of the spirit'.[24]
Then he ordered the guards to beat the defenceless POWs.

During the Second World War some nations left much more latitude to
individual guards in their behaviour towards the prisoners in their camps
than others. There are few, if any, accounts of Soviet guards showing
kindness or sympathy towards prisoners, though Japanese POWs in Soviet camps were struck by the fact that they were not treated as racially
inferior. Plainly the guards in the Nazi death camps were as sadistic as the

---

[22] Robert Havers, 'The Changi POW Camp and the Burma-Thailand Railway', below,
pp. 22–23.
[23] Mitchell, *Forty-Two Months in Durance Vile*, p. 152.
[24] Fletcher-Cooke, *The Emperor's Guest*, p. 228.

Soviets. But the behaviour of German guards towards their western captives did vary considerably from camp to camp and individual to individual. Some did their best to protect and feed POWs.

In the Japanese case there were similar wide variations, with some guards impressing POWs by their help and sympathy and others treating them with great brutality.[25] No doubt this was because guards were not selected for their sadistic characteristics, as they were in the Gulag Archipelago or in the Nazi extermination camps, and because the Japanese system allowed junior officers and other ranks a good deal of latitude. Thus the guards reflected the tensions within Japan between those who hated the west for its arrogance and those who believed Japan had benefited from western culture and technology.[26] Unfortunately superior officers were often old and out of touch, and their administrative abilities were poor.[27] Even if senior officers did not depersonalise the POWs, their subordinates were allowed to do so.

Allied treatment of Japanese soldiers also fell well below established norms. The Australian army had to struggle hard to persuade its soldiers to take prisoners so that they could be interrogated.[28] The Japanese army rightly believed that few of its soldiers would surrender. It taught them that their lives had value only so far as they could assist in the great struggle they were waging against the colonial powers. Allied unwillingness to take Japanese prisoners was caused in part by the belief that even wounded Japanese might still try to kill them. Though this conflict was less of a *War Without Mercy* than the German-Soviet theatre,[29] it was, nevertheless, fought with great bitterness and ferocity on both sides. For example, both sides took not only to killing enemy wounded but also to killing sailors struggling in the water after their ships were sunk.[30]

Treatment of prisoners in wartime is determined to some extent by the interaction between belligerents and the efficacy of deterrence. This naturally ceases to operate once the war has ended. Its efficacy in wartime ebbs and flows with the progress of the conflict and with states' concern about the

[25] Kinvig, 'Allied POWs and the Burma-Thailand Railway', below, pp. 51–52.

[26] Harumi Furuya, 'Japan's Racial Identity in the Second World War', below, p. 121; Townsend, 'Culture, Race and Power in Japan's Wartime Empire', below, pp. 105–6.

[27] Kinvig, 'Allied Pows and the Burma-Thailand Railway', below, pp. 49–50.

[28] Kent Fedorowich, 'Understanding the Enemy: Military Intelligence, Political Warfare and Japanese POWs in Australia', below, pp. 59–86.

[29] John Dower, *War Without Mercy: Race and Power in the Pacific War* (London, 1986); George P. Shultz, *Turmoil and Triumph* (New York, 1993), p. 173.

[30] Ibid., p. 61 passim. Bernard Edwards, *Blood and Bushido: Japanese Atrocities at Sea, 1941–45* (Worcester, 1991).

wellbeing of their own POWs. It can also operate at different levels. Individuals may be deterred from injuring POWs by their fear of the punishment they may receive from the enemy at the end of a conflict. On the other hand, their government may be impervious to such threats.

In the Second World War the efficacy of deterrence was much more limited than it had been twenty years before. The Germans and Russians fought a war to the death. Similarly, at the start of the war in the Far East, deterrence was ineffective in protecting Allied POWs in Japanese hands, or in ensuring that Japanese would be captured rather than killed if they fell into Allied hands. As the fighting swung in the Allies' favour, so deterrence began to influence the behaviour of individual Japanese officers and guards towards POWs. Senior officers apologised for previous maltreatment, Korean guards began to make their peace with those whom they saw as the likely victors, rations began to improve and Red Cross parcels were more frequently delivered in some camps.[31] But the military government in Tokyo was less emollient and the treatment of POWs in Japan itself changed less than in overseas camps. The POWs were sometimes told by their guards that, under orders from Tokyo, they were preparing to kill them in the event of Japan's defeat.[32] The prisoners felt that they were saved by the atomic bombs on Hiroshima and Nagasaki.

After the surrender of Japan, the Allies eventually repatriated those Japanese who were not to face war crimes trials. But Moscow had other priorities. The Soviet Union had declared war on the Japanese just before their surrender and had overrun Manchuria, capturing tens of thousands of Japanese soldiers and civilians. Once again neither deterrence nor international law could operate to protect them. Perhaps 600,000 were carried off into the Soviet Union as slaves to help the Soviets recover from the devastation and impoverishment brought by the war.[33] Their conditions uncannily mirrored the sufferings that other Japanese armies had wreaked on Allied POWs. In contrast, Communist and Nationalist Chinese treated Japanese POWs favourably after 1945, perhaps in the hope of improving post-war relations with Japan.[34]

The appalling outcome of the interaction between the west and Japan in the century after Commodore Perry's intervention is a salutary reminder

---

[31] Mitchell, *Forty-Two Months in Durance Vile*, pp. 198, 208 and 210.

[32] Ibid.

[33] Hideo Kobayashi, 'The Post-War Treatment of Japanese Overseas Nationals', below, pp. 163–72.

[34] Ibid.

to statesmen of the difficulties and dangers involved in dealing with deeply sensitive foreign cultures. Many Europeans were not hostile to Japan. The British were delighted by the Japanese victory over Russia in 1905 and, even if they disliked Japanese rule over Korea, they generally kept quiet about their feelings to avoid offending their ally. Commentators and politicians often sympathised with Japan's economic troubles, particularly at the onset of the Great Depression; some were even willing to condemn the League of Nations for its criticism of Japanese behaviour in Manchuria.[35] The Japanese armed forces were admired by some foreign military commentators for their courage and initiative.[36]

Yet the assumed superiority of western civilisation, western criticism of Japanese behaviour and western exclusion of Japanese goods from their markets still rankled in Japan. It would have been wise for the Australians to drop their opposition to the racial equality clause in the League Covenant. It would have been equally wise for Washington to encourage the British to maintain the Anglo-Japanese alliance at the Washington conference in 1921.[37] Japan was also a victim of the misguided protectionist policies of western governments in the 1930s. Of course Japanese policy might have been the same even without these particular slights. The wars against China in 1895 and Russia ten years later showed that, almost from the beginning of its modernisation programme, Tokyo was set on a programme of territorial expansion, a determination fortified in the 1930s by the effects of the Great Depression on the Japanese economy and society.

But there seems to have been a link between humiliation and cruelty. Certainly many of the Allied POWs felt that personal slights which they had suffered at European hands encouraged individual guards to want to humiliate and maltreat the POWs and Asians who fell under their control. They also knew that the Korean guards wreaked vengeance for their humiliation at Japanese hands.[38] The results were devastating for all those involved in the Far Eastern conflict and they still increase tensions and suspicions between the Asian countries over half a century later.

---

[35] *Parliamentary Debates, House of Lords*, 1933, column 215, comments by the Earl of Halsbury.

[36] Captain M. D. Kennedy, *The Military Side of Japanese Life* (London, 1924); Major-General F. S. G. Piggott, *Broken Thread: An Autobiography* (Aldershot, 1950).

[37] Yoichi Kibata, 'Japanese Treatment of British Prisoners of War: The Historical Context', below, pp. 135–47.

[38] Donald Smith, *And All the Trumpets* (London, 1954), p. 119; Kenneth Harrison, *Road to Hiroshima* (Adelaide, 1966), p. 144.

Fortunately there are growing signs of reconciliation as former enemies struggle to understand past policies and to forgive past sufferings.[39]

This book places the Japanese treatment of POWs in its context in Japanese history, in the history of race relations, culture, international law and military history. It tries not only to illuminate the sufferings of the POWs and other Asian peoples, but to show how they related to the interaction between eastern and western societies over the last 200 years. While the Japanese and British contributors inevitably have different viewpoints, both groups see the book as part of the continuing effort to understand and illuminate the darkest corner of their countries' relations in the twentieth century.

[39] Kazuaki Saito, "Towards Reconciliation: Japanese Reaction to Ernest Gordon', below, pp. 173–84.

# The Japanese Army and Prisoners of War

## Philip Towle

The treatment by the Japanese of European and Asian prisoners during the Second World War greatly increased the hatred between Japan and its enemies.[1] It is still a cause of discord between Japan and its former antagonists half a century later.[2] Such behaviour was not predicted by those British officers who had lived with the Japanese army and knew it very well in the 1920s and 1930s.[3] It was also in dramatic contrast with the excellent treatment by the Japanese of Russian prisoners during the Russo-Japanese War of 1904 to 1905.[4] There are many factors which explain this change in Japanese behaviour. This essay looks at three of these which relate to military affairs: the influence of the German army on Japanese attitudes towards guerrilla warfare; the effect of the bitter warfare between the Japanese and the Chinese during the 1930s; and the predicament faced by the Japanese in Malaya and elsewhere after the expansion of their empire in 1942.

From its foundation in 1871 the government of the German Empire took the view that guerrilla warfare was illicit, that guerrillas deserved no protection from the law and that civilians giving them succour should be punished. The founder of the empire, Count Bismarck, complained constantly during the Franco-Prussian War that German soldiers were too kind to French guerrillas and insisted that guerrillas should not be given prisoner of war status.[5] He told the French Foreign Minister, Jules Favre, 'We can only recognise soldiers under a regular discipline. The others are beyond the law'. When the Frenchman protested that his countrymen had a right

---

[1] See, for example, *The Memoirs of Cordell Hull*, ii (London, 1948), p. 1589; John Dower, *War Without Mercy: Race and Power in the Pacific War* (London, 1986).

[2] 'POWs Attack Emperor's Speech', *The Times*, 28 May 1998; 'Defending War Crimes', Korean *Newsreview*, 30 May 1998, p. 34.

[3] F. S. G. Piggott, *Broken Thread* (Aldershot, 1950), epilogue.

[4] Philip Towle, 'Japanese Treatment of Prisoners of War in 1904–1905', *Military Affairs*, October 1975.

[5] M. Busch, *Bismarck: Some Secret Pages of his History* (London, 1899), pp. 49, 78 and 79. When Bismarck heard that rumours that Garibaldi and his Italian volunteers had been taken, he demanded that all 13,000 should be shot, ibid., p. 133.

to defend their homes, the German statesman dismissed this as romantic nonsense.[6]

Subsequently, the United States army fighting nationalist opposition in the Philippincs, and the British forces attacking Boer Commandos in South Africa, insisted that their soldiers should take guerrillas prisoner and should not torture or kill civilians who supported them. However, the German armed forces never wavered from the Bismarckian view established in 1871.[7] During the First World War the German army shot civilian hostages and burnt towns and villages where *franc-tireurs* operated. On 12 September 1914, for example, the German authorities in Rheims placarded the walls with the names of the hostages taken and warned that 'on the slightest attempt at disorder these hostages will be hanged'. If the inhabitants tried to resist, 'the city will be entirely or partially burnt and its inhabitants hanged'. Many villages were destroyed as a consequence of such threats. Private Hassemy of the German 8 Army Corps recorded in his notebook, 'the whole village [of Sommepy] burned, the French thrown into the blazing houses, civilians burnt with the rest'. The Leipzig trials after the First World War, the forerunners of the Nuremberg and Tokyo trials, were in part concerned with the treatment by the Germans of Belgian children who had been caught sabotaging communications. One defendant, Ramdohr, had arrested children between the ages of nine and twelve and had them tortured to end the sabotage of the railways. The boys involved gave evidence of their suffering but Ramdohr was released, for lack of evidence, to the applause of the courtroom.[8]

In the Second World War the treatment by the Nazis of guerrillas and of the civilians suspected of supporting them was far more ferocious – part of a general policy of exterminating or enslaving the enemies of the Reich. From the Pyrenees to the Adriatic guerrilla warfare broke out against the conquerors. Everywhere it was savagely repressed. For example, Mark Mazower, the historian of the German occupation of Greece, has found that the destruction of whole villages had become so much a matter of routine that those involved could not remember individual cases. In the Soviet Union, Yugoslavia and Poland the practice was the same. Not only

---

[6] See Jules Favre, *The Government of National Defence* (London, 1873), p. 114.

[7] *Documents on Prisoners of War*, Naval War College International Law Reports, 60 (Newport, Rhode Island, 1979), p. 67.

[8] J. O. P. Bland, trans., *Germany's Violations of the Laws of War, 1914–1915: Compiled under the Auspices of the French Ministry of Foreign Affairs* (London, 1915), pp. 102, 155. Many such reports were later dismissed as propaganda but the nature of the evidence makes it unlikely that the general picture presented in Bland's book was entirely fabricated. On the Leipzig trials see James F. Willis, *Prologue to Nuremberg* (Westport, Connecticut, 1982), p. 134.

were guerrillas killed but so were French and other 'home guards', local militiamen who had some type of uniform but not enough to satisfy the conquerors.[9]

Many contemporaries believed that German example had an impact on events in East Asia in the 1930s and 1940s. The Germans replaced the French as the advisers to the Japanese army at its formative period in the 1880s and the Japanese apparently imbibed the German attitudes towards guerrilla warfare. Even after the First World War and the defeat of Germany, it was the German army which most impressed the Japanese over the decades. In the 1930s men like Hiroshi Oshima, who was military attaché and then ambassador in Berlin, linked the two armies, idealising the military and totalitarian tradition. So strong was this bond that it survived even though the Germans had provided advisers and arms to Japan's Chinese enemies.[10] The British sent dozens of language officers to Japan and some of these were socially close to the Japanese. But the British army was too small to influence the Japanese, who were not, in any case, impressed by the British forces during joint operations in China at the start of the First World War. Therefore British tactics for dealing with guerrillas, and the constraints under which the British had to operate, had no chance of influencing the Japanese army. At first this was not obvious to outside observers because the Russians fought a purely conventional war against the Japanese in 1904–5. Russian POWs were treated in an exemplary fashion by their Japanese captors, who scrupulously carried out the Hague Convention, concerning the treatment of prisoners, to which Tokyo had become a party.[11]

It was after the Russo-Japanese War, when the Korean peninsula was gradually absorbed into the Japanese empire, that the Japanese military attitude towards guerrillas became increasingly clear. The Koreans resisted

[9] Mark Mazower, *Inside Hitler's Greece: The Experience of Occupation, 1941–44* (New Haven, 1993). For a description of the guerrilla war in Yugoslavia see Milovan Djilas, *Wartime: With Tito and the Partisans* (London, 1977). On Albania see David Smiley, *Albanian Assignment* (London, 1985). On the execution of French 'Home Guard' see A. Costes ed., *La delegation Francais auprès de la Commission Allemande d'Armistice* (Paris, 1947–1957), iv, p. 342.

[10] For German influence on the Japanese army see Ernst L. Presseisen, *Before Aggression* (Tucson, Arizona, 1965), particularly p. 110; L. A. Humphreys, *The Way of the Heavenly Sword: The Japanese Army in the 1920s* (Stamford, California, 1995), pp. 99, 203: Roger F. Hackett, *Yamagata Aritomo in the Rise of Modern Japan, 1838–1922* (Cambridge, Massachusetts, 1971), pp. 82, 103. For Hiroshi Oshima see Carl Boyd, 'Japanese Military Effectiveness', in Allan R. Millett and Williamson Murray, *Military Effectiveness*, ii (Boston, 1988), p. 145. For German relations with Japan and China in the 1930s see John P. Fox, *Germany and the Far Eastern Crisis, 1931–1938* (Oxford, 1982).

[11] *Documents on Prisoners of War*, p. 231, 'Japanese Regulations for the Treatment of Prisoners of War'.

Japanese control by the limited means at their disposal, including riots and assassination attempts against pro-Japanese Koreans. They also formed the partisan groups of the so-called Righteous Armies, which at their height in 1908 numbered nearly 70,000 men. The Japanese reaction was immediate and dramatic. All the towns and villages suspected of supporting the guer-rillas were burnt. The British journalist, F. A. McKenzie reported, 'day after day we travelled through a succession of burned-out villages, deserted towns and forsaken country'. A journalist travelling through the Orange Free State or Transvaal during the Boer War would have seen the same sort of picture after the British 'cleared' the country. But the British generally housed those whose homes had been destroyed in temporary camps during the war. As soon as the fighting was over, they paid massive compensation to the Boers and helped them to restore their homes and farms. In other words, Japanese anti-guerrilla techniques were hardly unusual but they were carried out with the same sort of brutality and indifference to the suffering they caused that the Germans showed in their campaigns.[12]

Sir Ian Hamilton, who had served In South Africa and then as one of the senior British attachés with the Japanese forces during the Russo-Japanese War, appeared in his published writings to be pro-Japanese. In private, he quickly became critical of Japanese treatment of the conquered peoples. He complained to L. S. Amery of *The Times* that the paper was biased in favour of Japan; 'when one considers the happy contented pros-perous people who live in Manchuria under Chinese rule and contrasts that state of things with the bloody tyranny and cruel bullying and oppression which goes on the other side of the Yalu, it is truly appalling that kowtowing to Japan should be carried to such lengths'. In 1910 a missionary, Lord William Gascoyne-Cecil, noted similarly,

> except for the wisdom and gentleness of Prince Ito [the Japanese ruler of Korea], there was nothing but oppression and suffering for the Koreans. The Japanese army had learnt not only their military art but their statecraft in Germany, and the latter is traditionally harsh. Break, crush and bully are the maxims which found general acceptance in the Prussian Court ... Prince Ito could not control the Japanese soldiers, and the moans of the oppressed Koreans echoed throughout her land.

An American journalist wrote in 1911 of his travels in Manchuria and Korea,

---

[12] On Korean resistance see Ki-baik Lee, *A New History of Korea* (Seoul, 1984), p. 314. F. A. McKenzie, *The Tragedy of Korea* (London, 1908), p. 191. On British anti-guerrilla oper-ations during the Boer War see L. S. Amery ed., *The Times History of the War in South Africa* (London, 1907); Christian Rudolf de Wet, *Three Years War* (London, 1902). On British treatment of the Boers after the war see G. B. Beak, *Aftermath of War* (London, 1906).

'never a day passed that I did not see rough and often violent treatment of Koreans and Manchus by Japanese soldiers, police and the lower class of labor employed'.[13]

British officials were well aware of what was going on and reported it extensively to London. The British ambassador in Tokyo, Sir Claude Mac-Donald, publicly warned the Japanese early in 1906 that their forces' behaviour in Korea was dividing London and Tokyo. MacDonald claimed that Count Okuma had told him he sympathised with the ambassador's views and that Prince Ito would do the same. A British official in Korea itself commented, 'all the ... foreigners who employ native labour agree that the Korean is ... easy to get on with and it would thus appear that there must be something radically wrong with the Japanese methods of dealing with these people'.[14]

Wrong or not to British eyes, Japanese methods were successful in the long run. By 1910 17,600 guerrillas had been killed and the numbers in the various bands of partisans had dwindled away.[15] In later years thousands of Koreans joined the Japanese forces and were used as guards to look after British and other prisoners who fell into Japanese hands. They were noted for their ferocity and brutality towards the prisoners. The Japanese army, in turn, learnt that repression might increase the dislike of the colonial people for their conquerors but in some circumstances it could destroy their power to resist and, indeed, force them to cooperate.[16]

In the 1930s the Japanese army began to expand the empire into Manchuria and subsequently into the whole of China. The operations there brought the Japanese army up against guerrilla warfare on a far larger scale, where brutality alone proved inadequate to crush the resistance. In fighting against guerrillas conventional forces are frustrated by their inability to 'come to grips with the enemy', their numbers are worn down by attrition and they are infuriated by the support which the local people willingly or unwillingly give to the partisans. In Spain and Prussia during the Napoleonic Wars, in France in 1870 and in China in the 1930s, the natural tendency was for brutalities to grow in a spiral of hatred between the conventional forces and the guerrillas. An account written by an Italian, who claimed to

---

[13] Lieutenant-General Sir Ian Hamilton, *A Staff Officer's Scrap-Book during the Russo-Japanese War* (London, 1906). See also the Hamilton papers, King's College, London, 7/3/17/2; Lord William Gascoyne-Cecil, *Changing China* (London, 1910), p. 235; Angus Hamilton, *Korea* (London, 1904), p. 128; and Price Collier, *The West in the East* (London, 1911), p. 454.

[14] PRO FO 371/477 and FO 371/179.

[15] Lee, *New History of Korea*, p. 317.

[16] On Korean guards of the POWs see L. l. Baynes, *Kept: The Other Side of Tenko* (Lewes, 1984), p. 39; Donald Smith, *And All the Trumpets* (London, 1954), p. 118.

have worked as an agent for the Japanese, described a typical incident in Manchuria where guerrillas had derailed a Japanese train:

> with over 200 Japanese soldiers and gendarmes loose in the countryside, an orgy of bestiality was spreading horror and terror everywhere in the region. Not a home was spared. Every conceivable form of outrage was perpetrated. Hundreds of Chinese and Russians were massacred, their homes ransacked and set on fire; scores of young girls, some less than ten years old, five of whom died, were assaulted.

The parallels with German behaviour in France and Belgium in 1914 are very clear. Hugh Byas, who was a correspondent in Tokyo from 1914 to 1922 and again from 1926 to 1941, pointed out that Captain Masahiko Amakasu, the man chosen to be chief of the Japanese police in Manchuria, had murdered a socialist writer, Sakae Osugi, together with Osugi's wife and young nephew, while they were in prison in 1923. Byas also referred to the case of two Japanese soldiers who became heroes because they held a competition to see who would be the first to kill 250 Chinese with two-handed swords. Clearly the toughest and most xenophobic were chosen for repressing Chinese insurgents.[17]

In northern China the Japanese confronted the people's war doctrines being developed by Mao Tse-tung and his Communist associates. Mao had begun to evolve these in the ferocious struggle between the Communists and the Nationalist Chinese of the Kuomintang which had already devastated large areas of the country even before the Japanese invasion.[18] As its name implies, people's war mobilises the mass of peasants, more systematically in support of the guerrillas than previous partisan movements had done, by promising to transform their lives through economic and social reforms. Guerrillas initially went out into the villages and won over the peasantry by helping them with their work and spreading propaganda. Then they encouraged the peasantry to attack the Kuomintang or the Japanese invaders. The effect was to place the peasantry even more firmly in the firing line than had been the case in previous insurgencies.

In Mao the imperial armies clashed with an enemy who was quite as ruthless and determined as themselves. For both sides the ends justified any means, something which Mao made clear in his lectures to the Communist

---

[17] Amleto Vespa, *Secret Agent of Japan: A Handbook of Japanese Imperialism* (London, 1938), p. 111; Hugh Byas, *The Japanese Enemy* (London, 1942), pp. 53, 54. Contrast the Japanese view of their operations in Ashihei Hino, *War and the Soldier* (London, 1940), pp. 14, 179, 572.

[18] For western observers with the Communists see Edgar Snow, *Red Star over China* (London, 1937); Agnes Smedley, *China Fights Back: An American Woman with the Eighth Route Army* (London, 1938). See also Meirion and Susie Harries, *Soldiers of the Sun* (London, 1991), p. 214.

cadres at his base in Yenan.[19] While Christian doctrine had for hundreds of years in the west laid down that a war could only be just if it were fought for just ends *and with just means*, Mao divided war into only two sorts; 'all wars that are progressive are just and all wars that impede progress are unjust'.[20] The methods used in warfare were irrelevant to the question of justice or, to put it another way, all means were justified if your side was 'progressive'. Mao gave the impression that he was involved in a chess game and that Japanese cruelties simply played into the hands of the Communist Party.[21]

Under the pressure of events in China, Japanese army training, which had always been very tough, had become thoroughly brutalised by the end of the 1930s. John Morris, who taught English in Japan, recorded afterwards, 'an open space outside one of the schools where I taught was a practice ground for artillery units and on several occasions I saw conscripts knocked unconscious by non-commissioned officers. This was done in the presence of the higher ranks so I can only assume such behaviour was condoned'. Japanese soldiers were routinely beaten by officers for petty offences and sometimes forced to bayonet prisoners as the culmination of their indoctrination. In Tsingtao it seems that ordinary Chinese criminals were despatched in this way. Similarly, Field Marshal Slim recalled that, after one of the early battles in Burma during the Second World War, twelve British wounded 'were kept till next day when, tied to trees, they were used by the Japanese to demonstrate bayonet fighting to the villagers'.[22] The Japanese army was imbued with an exceptional fighting spirit and the men showed great individual initiative but, perhaps to avoid inhibiting this, senior officers were unable or unwilling to constrain the ordinary soldier on the battlefield or afterwards.

Japanese soldiers, like their contemporaries in the Nazi army, were deliberately trained to extinguish any humanitarian instincts, to depersonalise themselves, their colleagues and, above all, the enemy. By no means every conscript accepted this indoctrination but many agreed with their colleague who asserted later, 'in the desperation of war, men cease being human. Pillage, arson, and murder are everyday affairs. The soldier unhesitatingly shoots mother and child who, with hands joined in supplication, beg to

[19] *Selected Works of Mao Tse-Tung*, ii (Peking, 1967).

[20] Ibid., p. 150.

[21] Ibid., pp. 81, 117, 167.

[22] Otis Cary, *Eyewitness to History: The First Americans in Postwar Asia* (Tokyo, 1975), p. 196; Field Marshal Viscount Slim, *Defeat into Victory* (London, 1962), p. 31; John Morris, *Traveller from Tokyo* (Harmondsworth, 1946), p. 212.

be spared'.[23] Soldiers also denied that it was possible for restrictions or laws of war to operate; 'once war has started, there is no way for human beings caught in it to avoid doing cruel things. It is too late to escape'.[24] The army's determination to make soldiers fight until they were killed, to refuse to surrender in any circumstances, and to regard their lives as useless once they were wounded, reinforced these attitudes. So did the careful selection of soldiers from rural areas, rather than from cities such as Tokyo where the recruiters feared different values were widespread.

Yet the Japanese deeply resented western criticism of their behaviour in China during the 1930s. Such resentment is not unusual in the cases of nations involved in fighting guerrillas, though it seems to have been particularly strong in Japan, both because of the strength of Japanese patriotism and because it was seen as patronising and racist coming from colonial powers, such as Britain and France. Certainly international criticism was unable to persuade them to change their behaviour in the 1930s. Instead, they warned British sympathisers that their government was blamed for generating criticism at the League of Nations and that this was creating bitter hatred against them amongst the Japanese population.[25]

At the end of 1941 this hatred burst out into the open when Japanese armies began the conquest of Hong Kong, the Philippines, Malaya and the Dutch East Indies. After the rapid conquest of Malaya and Singapore, they were faced with four possible types of resistance. First, from the Chinese living in the towns who felt loyalty to their fellow countrymen struggling against Japan in China itself and were tempted into active or passive resistance. Secondly, from Chinese, predominantly Communist, guerrillas operating in the jungles. Thirdly, from the handful of British troops who had not surrendered and operated with the Communist Chinese in the jungle.[26] Finally, they had to control the very large number of Allied prisoners of war, now in their hands, who believed it was legitimate to escape and to resist their conquerors in any way possible. All of these groups attempted fitfully to coordinate their resistance. Their failure was in large part due to Japanese repression.

Struggling against the Chinese, the British in India and US forces spread across the Pacific, the Japanese armed forces were stretched to the limit.

[23] *Cries For Peace: Experiences of Japanese Victims of World War II* (Tokyo, 1978), pp. 130, 133.
[24] Ibid., p. 135.
[25] Captain M. D. Kennedy, *The Problem of Japan* (London, 1935), p. 11; Byas, *The Japanese Enemy*, p. 68; Tota Ishimaru, *Japan Must Fight Britain* (London, 1936), p. 68.
[26] F. Spencer Chapman, *The Jungle is Neutral* (London, 1950). See also Charles Cruickshank, *SOE in the Far East* (Oxford, 1983), chapter eight.

To preempt threats from conquered peoples they reacted with utmost brutality to any signs of resistance, while trying to minimise Allied fury at their behaviour. Preemptive brutality is often used by armed forces to hide their weaknesses. The British, for example, reacted with ferocity during the Easter Rising in Ireland in 1916, when their forces were stretched to the limit in the war against Germany.[27] Similarly, General Dyer, the commander of British forces in Amritsar in 1919, defended his shooting of Indian demonstrators on the grounds that this was the only way for his small force to quell a mob of thousands and to prevent a general insurgency.[28]

As far as the POWs were concerned, the Japanese government only slightly adapted the methods it had evolved during the war against the Chinese. Captured Chinese had not been considered prisoners of war and no information had been kept on their treatment as required by international law. Now Japan told the Allies that it would abide by international agreements. A prisoner of war bureau was established but, at the same time, Prime Minister Tojo told those in charge of the prisoners that 'international law should be interpreted from the view point of executing the war according to our own opinions'. In practice this meant that the methods developed in China were continued, while the Allies were supposed to be pacified in January 1942 by the assurance that Japan strictly observed the Geneva Convention of July 1929.[29]

Asians living in the towns were terrorised into subservience to the Japanese empire. The massacre of civilians had become routine after the capture of a major town. The Allies estimated that some 200,000 had been killed at Nanking alone. When Singapore was taken, British soldiers were forced to bury the bodies of those murdered:

> they marched us out on work parties to the beaches near Changi. There, lying grotesquely entangled in rolls of barbed wire, were hundreds of bodies of Chinese men [civilians], women and even youngsters of all ages. Their hands were still bound together on long ropes. They had been herded together into the water, and then either shot or bayoneted.

---

[27] Brock Millman, 'British Home Planning and Civil Dissent, 1917–1918', *War in History*, April 1998, p. 216.

[28] A. Draper, *The Amritsar Massacre: Twilight of the Raj* (London, 1985). General Dyer, the officer responsible for ordering troops to fire on an Indian crowd commented, 'I had the choice of carrying out a very distasteful and horrible duty or of neglecting to do my duty, of suppressing disorder or of becoming responsible for all future bloodshed'. See also Lieutenant-Colonel A. A. Irvine, *Land of No Regrets* (London, 1938), p. 235; Carol Mather, *Aftermath of War: Everyone Must Go Home* (London, 1992), p. 162, for British orders to shoot Cossacks who refused to be repatriated at the end of the Second World War.

[29] *Documents on Prisoners of War*, pp. 440, 454.

Burying the decomposing bodies took three weeks. General A. E. Percival, the British commander who surrendered Singapore, later argued that those massacred belonged to the Kuomintang, though many were evidently far too young to have been active members.[30]

The Japanese were not satisfied with the fear that their initial conquest and the massacres created. Allied prisoners of war were aware that very large numbers of Chinese were also imprisoned. Groups of prisoners were told that one of them would be executed the next day so that all would be tormented by fear; 'then in the morning another head would appear on a pole in the streets'.[31] Chinese men and women accused of theft were tied naked in public places for several days before being decapitated in front of the assembled Allied prisoners and local population. Japanese methods were similar in their other conquests outside Malaya. Indonesian prisoners were buried up to their necks and allowed to die over a number of days. Torture was frequently applied, particularly water torture and hanging people by their thumbs. Tens of thousands of Tamils, who were living in Malaya, were marched away into the jungles to help the prisoners of war build the railway to Burma. Many of the men, women and children died of cholera and other diseases. All these methods undoubtedly cowed the Chinese population but the general brutality appeared to the Allied prisoners to have alienated many, even amongst the Malays and Tamils, who might otherwise have sympathised with the Japanese struggle against the Europeans. Donald Smith, one of the POWs, recalled in his memoirs how, when a Malay was spitting at the British soldiers being marched into captivity, 'the Japanese guard, without a word, brought his rifle-butt down viciously on the back of the native's head. The Malay fell unconscious, and the Japanese in the column behind us kicked him out of his path'.[32]

Guerrilla resistance to the Japanese continued in China and the rest of Asia. In two and a half years the Malayan guerrillas claimed to have killed 2485 Japanese soldiers and seriously wounded 2600. The brutality of Japanese reaction against the civilian population in Malaya was graphically recorded by two of the British officers given the task of cooperating with

---

[30] Russell Braddon, *The Naked Island* (London, 1951), p. 101. On the Hong Kong massacre see Charles G. Roland, 'Massacre and Rape in Hong Kong: Two Case Studies Involving Medical Personnel and Patients', *Journal of Contemporary History*, January 1997. On Singapore see Jack Cosford, *Line of Lost Lives* (Northampton, 1988), p. 27; Jack Edwards and Jimmy Walter, *Banzai You Bastards!* (London, 1990), p. 54.

[31] On treatment of the Chinese see Braddon, *Naked Island*, p. 111; Peter Hartley, *Escape to Captivity* (London, 1952), p. 77; Arthur Lane, *One God, Too Many Devils* (Stockport, 1989), pp. 126, 137.

[32] Smith, *And All the Trumpets* ( London, 1954), p. 38.

the resistance after the surrender of Singapore, F. Spencer Chapman and John Cross. Chapman recorded in *The Jungle is Neutral*:

> The Japanese were in the habit of collecting all the people of a suspected kampong into one kongsi house. They would then give them lectures and afterwards, in their capricious way, either tommy gun or bayonet them, or let them go free. Once further north, they had driven over a hundred Chinese, including old men, women and children, into an atap shed and had then burned them to death.

Such capriciousness was by no means unique to the Japanese army. A US military interpreter commented on the oscillation in the behaviour of American troops, sometimes sharing cigarettes with captured Japanese but in other circumstances murdering them.[33]

Maoist guerrilla doctrine was that the 'fish', the guerrillas, should live in the 'sea' provided by the peasants. But the Japanese simply drained the sea. 'Young able bodied men were seen no more … girls, even children of twelve or thirteen years, were often raped or taken away to fill the military brothels. An enormous number of Chinese were tommy gunned or bayoneted, others were driven into atap houses and burned alive.' Both the brutality and the capriciousness, which Chapman noted, may have helped to prevent more widespread insurgency.[34]

The Japanese use of torture on captured guerrillas and suspects was also very effective. At the so-called 'double tenth trial' after the war, the Japanese defendants argued that they had a 'natural right' to extort information about resistance from people living in conquered areas. In his memoirs, John Cross described how the guerrillas' operations were often seriously compromised as a result because the Japanese learnt of the whereabouts of their hideouts, the nature of their future plans and the names of the villages which had willingly or unwillingly cooperated with them. In the circumstances, despite the casualties the guerrillas claimed to have inflicted, their form of warfare does not seem to have been either widespread or successful. A number of the very small forces of Allied soldiers who did not immediately surrender after the fall of Singapore abandoned their plans to operate as guerrillas because of the destruction that they found this would cause the civilian population. Van Rennan and his band

---

[33] Chapman, *The Jungle is Neutral*, pp. 105, 278. Figures for Japanese soldiers allegedly killed by guerrillas in Malaya are from John Cross, *Red Jungle* (London, 1957), p. 188. For US capriciousness see Cary, *Eyewitness*, pp. 37–38.

[34] Chapman, *The Jungle is Neutral*, p. 278.

surrendered after all the men in a village of 200 were killed and the women mutilated.[35]

Brutality also prevented Allied prisoners of war escaping and made them work for their captors. The prisoners knew that they would be executed if they tried to escape. The Malays and other civilians were equally aware that their villages would be obliterated if they gave the slightest sign of assisting escapers. The result was that, however much most prisoners thought of escaping, they knew that the risks were great and the chances of success slight.[36]

The Japanese on their side realised that the tens of thousands of European, American and Australian soldiers who had surrendered might try to escape but they had few guards to contain them because they wished to use their best soldiers for the wars in Burma, China and elsewhere. Generally they employed low-grade Japanese, Koreans and renegade Sikhs. The number of POW accounts which mention meeting Japanese guards who had been educated in the USA suggests that they were regarded with suspicion, being given the job of guarding POWs because they were considered too unreliable for other purposes. If this is true, events sometimes proved it justified. One Japanese-American may have been executed as a spy for fraternising with POWs working in the Taiwanese copper mines, another allowed POWs to forage for food in Singapore. However brutal the Koreans usually were towards the POWs, some were increasingly unreliable as the war moved against Japan. One tried to persuade POWs in Changi to seize an aircraft and escape to safety, another led a futile effort to escape to Burma.[37]

The Japanese also dispersed the prisoners in support of their war effort, building the Burma railway and other railways in the Dutch East Indies, mining for copper in Taiwan and for coal in Japan. Finally they deliberately spread the prisoners around their empire in order to demonstrate to Koreans and others, including their own people, how the white men could be defeated and humiliated.

So effective was their policy of repression that very often the prisoners could be left virtually unguarded while involved in their unremitting toil. They were weakened and demoralised by brutality, shortage of food and

---

[35] Cross, *Red Jungle*, p. 114. Van Rennan was later executed for escaping from camp, Braddon, *Naked Island*, p. 136. Kenneth Harrison, *The Brave Japanese* (London, 1967), pp. 119–23. For Japanese defence of the use of torture see Colin Sleeman and S. C. Silkin, *Trial of Sumida Haruzo and Twenty Others* (London, 1951), p. 226.

[36] Walter Irvine Summons, *Twice Their Prisoner* (Melbourne, 1946), p. 114 and 165.

[37] On attempts by the Korean guards to encourage POWs to escape see G. Pharaoh Adams, *No Time for Geishas* (London, 1973), p. 91; Braddon, *Naked Island*, p. 252. On Japanese educated in the US see Summons, *Twice Their Prisoner*, p. 149.

disease. On occasions, the prisoners actually carried the guards' loaded weapons for them even when they were alone and isolated in the jungle. Pharaoh Adams was left with a small party of prisoners and a single Korean guard who gave him his rifle to carry while they drove cows through the jungle. Adams and the rest of the prisoners discussed murdering the guard and escaping into the jungle but eventually decided it was too risky.[38] The POWs might see themselves as helpless, downtrodden victims but, to the Japanese, they were a sullen, mutinous mob, disgraced by surrender but threatening to the end.

Some camp guards were murdered by the prisoners. Donald Smith claimed that the Gurkhas routinely killed renegade Sikhs. Arthur Lane killed a Japanese guard who was attempting to rape a young Australian, the body of the Japanese, like those of other Sikh and Korean guards killed from time to time, being hidden in the sewage. An RAF doctor, Aidan MacCarthy, helped drown a particularly unpopular Korean guard after a shipwreck on the way to Japan. Dr Stanley Pavillard infected the most vicious Japanese guards with amoebic dysentery so that they would be invalided away from the camps. Thomas Pounder watched as one of his colleagues managed to rock a beam on which a Japanese guard was balancing and throw him to his death. There are also accounts where larger, planned enterprises were conceived. MacCarthy discussed with his fellow officers the possibility of taking over the ship on which he and another 1200 prisoners were being transported. The problem was not the strength of the guards but the slowness of the ship and the threat to the lives of the other prisoners if the Japanese navy recaptured them. Donald Smith and others pondered the possibility of a mass rising at the Changi camp in Singapore where most of the POWs were concentrated.[39]

Passive resistance was practised and frequently improved the prisoners' morale, even if it did little to hamper their captors. Prisoners routinely sabotaged shells which they were made to carry. They tried to make the railways they were forced to build in Thailand and the Dutch East Indies as weak as possible, something which they regretted when they had to use them themselves. They bumped around the wounded Japanese soldiers they were compelled to carry over the mountains from Burma into Thailand.

---

[38] Pharaoh Adams, *No Time for Geishas*, p. 89.
[39] Smith, *And All The Trumpets*, p. 64; Kenneth Harrison, *Brave Japanese*, p. 177; Aidan MacCarthy, *A Doctor's War* (London, 1979), p. 86; Stanley S. Pavillard, *Bamboo Doctor* (London, 1960), p. 104; Arthur Lane, *One God Too Many Devils*, p. 193. The plan to seize the Japanese ship was replicated by the German POWs' plan to seize the *Pasteur* and take it to Singapore, see Matthew Barry Sullivan, *Thresholds of Peace* (London, 1979), p. 220.

They worked as slowly as they could on the railways, in the copper mines of Taiwan and in the dockyards and coal mines of Japan. There were examples of more active sabotage, of explosions on the completed railway and the destruction of trains and supply dumps. But again these were isolated.[40]

The Japanese feared that the POWs might be much more successful. On 28 November 1943 six Japanese oil tankers were sabotaged in Singapore harbour. The raid was carried out from Australia but the Japanese suspected that it was master-minded by civilians interned in Changi gaol. This led to the torture of many of them, the incarceration of a large number of men and women in a tiny cell, where the lavatory provided the only drinking water, and where they could hear the screams of those being tortured. Fourteen Europeans died and twenty-one Japanese guards were tried for their murder after the war. The torture they had used was 'successful' in forcing the victims to confess to actions they had not committed but otherwise revealed its futility.[41]

Senior Japanese officers and officials were aware of the level of brutality practised on the prisoners and Asians, and even encouraged it to a greater or lesser degree. The Hayashi Division in Burma, for example, issued 'Notes for the Interrogation of Prisoners of War' which advised those involved only to use kicking, beating and other tortures as a last resort. As Spencer Chapman's comments quoted above show, everything depended on the attitudes or mood of the junior officers. Some guards were actually liked and befriended by the prisoners, others were feared and loathed for their sadism. Most accounts by prisoners of war describe incidents of genuine humanity shown to them as well as cases of appalling brutality. They also often make clear that senior officers began to intervene towards the end of the war when it was likely that Japan would lose and that some would be forced to answer for their behaviour.[42]

After the Japanese surrender, this attitude ensured that guerrilla warfare would not be used against Allied forces. This surprised the Allies who assumed, from the determination and courage with which the Japanese had

[40] J. Cosford, *Line of Lost Lives* (Northampton, 1988), p. 148; Arthur Lane, *One God Too Many Devils*, pp. 207, 224.

[41] Sleeman and Silkin, *Trial of Sumida Haruzo*.

[42] *Documents on Prisoners of War*, p. 452. On variations in guards' behaviour see Summons, *Twice Their Prisoner*, p. 109; Kenneth Harrison, *Road to Hiroshima* (Adelaide, 1983), pp. 109, 117, 143; Ken Attiwill, *Rising Sunset* (London, 1957), p. 113; Alfred Allbury, *Bamboo and Bushido* (London, 1955), p. 98; David Michel, *A Boy's War* (Singapore, 1993), pp. 54–55; Reginald Burton, *Road to the Three Pagodas* (London, 1963), pp. 51, 109, 138; Stanley Pavillard, *Bamboo Doctor*, pp. 81, 89.

fought, that they would continue to fight after their conventional army had been defeated. There were feeble attempts of this kind in outlying areas, as Hiroo Onoda recorded, but fortunately there was no futile resistance of this kind in Japan and the tens of thousands of Allied troops serving in the occupation forces were mainly involved in discovering hidden weapons and helping feed the conquered people. To the very end both the Germans and Japanese maintained the traditional military attitude towards guerrillas rather than the romantic civilian one.[43]

Japanese brutality had served a number of purposes after the expansion of their empire in 1942. By then German influence and their own experience in Korea and China had convinced the Japanese army that the harshest measures enabled them to assert dominance. Brutality meant that POWs could be lightly guarded, that Malays and other Asian peoples were terrified of helping the POWs, that Chinese and British guerrilla resistance in Malaya was seriously hampered, and that the POWs and conscripted Asians had to work to the benefit of the Japanese war effort. In this way, Japanese soldiers were indoctrinated with the view that repression and indifference to human suffering were essential to their profession. The disadvantage of such training and the methods the army employed was the hatred of the Chinese, Indonesians and Malays, who might have supported the Co-Prosperity Sphere because it offered liberation from the European colonialists.

Other armed forces have used preemptive brutality when they were weak, and other armies have sometimes behaved capriciously and ferociously towards prisoners and others killed guerrillas and murdered their civilian supporters. What was abnormal about Japanese behaviour (and indeed of German behaviour in the Second World War) was the untrammelled nature of this brutality. There were no forces working to inhibit the repression described, except the goodwill of the individual Japanese soldier or officer. Plainly liberal democratic societies, with widespread journalistic coverage of the operations by government forces, are less likely to allow torture and murder. Of course, much can be hidden by the armed forces, as it was during the British counter-insurgency campaign in Palestine in the 1930s.[44] Similarly, even with press coverage of the French war in Algerian in the 1950s or of US operations in Vietnam in the 1960s, it took time before the torture of suspects and the murder of civilians was widely reported

---

[43] Hiroo Onoda, *No Surrender: My Thirty-Year War* (London, 1975); Philip Towle, *Enforced Disarmament* (Oxford, 1997), p. 152.
[44] Lane, *One God Too Many Devils*, chapter 2.

in either case. The French and US people were reluctant to believe in the depravity of their army and of the young conscripts involved.[45]

In the 1930s and 1940s Japan was an isolated authoritarian society, press coverage of the conflict and of the treatment of POWs was under strict control, the Japanese army was decentralised, allowing low-grade officers and other ranks to behave as they thought fit, and brutality was endemic in army training. If the brutality of British troops towards Palestinians in the 1930s had been revealed to the public, it would have led to bitter criticism in the press and enquiries in Parliament. In the 1950s French military brutality in Algeria helped to erode domestic support for the war and this was even more the case with the United States in Vietnam ten years later.

Japan was dominated in the 1930s by a military clique who believed that victory should be achieved at whatever cost. The whole army was imbued with the notion that the end justified the means. The only criticism in the 1930s came from the League of Nations and the western press, but this simply evoked bitter resentment and the determination to attack the European empires in Asia. By 1941 there was no criticism that the Japanese army would listen to and the only state capable of influencing Japan was Nazi Germany. Japan should have been liberating Asians from European rule, yet the worst cruelties, such as chemical and biological warfare, torture and mass murder, were actually perpetrated in China and against other Asian peoples.

---

[45] On the French operations in Vietnam see Phillipe de Pirey, *Operation Waste* (London, 1954), p. 56; and Henry Ainlie, *In Order to Die* (London, 1955), p. 30. On Algeria see Pierre Leulliette, *St Michael and the Dragon* (London, 1961), p. 3. See also Simone de Beauvoir and Gisèle Halimi, *Djamila Boupacha* (London, 1962). On the US in Vietnam see Lieutenant General W. R. Piers, *The My Lai Inquiry* (New York, 1979), p. 230.

# 2

# The Changi POW Camp and the Burma-Thailand Railway

### Robert Havers

On Sunday 2 May 1943, an Australian army officer, Captain Alan Rogers, noted in his personal diary an account of his activities during the past week: 'On Wednesday night we were fortunate enough to get tickets to the palladium and to see *I Killed the Count* – a good play and magnificently acted'.[1] It might appear that Captain Rogers was enjoying his war, in London or elsewhere, far removed from combat and the grim realities of the front line. Rogers, however, was certainly not in the front line, nor was he in London. In fact Captain Rogers had served with the Australian forces in the jungles of Malaya and at the siege of the 'impregnable fortress' of Singapore. He endured the Singapore surrender, described by Winston Churchill as 'the worst disaster and largest capitulation in British history', and survived the following three and half years as a prisoner of the Japanese.[2] Captain Rogers' diary is a record of events that happened inside the 'most notorious prisoner of war camp in Asia': at Changi on Singapore.[3]

Changi was the principal POW camp in Japanese-held South-East Asia. From Changi men began the arduous journey, by sea or more usually by rail, to work on the Burma-Thailand railway. While the appalling conditions on the railway are well known, indeed provide the raw materials from which popular perceptions of Japanese-held POWs are drawn, the altogether different conditions at Changi have, by contrast, received little attention. In 1946 Rohan Rivett published *Behind Bamboo*, one of the first accounts of captivity at the hands of the Japanese. He wrote: 'At Changi we found a far greater degree of freedom and comfort than we had ever known in Batavia'.[4] Kenneth Harrison was captured on the Malayan mainland and

---

[1] Australian War Memorial, henceforth AWM, PR85/145, A. W. Rogers, Captain, Australian Army Medical Corps, diary entry for 29 May 1943.

[2] Winston Churchill, *History of the Second World War*, iv, *The Hinge of Fate* (London, 1951), p. 81.

[3] Quoted from the back cover of the 1994 paperback edition of James Clavell, *King Rat* (London, 1962).

[4] Rohan D. Rivett, *Behind Bamboo* (Ringwood, Victoria, 1946), p. 158.

held at Kuala Lumpur. He wrote subsequently of his first encounter with Changi and considered that 'Changi itself was rather incredible to us Pudu [Pudu gaol in Kuala Lumpur] men, and in many ways [it]could have been called a POW's paradise'.[5] Lieutenant-Colonel E. E. 'Weary' Dunlop was captured in Sumatra, some weeks after the surrender at Singapore. Dunlop was eventually sent to work on the railway where he made his name as an outstandingly resourceful officer and doctor. In common with thousands of other POWs, Dunlop passed through Changi *en route* to the railway. On 7 January 1943 he commented on his initial sight of the camp:

> As we moved on we noticed splendid stone buildings in a beautiful part of the Island filled with British and Australian troops and – an astonishing sight – diggers *on guard* controlling traffic at points. All these troops are very well dressed, very spick and span, officers with sticks and ever so much saluting.[6]

Despite testimony such as this, Changi is frequently included in more homogenous interpretations of the treatment of Japanese-held POWs. On occasion, Changi is described as being peculiarly brutal in its own right, a place where of the 'nearly 150,000 young men' captured at the fall of Singapore 'only one in fifteen was to survive the three and a half long years to VJ day.'[7] This figure is doubly misleading. The number of men captured at Singapore was far less than 150,000, and certainly all but 10,000 men did not die as POWs.[8] Although many men did die, they died on the railway and not while at Changi. Descriptions such as 'one of the most infamous Japanese POW camps' owe more to the worst excesses experienced on the railway than to the conditions pertaining at Changi itself and have combined to foster a 'myth' of Changi.[9] In fact, by May 1944, the month the POW hospital moved to Kranji in Singapore and the main camp relocated to Changi gaol, 680 men had died at Changi.[10] This figure, while

---

[5] Kenneth Harrison, *The Brave Japanese* (London, 1967), p. 132.

[6] E. E. Dunlop, *The War Diaries of Weary Dunlop* (London, 1990), p. 160, author's italics.

[7] Quoted from the back cover of the 1977 paperback edition of Clavell, *King Rat*.

[8] Total British losses in manpower during the Malayan campaign were 138,708 of whom 130,000 became POWs. Of these 38,496 were British, 18,490 Australian, 67,340 Indian and 14,382 locally recruited volunteers. These figures are quoted from Major-General S. W. Woodburn Kirby, *The War Against Japan*, i, *The Loss of Singapore* (London, 1957), p. 473. This is part of the British official *History of the Second World War*. The figures are disputed by Peter Elphick's more recent study, *Singapore: The Pregnable Fortress* (London, 1995). Elphick considered that the Allied forces involved in Malaya and Singapore amounted to 86,895 all nationalities, ibid., p. 185.

[9] Quoted from the back cover of the 1993 Penguin edition of Russell Braddon, *The Naked Island* (London, 1951).

[10] Public Record Office, British and Australian POW Camp, Changi, WO 222/1352–55.

still significant, is obviously indicative of a fundamentally different regime to that experienced on the railway. Although the erosion of the ration scale, over the course of the war, left many prisoners malnourished by September 1945, overt, premeditated Japanese brutality was generally absent at Changi. The only manifestation of coercion, on a large scale, occurred when the Japanese attempted to extract from the prisoners a declaration promising not to attempt escape.[11] Even this event was comparatively innocuous when set against the conditions on the railway.

As is evident from the above quotations, Changi is often mentioned within the extensive literature concerned with POWs. What is significant is that it is frequently misrepresented and that little is known about the reality of life at Changi itself. For these reasons Changi is deserving of recognition and study in its own right. Ironically, while Changi might not be deserving of its apparently fearsome reputation, its role within the POW experience is significant and does need to be examined, with greater emphasis placed on what happened specifically at Changi. As Captain Rogers' diary suggests, life at Changi was almost more outlandish in reality than many of the myths that currently surround it. Even at the time, the experience of Changi was difficult to reconcile with more traditional images of POW camps. General Percival, the former General Officer Commanding (GOC) Malaya, and the man who signed the Singapore surrender, had difficulty in adequately capturing the nature of Changi. In a post-war letter concerned with events during the war, Percival felt compelled to emphasise this fact:

> The Changi camp was not like an ordinary POW camp surrounded by barbed wire with a staff and guards of the detaining power. It covered a considerable area of ground, bounded on one side by barbed wire and on the other sides by the sea and was divided into sub areas each under a British commander assisted by a British staff. The whole was under my general administrative control assisted by the staff of headquarters, Malaya Command. We had our own Military police. The Japanese commander had an officer at the entrance to the area and issued his instructions through my headquarters.[12]

The nature of this Japanese control meant that the POWs in Changi were afforded, initially at least, a far greater degree of freedom than they might otherwise have expected as prisoners. This freedom extended to their

[11] See R. P. W. Havers, 'The Selarang Barrack Square Incident', *Imperial War Museum Review*, 11, Autumn 1997.

[12] Percival to Major-General Sir Guy Glover, letter dated 8 January 1946, Recognition of Promotions of British Other Ranks made whilst POW under Japanese Control, WO 32/ 11684.

movements and, crucially, to the manner in which they organised themselves to face the undoubted challenges of captivity.

While Changi is not deserving of its sinister reputation, the reality of the POW experience at Changi is deserving of a wider appreciation. This, at times, was almost more outlandish than the wildest of myths. Similarly the impact that this peculiar existence had on those held there also requires examination. Ironically, such myths as attached themselves to Changi were created by those who experienced it at the time rather than subsequently. That is to say that conditions at Changi did not equate to the type of confinement that the POWs themselves were expecting. Even as they experienced Changi on a daily basis, their contemporary diaries bear witness to a continuing incredulity at their situation. The belief that Changi was 'special' and 'unique' was widespread and, in turn, this belief both encouraged and demanded activities and initiatives that would have been unthinkable in more conventional prison camp environments. The construction of theatres and 'The University of Changi' (an ambitious education scheme), for example, themselves then became further evidence of the 'fantastic' element of Changi that had, paradoxically, been responsible for their conception in the first place.

This essay aims to provide an insight into some of the peculiarities of life at Changi POW camp, as it existed between February 1942 and May 1944; to examine how these conditions influenced POW attitudes to captivity and also explore some of the less obvious links between Changi, one of the least well known, and most misunderstood, components of the Far Eastern prisoner of war experience, and, conversely, the most well known, the Burma-Thailand railway.

On 15 February 1942 the British forces at Singapore surrendered to the Japanese, a mere seventy days after the Japanese invasion of Malaya. Unprepared to deal with so many prisoners of war, the Japanese simply ordered all surrendered British personnel to proceed, *en masse*, to Changi, the large British army complex east of Changi gaol. Before the war, Changi had been considered 'one of the most modern and best equipped military bases anywhere in the world'. Despite suffering repeated artillery bombardment during the battle for Singapore island, it was largely unscathed. [13] Changi's incarnation as a POW camp lasted from February 1942 to May 1944 and was characterised as much by the fluidity of its boundaries as by its transitory and diverse population. In the immediate aftermath of the surrender, in February 1942, Changi contained 45,562 POWs, mainly British and Australian, to be joined by Dutch troops after the fall of the Dutch

---

[13] Squadron-Leader H. A. Probert, *The History of Changi* (Singapore, 1965), p. 34.

East Indies. By October the number of POWs had fallen to 15,744 and by June 1943 just 5359 remained, the lowest total for the whole war.[14] The number of men at Changi ebbed and flowed in proportion to Japanese demands for labour and, initially, large numbers were employed on working parties in Singapore town. Later, as Japanese requirements grew larger, groups known as 'Forces' were despatched to a variety of destinations that included Taiwan, Japan and of course the Burma-Thailand Railway itself which required huge numbers of POWs. Changi served as a transit camp and prisoners captured in Java and Sumatra were housed there temporarily, spending varying lengths of time before moving on. By the summer of 1943 the labour requirements of the railway were such that the remaining men at Changi occupied just a few barrack buildings. With the return of many men from Thailand and Burma, in autumn 1943, together with Japanese demands on the existing space for their own personnel, a reappraisal of the camp housing situation was required.[15] In May 1944 the entire POW body was moved into Changi gaol, displacing the civilian internees held there since the British surrender. The time spent by the POWs at Changi gaol, from where they were finally liberated in September 1945, is beyond the scope of this essay but the origins of the 'infamous' tag attached to Changi may also be rooted, partially at least, in the reputation that the gaol earned in its own right, before and after the war.

The Changi POW camp challenged the preconceptions of every prisoner who spent time there. The diary of an 'anonymous Australian officer' contains these comments on his first impressions of captivity and of Changi. His unit 'had been given the job of providing the medical services for the camp ... and as a consequence it was arranged that we should proceed as a complete field ambulance, including all our transport and gear as usual'.[16] He continued that:

> Bert ... was with me in the car and one remark to me typifies, I think, what must have been in all our minds at the time. He said 'well I never really thought that we would end up as prisoners of war, but if I ever think about it at all, I visualised something quite different from this. If anyone had told me that as prisoners, we would be driving out to our prison camp in our own cars,

[14] British and Australian POW Camp, Changi, WO 222/1352, 1352.

[15] Only the survivors of H and F Forces returned to Changi. The survivors of other groups either remained in Thailand or moved to Japan. See David Nelson, *The Story of Changi* (Perth, 1974), 'Chronology of Important Events and Moves of Working Parties from Changi', AWM, 54 554/11/29 and 'AIF War Diary', AWM, 54 554/11/39, for an exhaustive list of which groupings went where and for how long.

[16] AWM, 3DRL/6355, Australian officer in Changi (anon.), p. 1.

complete with our own equipment, and all our belongings, without even a Japanese guard to accompany us, they would have laughed him down.[17]

On his arrival at Selarang barracks, where the Australian POWs were originally billeted, this officer wrote that:

> I might also say that this was my first visit to Changi and we were amazed at the colossal amount of money that must have been spent on the ... buildings. The general layout, the quarters for married officers, the elaborate almost palatial buildings for the officers' and sergeants' messes, was an eye-opener to most of us. The place was a much grander scale than the Malay Regiment at Port Dickinson, but as far as I could gather, nothing outstanding compared with other barrack accommodation on Singapore island. No doubt we were all feeling a bit embittered at the time, but we could not help feeling that if less money had been spent on palatial buildings and more used on real defences things might have been different.[18]

CSM Romney wrote in his letter diary of the ambiguities and contradictions that he noticed at Changi, commenting that:

> It is not always easy to realise that we are prisoners, for this is one of the most delightful parts of the island, the area is very large, and although there is wire fencing it is so far away from sight that there is not a continual reminder of our lack of freedom. Let me describe it to you. There is a large sea frontage extending as far as the eye can see, the water glistening smoothly in the early morning sun, a large island the other side of the strait and the Johore coastline little more than a mile away. Within the area a wealth of bougainvillaea, delicately-tinted temple flowers, and bright yellow cassia, and some of the loveliest trees on the island. It is not to be wondered at that in peacetime this was one of the ... most popular military stations in the world.[19]

Bombardier Parry thought 'hey! we are just like the Ities no guards or Nips anywhere – maybe we've won after all?'[20] Initially the POWs were allowed to roam at will over a large proportion of the Changi base before the Japanese eventually imposed the minimum of restrictions and sub-divided the camp into areas. This meant that a group or individual now needed to be in possession of an official flag that was to be carried when men proceeded from one area to another. The Japanese also decided to erect a wire fence around each area and around the camp as a whole. The construction of

---

[17] AWM, 3DRL/6355, Australian officer in Changi (anon.), p. 2.
[18] Ibid., p. 3.
[19] Imperial War Museum (henceforth IWM), PH Romney, 81/7/1, CSM, Selangor Battalion, Federated Malay States Volunteer Force, diary entry for 1 April 1942.
[20] IWM, 86/35/1, E. W. Parry, gunner, 88th Field Regiment, Royal Artillery, diary entry for 16 February 1942.

this fence was also a source of considerable wonder to the POWs who 'commenced wiring ourselves in under IJA orders' in early March. 'The last few days', wrote Sergeant Roxburgh, 'working parties have been finishing a barbwire barricade around the whole camp. It consists of two lines of double apron fence with a triple concertina fence in between them'.[21] Roxburgh thought that 'it is so good a job that a cat could hardly get through. When we go outside the camp area one of our officers is put in charge of us'.[22] The incongruous fact of the POWs themselves performing the wiring in task was all too apparent. Private J. Houghton wrote that, 'this [Changi] is the funniest Camp in the world. We had to wire ourselves in with barbed wire so that we could not escape'.[23] Captain Dickson's experience of the wiring-in procedure was even stranger, as his commanding officer was obliged to source his own wire, as well as to put it up.[24] S. Dawson, writing in 1946, wrote that 'the early days were perhaps unique in prisoner of war history and we were not unappreciative of the many advantages we enjoyed'.[25] Allied intelligence reports obtained from captured Japanese personnel provided some information on what was happening in Singapore, although the conditions must have seemed equally perplexing when viewed from outside:

> Prisoner of war JA (USA) 100050 states that … while on six hour leave [in April 1942] he had seen three large two storey barracks, each capable of housing 500 to 600 men under Japanese army standards. White POWs could be seen at the windows and one stood guard at the front of the barracks. There was no fence or wall around the camp.[26]

The absence of Japanese direction, except at the highest level, left the POWs to their own devices. Once the Japanese had provided food material, for example, the subsequent cooking and division of meals were left entirely to the POWs themselves. The imposition of discipline was also left to the British authorities. POWs were encouraged, indirectly, to comply with the Japanese wishes by the knowledge that failure to do so 'seriously hampers all efforts of the Commander [from August 1942, this was

[21] AWM, PR84/117, James A. Roxburgh, Sergeant, 2/30th Battalion, AIF, diary entry for 15 March 1942.

[22] Ibid., 15 March 1942.

[23] IWM, 93/8/1, J. R. Houghton, Private, the Loyal Regiment, diary entry for 3 March 1942.

[24] IWM, E. C. Dickson, Captain, 88th Field Regiment, Royal Artillery, 11th Indian Division, diary entry for 8 March 1942.

[25] IWM, S. Dawson, memoir written in 1946, covering service with 18th Division Field Workshop, RAOC, . 39.

[26] PRO, WO 208/ 3485, Allied POWs in Japanese Hands, 24 August 1944.

Lieutenant-Colonel E. B. Holmes, the Manchester Regiment] British & Australian troops, to obtain better treatment for all POWs'.[27] This method of ensuring compliance with Japanese directions was a subtler one than traditional army methods. The British authorities walked a fine line at Changi in the knowledge that consistent or serious transgressions on the part of individual POWs would render them liable to punishment by the Japanese, a fate generally to be avoided, and also the threat that an apparent inability on the part of the POW authorities to maintain control invited greater Japanese interference in POW matters. In November 1942 the Japanese instituted roll call parades for the first time.[28] These roll calls were to occur at 1315 hrs and 2000 hrs and all ranks were to be present with 'no exceptions save in the case of personnel sick in quarters'.[29] The POWs were advised that failure to attend would result in the Japanese assuming that the individual concerned was attempting to escape and that 'experience has proved that explanation[s] will not be accepted by the IJA'.[30] The adherence to rules and regulations was an insurance for the POWs against what Lieutenant-Colonel F. G. 'Black Jack' Galleghan, the senior Australian officer after August 1942, termed the 'illogical temper and brutality of the Japanese'.[31]

Despite these considerations, life at Changi was still comparatively unrestricted. Colonel Shorland considered:

> The sense of relief from the War was still on everybody. Wrongly no doubt, but all were tired with overwork and lack of sleep and a carefree life in Changi seemed unexpectedly good. So for a few days we enjoyed the fresh air, the peace and the sea and the problems of organisation were left to solve themselves. We got into a slipshod and unhappy way of life and all suffered in consequence.[32]

By contrast W. Sowter, serving with the Royal Army Service Corps, said that:

> One good feature of this camp is that we can do practically what we like without interference from the Japanese. The camp is administered entirely by our own officers and we can wander at will over a very large area and the only sign of

[27] AWM, PR 86/ 187, AIF Routine Orders, no. 2, Discipline-Saluting, 11 October 1942, MC A/57/2684.

[28] AWM, PR00016–2, Alexander Thompson, Major, AIF Camp Quartermaster, diary entry for 13 November 1942.

[29] AWM, PR86/187, AIF Routine Order, no. 31, MC A/63/349, 13 November 1942.

[30] AWM, PR86/187, AIF Routine Order, no. 42, 16 November 1942.

[31] AWM, 54:554/11/4, Interim Report by F. G. Galleghan.

[32] IWM, G. H. Shorland, Colonel, Royal Artillery (regular soldier), diary entry for 15 March 1942.

guards we see is a couple of Japs with rifles who patrol the roads (quite un-necessarily) and are seen perhaps once or twice during the day.[33]

Despite the occasional 'slipshod' element, the level of independence afforded those held at Changi enabled the POWs to exercise a crucial degree of self-determination that prevented the development of a passive 'captive' attitude. This was especially important in the context of Changi which was also different from other POW camps in another very important respect.

A central tenet of POW existence, certainly in the way in which the experience has been represented, is that of the significant role played by the hope of escape in the lives of those held captive. Escape for a POW is both a practical and a psychological refuge since prisoners necessarily spend much time thinking about the day when they will leave the POW camp behind. Escape is the only way in which a POW can influence his own future to any meaningful extent. Escape, in whatever form, is generally the only decisive expression of self-determination that a prisoner can make, the alternative being a passive wait for release. The many films and books that attempt to recreate and represent the experiences of POWs frequently focus on escape, and the process that led to escape attempts, whether successful or not. Even the well-known film, *The Bridge on the River Kwai*, which purports to detail life on the Burma-Thailand railway, features a successful escape, albeit a somewhat implausible one. For the Allied servicemen at Changi escape was not a realistic option. Even those who had little idea about the geography of Singapore and Malaya could understand that they were detained on an island that was itself surrounded by hostile territory, and that their skin colour and physical features marked them out. Crucially, from the very beginning, life at Changi was deprived of a staple prop of POW existence. While escapes are mentioned in contemporary accounts, they were restricted to the early months and are reported as being uniformly unsuccessful, the exception being accounts of men absconding from Changi and joining up with guerrilla forces operating in the jungle of the Malayan mainland, with varying degrees of success.

By way of compensation, the men at Changi had, for the first two years of captivity, considerable freedom and physical space within which to utilise their apparently boundless ingenuity. This well-spring of latent talent, drawn from an immensely diverse cross-section of British, Australian and Dutch society, led to the lavish theatre productions mentioned by Captain Rogers, the establishment of a rubber 'factory' and a broom factory and the manu-facture of a vitamin substitute derived from the abundant local lalang grass,

[33] IWM, W. W. Sowter, Royal Army Service Corps, diary entry for 24 December 1942.

to name but a few of the many innovations.[34] Major Shean, in fact, had very few complaints about his situation, other than the simple fact of being held as a POW. This predicament was even less of a concern to some of his fellow officers. Shean noted that:

> Perhaps the only advantage of being here is that one has time to think and to analyse one's character and try and correct the faults which one always knew existed but couldn't do anything about. Imprisonment is not too bad, also, for those chaps with creative hobbies who in normal life have little spare time. Some chaps are like schoolboys on holiday and with nothing but scraps of material make the most wonderful things such as musical instruments, steam engines, electric clocks … I certainly envy them. They potter along with their hands and have no time to bother their heads with morbid thoughts or introspection.[35]

The comparatively open nature of Changi provided practical relief from many of the harsher realities of confinement. The River Valley camp, where large numbers of men from Changi lived whilst employed on working parties around Singapore town and island, was described by Major Shean, after a brief visit, as 'a bloody camp … no liberty and Jap and Sikh sentries all round and no view … altogether it's much worse than Changi'.[36] Shean was able to make a distinction between Changi and the conditions he saw on display at River Valley and realise that his existence at the former was far preferable. Crucially, the reasons upon which this judgement was based – 'no liberty … sentries all round' – are not in themselves unreasonable constituent elements for any POW camp and would seem, rather, to be prerequisites for such an institution. Only by comparison with the favourable conditions at Changi can these staples of containment appear unreasonable.

The arrival of men who had endured somewhat different conditions as POWs also served to highlight the comparative comforts of Changi and both to reinforce and to confirm its unreal elements. Captain Yates arrived in Singapore in September 1942. His first impressions are instructive: 'Changi camp appeared to us to be a POW's paradise … the only guards were on the road between the areas and one might go for days without

---

[34] The POW population grew ever more diverse as the war progressed. In 1945 Captain Horner noted the results of a census: 'nationalities in Changi gaol camp as at 1 June 45: British 3845, Australian 3006, Canadian 9, South African 2, New Zealand 8, Americans 47, Dutch 1963, Danish 3, Norwegians 2, Czech 1, Indian 1, Italian 19 and French 1', IWM, Horner, diary entry for 6 June 1945.

[35] IWM, D. M. Shean, Major, East Yorkshire Regiment serving in Q Branch Malaya Command, diary entry for 6 May 1943.

[36] Ibid., 26 September 1942.

even seeing a Japanese'.[37] Yates noted that: 'some lived in positive luxury with salvaged furniture, messes and concert halls. The entire camp administration was in British hands and a complete military organisation existed headed by Malaya Command with red arm bands'.[38] On 7 January 1943, Corporal Albert Thompson also arrived from Java. His impressions of Changi are in stark contrast to his previous experiences of captivity at the hands of the Japanese:

> After forty minutes run from the docks we eventually came to 'Changi'. Thought we were going to 'Changi' jail at first. What a surprise when we turned into a camp with a huge parade ground in the centre – the Jap. guard immediately unfixed bayonets, counted us and cleared out. Well there are camps everywhere here and no Nips and no barb wire – what a time these people must be having. No scraping and bowing, no lashing and no interference whatever. We arrived here at 2200 hours moved to a temporary camp had tea and went to bed in a tent and it was glorious with a keen fresh wind blowing in the open no one to worry you, it was glorious believe me after the boat. Evidently the camps here are run under their own steam.[39]

Lance Corporal Kenneth Heyes arrived on the same day as Thompson. After landing in Singapore he was driven

> about fifteen miles north to large area in which there is nothing but prisoners, it was originally a British camp. Main road goes right through and one has to get leave pass to visit other camp all nationalities, about four miles away are all the Aussie prisoners ... billeted in a large three storey barracks, good room and showers every other camp is patrolled by MPs ...[40]

These men found Changi to be beyond their own experiences of captivity and fundamentally at odds with conventional notions of incarceration.

Despite the reactions of these men to their first glimpse of Changi, the conditions under which they had been held in Java were also reported, amongst the long-term Changi residents, to be comparatively good and inevitably sparked off much debate and rumour.[41] Lieutenant Orr compared conditions in Changi unfavourably with what he heard went on in Java lamenting that 'if they [the Japanese] can bring troops from Java they can

[37] IWM, H. D. A. Yates, Captain, Royal Army Ordinance Corps, MS journal written shortly before the Japanese surrender in 1945, p. 37.
[38] Ibid.
[39] AWM, PR89/167, A. G. Thompson, Corporal, 2/6th Field Company, Royal Australian Engineers, diary entry for 7 January 1943.
[40] AWM, PR86/232, Kenneth Heyes, Lance-Corporal, 1st Australian Corps Troop Supply Column, diary entry for 7 January 1943.
[41] AWM, PR00016–2, Thompson, diary entry for 14 September 1943.

bring food' from where it was believed to be plentiful.[42] Major Shean had also heard that the POWs in Java had been living on 'milk and honey'.[43] By contrast, Major Gillies, a doctor, was better informed about Java and also about the privileges of life at Changi, noting that 'the Java people are only passing through but we got all their sick and they have plenty of them. Quite evidently we have had a cushy time here compared with Java'.[44]

By the end of April 1943 the population of Changi had dropped drastically as thousands were sent to work on the railway. Those remaining were obliged to relocate to other areas and, amid the movement, men were able to venture to areas that they had not previously visited. Whilst exploring, Captain Rogers made an interesting discovery:

> Personally, this week has been rather full, Monday night Harold and I went over to Southern area to hear a concert there. It was typically English and though the orchestra was shocking, we were well entertained. Now this will rock you – there is, in this half starved, desolate, under-fed joint a restaurant running. Over in 18 Division, run by the Dutch, who receive practically no pay from the IJA, and they have adopted this way of getting money to contribute to the hospital. We had heard that Greenwood's swing band would be playing there, but unfortunately, on Tuesday night when we went there, they had finished their season. However it was a most peculiar evening. I have been in some queer dives, but this must rank as among the queerest. The building was divided into two, on one side being a large bar arrangement patronised by the other ranks and another smaller portion with a few tables and forms separated from the larger part by a partition of palm leaves, reserved for officers. It was a cross between a cheap bar and a coffee lounge and the customers were Dutch, British, Americans and Australians, and I might add a very rare mixture of each. Anyhow, we … had a sandwich each, three cups of coffee and two slices of toast with herrings on – my night cost me 39 cents – not much perhaps, but I am now stony, and we will not be paid for at least another twelve days. But what is the odds? It was a welcome break and we all enjoyed it. Grog can be purchased there at times, the 'white wine' costing 40 cents per bottle, and the better 'red wine', which takes at least a fortnight to mature, costing slightly more. Fortunately we did not know about the grog, otherwise we may have had the pleasure of a hangover the following morning.[45]

Rogers was not alone in appreciating this 'peculiar' restaurant, nor in being surprised and impressed by its ambition. The 'anonymous Australian

[42] AWM, Lindsay Orr, Lieutenant, Australian Army Service Corps, diary entry for 15 September 1943.
[43] IWM, Shean, diary entry for 16 September 1943.
[44] IWM, D. W. Gillies, Major, Royal Army Medical Corps, diary entry for 24 October 1942.
[45] AWM, Rogers, diary entry for 26 April 1943.

officer' also commented on the restaurant and his notes are reproduced in full:

> With the cleaning out of 18th Division and Southern Area all the troops remaining there are being moved to Selarang. With them goes one of our lately discovered haunts – the Changi restaurant – known as 'Smokey Joe's'. The raison d'être of this place is that the IJA do not pay the Java parties at all; consequently 18th Division allowed the Dutch to start and run this restaurant, and all profits were dedicated to providing extra food for the Java parties. Recently John and I developed the habit of going there occasionally in the evenings … I was never able to get in there in the mornings although I believe it was better then and less crowded. Last Saturday night – almost the last night before the place closed down, it was an amazing night. The restaurant itself consists of an attap hut with one end partitioned off by palm leaf … for officers, and the whole place was packed to capacity. All the overflow were sitting about in the grass outside … most of the officers from the 18th Division were there for a final farewell before they went up country, and a fair crowd from the hospital and from Selarang also were there . It is too absurd for words when you come to think of it – the poor prisoners of war, instead of being cooped up in compounds, guarded by numerous guards, and afraid to lift a finger, simply coming from all parts of the area to spend a pleasant – if hot – evening at the 'café' with full musical accompaniment. The night was made all the more unforgettable by the fact that the only lights were coconut oil lamps, as the 18th Division electric light engine had been packed up to take up country with them. 'Smokey Joe's Cafe will go down in the annals of the history of Changi'.[46]

As can be seen, both men took great trouble to record the details of Smokey Joe's. Its impact on their daily lives, and on their perceptions of what it meant to be a POW, is obvious. The camp reorganisation obliged Smokey Joe's to close down, but it did reopen for business in the area of Selarang barracks. Despite the late discovery of such an establishment by some at Changi, the mere fact that it had existed at all was also a source of considerable comfort. The detailed representations of Smokey Joe's in several diaries go beyond just recording the fact of its being and, in addition, emphasise the pride apparent in being part of a group that could both conceive of and realise such an apparent paradox. In the context of the Singapore surrender, and the apparent Japanese superiority demonstrated during the Malayan campaign, these actions by the 'vanquished' POWs helped to redress the imbalance between captor and captive. Captain Rogers had been happy to dismiss some of the Dutch colonial troops as 'boongs' some months earlier, yet the discovery of the café, the embodiment of wit,

---

[46] AWM, anonymous Australian officer, diary entry for 27 April 1943.

imagination and ingenuity under the most trying of circumstances, allowed
Rogers, and all the POWs, to bask in the reflected glory of such an achievement. Irrespective of who was actually responsible, the café helped to define
a group identity above and beyond nationality, although not necessarily
beyond the constraints of rank. The practical boost in morale that Smokey
Joe's afforded was matched by the sense of pride apparent at the fact that
fellow POWs had the audacity and initiative to make it happen. These
considerations in tandem went some way toward welding the disparate
elements at Changi into a far more cohesive grouping and to demonstrate
that, for all its privations and deprivations, Changi and its prisoners still
had the power to elicit surprise from its own 'captive' population.

While the horrors of the railway were physically remote from Changi, the
shadow of its construction was always apparent. The freedoms of Changi,
which found expression in an enormous range of activities and initiatives,
were severely curtailed by the loss of so many men sent to labour on the
railway.[47] The large-scale departures changed the nature of the camp irrep-
arably. Men lost long-term friends and the camp itself lost individual skills
and the opportunity of utilising the huge pool of labour for its own benefit.
Signaller Coombs heard that he would be one of the men to head up-country
on F Force and noted that he was 'very relieved to be leaving Singapore
island'.[48] J. Houghton, by contrast, was similarly relieved to hear that he
was *not* one of the men detailed to leave on a party, believed to be going
to Japan.[49] Rumours as to the destination of the 'overseas' parties were rife.
Major Gillies noted that the 'most popular [rumoured destination was] the
Cameron highlands which is [a] health resort and hill station in Malaya
and [another choice] a place forty or fifty miles N. W. of Bangkok'.[50] At
the beginning of November Lieutenant Baillies wrote: 'We had word last
night to be prepared to move up country on Wednesday 4 November, so
presumably we are going to Siam. They say that travel broadens the mind.
Conditions will probably be worse, but I am rather glad of the change'.[51]
    Major Braganza did not wish to leave Changi, thinking 'I could not be
more comfortable and would like to have spent my POW days there'.[52]

[47] AWM, 54 554/11/39, AIF War Diary, p. 7.
[48] IWM, 88/62/1, C. Coombs, signaller, 9th Division Signals, diary entry for 23 October 1942.
[49] IWM, 93/8/1, J. R. Houghton, private, The Loyal Regiment, diary entry for 23 October 1942.
[50] IWM, Gillies, diary entry for 24 October 1942.
[51] IWM, W. M. Baillies, Lieutenant, Singapore Royal Artillery Volunteer Force, diary entry
for 1 November 1942.
[52] IWM, R. R. Braganza, Major, Surgeon, Indian Army Medical Service, diary entry for 24
March 1943.

Lieutenant-Colonel Wilkinson was also unhappy about the prospect of going, 'it is a great pity we are leaving Changi as we have so much to be thankful for here and God alone knows what the conditions will be like where we are going'. Colonel Shorland was also concerned and considered it 'a pity as life here had settled down to be quite bearable and all this change is disquieting'.[53] Less than a week later, Shorland lost his best friend to a working party, an event that put his current, comparatively comfortable, life into context. 'This is a very sad day ... I am left alone in the room with all the accumulated furniture and comforts of nine months hard scrounging'. He thought it 'wonderfully comfortable and roomy but very depressing. After living so long all cramped up one feels quite lonely to be back in an ordinary room'.[54]

At this early stage the dreadful fate of parties going to the railway was unknown but conditions at Changi were still sufficiently pleasant to cause men some concern at being obliged to leave. Captain Horner had his own views on the continuing exodus of POWs up-country when his friend was included on a detail to go north: 'Bill Cowell is going up-country – he hasn't been "yessing" well enough – Hells Bells these senior officers are bum, the whole bloody lot of them, the more I see of them the less respect I have'.[55] Horner at least had more of an idea of what was to come. When his turn came to be included in an 'up-country' party he was sufficiently well informed to speculate that he was to help 'superintend the making of a road or a railway', although the conditions under which he and his fellow officer POWs were to conduct this comparatively innocuous sounding task were as yet still unimagined.[56] Captain Malet was concerned to discover that he had been classified as being in condition 'A' and realised that he would, in all probability, be sent 'up to railway construction jobs in Siam'. Malet was concerned about this, considering 'God forbid I should qualify for that outfit [the railway]'. Malet, a locally recruited soldier with the Federated Malay States Volunteer Force, noted that many of his fellow officers had classified themselves as 'B', 'simply because they were over forty', something that Malet appeared to disagree with. He was sufficiently worried, however, to set aside his initial objections and note, 'if this is legal I'm going to try it – not to get out of fatigues which I enjoy- but to miss a possible up-country party'.[57]

---

[53] IWM, Shorland, diary entry for 30 October 1942.
[54] IWM, Shorland, diary entry for 5 November 1942.
[55] IWM, R. M. Horner, Captain, Royal Army Supply Corps, diary entry for 31 October 1942.
[56] IWM, Horner, diary entry for 9 May 1943.
[57] IWM, Malet, diary entry for 17 September 1942.

While some expressed excitement at what these moves might bring, no diarist indicated that it was because of unfavourable conditions pertaining at Changi. When Captain Malet was, as he had feared, detailed for an up-country party, his concerns, and those of the men set to accompany him, focused as much on what they were obliged to leave behind as on what the future might hold. News of his departure prompted him to write 'this is rather alarming as we feel we'll never have another climate as healthy as this and certainly never the convenience of a settlement such as this with barracks and married quarters'.[58] Captain Malet's concerns proved to be well founded. He never returned to Changi and died on the railway in June 1943.[59]

The demand for labour denuded Changi of thousands of the fittest men and had a significant impact on those left behind, for a variety of reasons. Colonel Shorland's comment that 'we have lost practically every fit man in the camp' would prove to have serious repercussions.[60] When, in April 1943, after the large-scale movements of troops out of Changi, the IJA granted permission for extra trailers to be used in hauling wood for fuel – vital in ensuring that cooking instruments were boiled to ward off dysentery – problems were encountered, firstly with defective trailers and, more significantly, through a lack of fit men to do the pulling.[61]

The departures also shed light on the internal dynamics of Changi's social structure and the extent to which divisions of rank were adhered to. Only with the departure of F Force did 'general duties' become the first charge on the services of 'batmen', rather than the more traditional batting activities; 'in such cases, officers [were to] reduce batting duties to a minimum otherwise only those unfit for any other duties will be employed as batmen'.[62] While the expenditure of any time and effort on these services might have appeared essentially trivial, the loss of such services was perceived to be of some importance. Major Shean, along with other officers in his mess, believed that they stood to suffer when 'Freeman [Shean's batman] was picked in a lottery to go [up-country] along with Dolman, our head gardener. But we had a protest mass meeting and eventually our two head cooks were detached as they were asking for a transfer anyway. This is the third time that I have been on the verge of losing Freeman and I hope this

[58] IWM, Malet, diary entry for 23 October 1942.
[59] Malet's diary was returned to his family and donated posthumously to the Imperial War Museum.
[60] IWM, Shorland, diary entry for 30 October 1942.
[61] AWM, Thompson, diary entry for 1 April 1943.
[62] AWM, PR86/187, AIR routine order, no. 149, 14 April 1943.

luck will hold'.[63] When the efficient utilisation of scarce rations was absolutely crucial, the willingness of Shean, and his fellow officers to lose two experienced cooks seems particularly shortsighted when set against the value of the duties that a batman could provide.

While life at Changi had appeared to be well regulated and efficient, it may be seen that there were still inequities and inefficiencies in the use of labour. These were grounded partly in a surplus of men, which soon evaporated, and also in a strict adherence to military tradition and discipline. The loss of virtually all the fit men in camp meant that the continued Japanese demand for labour would require that unfit troops be sent. H Force thus comprised 10 per cent Class III men. It now became necessary for officers to take the place of enlisted men in the gangs of POWs pulling trailers around the camp and also to take their turn working in the camp gardens, two activities in which they had not previously participated. On 30 April, Colonel Shorland commented that:

> We have now lost another 4000 odd, and the problem of keeping the hospital and the gardens and wood-cutting going is very difficult. Every fit man is out on trailer parties, carting round wood or rations. It appears inevitable that we shall have to take to some form of feeding on a larger basis than the present mess of twenty-one. If so it will be a tragedy as regards the garden and fowls, which are now doing us very well in a small mess. People are willing enough to work hard for themselves and friends or for the sick in hospital, but when once the basis become larger, the number of drones and anti-social people seems to get bigger, and at once dissatisfaction creeps in. There have been plenty of heart burnings [sic] over those to go away. Many rush off to get doctor's certificates, or find berths in cushy jobs to avoid moving out. As a result good useful people like David go away, and the useless and unpleasant bits of work who never do a thing stay behind to be waited on by the rest of us.[64]

Despite the additional burdens imposed by fewer available men, Colonel Shorland considered 'there are advantages to the reduced numbers about the place, even though it makes more work. The garden produce goes further and so do the eggs'.[65] Major Shean noted that:

> owing to the loss of so many men up country & overseas the o/c i/c British and Dutch cemetery cannot get enough labour to keep the place up. They called for volunteers from the area which holds about seventy officers we got seven volunteers ... its always the few of the old gang from this house which do all the volunteering and all the jobs. I believe S.A. [Southern Area] which has an

[63] IWM, Shean, diary entry for 3 May 1943.
[64] IWM, Shorland, diary entry for 30 April 1943.
[65] IWM, Shorland, diary entry for 4 July 1943.

officer population of approx. 350 produced three volunteers for the job! A few hours a week pottering in the cemetery and yet the buggers won't give up hogging it on their beds. [66]

Despite the enforced changes in the utilisation of what POW manpower remained, it was still insufficient for the Japanese who, in mid August 1943, expressed concern that POW behaviour was becoming 'slack' and that there were far too many 'healthy POWs remaining in lines'. The British authorities responded to this by ordering, finally, all fit POWs not otherwise employed to work on the extensive camp vegetable gardens.[67]

The construction of a new fence around part of the Changi area highlighted some of the manpower problems. Captain Rogers had an amusing story concerned with this event that serves to illustrate further both the contradictory nature of Changi and the extent to which the men held there appreciated it:

> Quite recently, the IJA came down to Divvy and said 'We want a working party', 'Can't do' says Divvy, 'No men', 'We want a party to put up another fence'. Says Divvy, 'The men who put up the fence have all gone away – how big do you want the fence?' 'Big enough to keep the prisoners in', was the answer, 'about two strands of wire.' [68]

Despite this jocularity, rumours were already circulating about the fate of those men who had left Changi. Lieutenant Orr noted in his diary that he had heard 'talk of 600 of F Force who went up country being dead through cholera, we all went to bed feeling sad'.[69] Changi was 'warned to expect heavy casualties' as the survivors returned. Major Shean was familiar with all the rumours and wrote:

> its quite obvious that H & F forces have been through unbelievable hell. Tanaka and Tagumi [Japanese officers in charge at Changi] were down to see the party arrive [back from the railway] and I gather were obviously horrified and embarrassed by the condition of the men. I'm not surprised as T. & T. have always appeared very sympathetic & quite reasonable.[70]

Shean thought that 'all the IJA appear to realise what a bad show it all is and are anxious to make amends'.[71]

The return of men from the railway, and the forthcoming move to Changi

---

[66] IWM, Shean, diary entry for 30 May 1943.
[67] AWM, Thompson, diary entry for 12 August 1943.
[68] AWM, Rogers, dairy entry for 21 May 1943.
[69] AWM, Orr, diary entry for 28 June 1943.
[70] IWM, Shean, 17 December 1943.
[71] Ibid.

gaol, once again brought home the reality of the war and of captivity to Changi in the most forceful manner. For those who suffered in Burma and Thailand however, the 'myth' of Changi had not faded and proved the single positive element in their cumulative experience of captivity upon which to focus. P. Allwood worked on the railway and recorded in his diary the following lines written by a fellow POW while at Kanu (probably Konyu).

> I'd be happy, oh so happy, if someone said to me
> We leave today at three, for Changi by the sea.
> No Nips yelling, jungle felling I'd be happy there,
> Here my ruddy bed's so buggy, it leaves the bamboos bare.
> At Changi by the sea, that's where I long to be,
> Where fags were issued free, and where we had meat for tea.
> I can't help thinking tonight, how my belt was always tight
> With Red Cross rations served in all fashions, everything was bright.
> The handcarts round the door of our old ration store were always on the go
>    and yet
> We grumbled so.
> Oh! I would never be a squealer, if I could breakfast off 'Mabela'
> And could get back, to my old shack, back in Changi by the sea.[72]

Life at the Changi POW camp does not conveniently dovetail with the received wisdom concerning the experiences of POWs of the Japanese, dominated as it is by accounts of life on the railway. For almost all of those who laboured in Burma and Thailand, however, Changi was an integral element of their experience of captivity. Changi was not a holiday camp where men simply idled and killed time between extravagant theatrical performances. Adequate food and medical supplies both dwindled as the war progressed and this took an inevitable toll on the health of those there and in particular those who returned, sick or injured, from the railway. In 1951 Roy Whitecross published *Slaves of the Son of Heaven* and he wrote then that 'compared to later times and places, Changi Camp was a haven of rest'.[73] Changi was, as Whitecross appreciated, only a haven of rest by *comparison* with the railway camps.

Despite this, Changi is important for a number of reasons. While it is impossible to gauge what the men who were sent to the railway took from Changi in terms of resilience, imagination and ingenuity, it is certain that these qualities, so vital in the struggle for survival in the jungles of Burma and Thailand, were on display in abundance in Changi itself. Changi also

---

[72] IWM, P. Allwood, 'Greater part of this diary written at Pratchai in September 1945, based mainly on contemporary notes'.

[73] Roy H. Whitecross, *Slaves of the Son of Heaven* (Sydney, 1951), p. 10.

provided an important mental, as well as physical, refuge. The knowledge that captivity did not only comprise the hellish conditions of the railway offered some hope in the face of daily brutality, hard labour and starvation. Allwood's carefully noted verse demonstrates that it was not always the unrealistic dream of home that sustained the prisoners in time of need. A return to Changi was, in fact, far more probable than an immediate return home and the fact that Changi held positive associations served only to reinforce its position as an attainable goal. Even if a return to Changi had never been an aspiration to those on the railway, then the actual return was sufficient to impress upon them that they were indeed fortunate. In April 1943 F Force departed for Thailand. Of the 7000 British and Australian troops who left, 3000 died on the railway. Glenleigh Skewes was one of the lucky ones and returned, sick and emaciated, to Changi:

> On arrival at the Garden & Wood area at Changi, we walked across a Padang of long turf, green and soft. At the other end we were shown into *new* attap huts erected by POWs ... for the return of F Force. We repeated to ourselves and to one another, 'brand new huts for us! and electric lighting too!' We could scarcely believe our eyes ...[74]

In 1980, ex-POW Stan Arneil wrote that 'the portrayal of the "dreaded Changi" brings a smile to the faces of many former POWs who longed for Changi as almost a heaven on earth compared to some of the dreadful places to which they were taken'.[75] Changi was a place that defied the preconceptions of those held there as prisoners, that redefined the boundaries of what it meant to be a POW and ultimately provided a refuge from one of the most horrific episodes of the Second World War.

---

[74] AWM, PR88/128, Glenleigh Skewes, private, 2/13th Australian General Hospital, diary, p. 113.
[75] Stan Arneil, *One Man's War* (Sydney, 1989), p. 3.

# 3

# Allied POWs and the Burma-Thailand Railway

## Clifford Kinvig

Japan's decision to invade Burma in 1942 and to add that country to its Greater East Asia Co-Prosperity Sphere led directly to three of the greatest military engineering projects of the Pacific War, one undertaken by the United States, one by Great Britain and one by Japan itself. Burma was then, and to some extent it remains today, a giant cul-de-sac, easily entered at its port and capital city Rangoon, but leading nowhere. Great mountain ranges, the southern extensions of the Himalayas, enclose it from easy landward contact with its neighbours, India, China and Thailand. All three projects were put in hand to enable control of Burma to be maintained or disputed. The manner in which each was undertaken was eloquent of the strategic circumstances of the powers concerned, but perhaps bespoke even more clearly the contrasts between their military cultures and their approach to war.

The first project, the building by the United States of the Ledo Road in northern Burma, was an attempt to reestablish a land supply route to the beleaguered Chinese, isolated and embattled since the Japanese occupied the southern part of the famous Burma Road. The new road linked Ledo in north-eastern India with the upper stretch of the Burma Road still in Chinese hands. It was pushed through dense jungles and over the slopes of the Himalayas. To its construction the American Army engineers applied their very considerable road-building skill, a huge quantity of advanced road-making machinery and a substantial force of largely Indian labour. By the time the Ledo Road was completed, in January 1945, it was virtually redundant; air supply was already providing the lion's share of the supplies needed by the armies of Yunnan. Despite this, once their industrial resources were mobilised for war, the Americans were easily able to make this largely superfluous effort, giving themselves fail-safe assurance that the Chinese armies would be supplied whatever the circumstances.[1]

The second major logistical undertaking was not a single but several road and rail-building efforts by which a line of communications was established

---

[1] During the first ten months of 1945 the completed road carried a total of 38,000 tons of supplies into Yunnan, while the 'Hump route' airlift was managing 39,000 tons each month.

and expanded between Bengal in British India and the three separate Allied war fronts in Burma. The capacity of the little tea gardens railway linking Calcutta with Dimapur and Ledo was increased tenfold by 6500 professional military engineers and a civil labour force of 15,000 and involved the laying of 480 kilometres of additional track. Major all-weather roads were built down to the British base at Imphal and then on to the fronts at Kalewa and in the Arakan. The road to Imphal, 'a truly magnificent engineering achievement, was of a quality and permanence beyond any other on the Burma front', wrote General Slim.[2] Once again the construction benefited from the latest caterpillar tracked, earth-moving equipment and a substantial Indian labour force, while the road to Arakan, where there was no stone available for road metal, was built with millions of bricks. Skilled brick-makers were imported from India, as were huge quantities of coal. Kilns were set up every twenty miles or so along the route. When the brick road sank in the monsoon rain, a fresh one was built on top of it. By this mixture of high and low technology, and with the aid of an Indian labour force of some 40,000, managed by the tea estates of India, the logistical basis of the ultimate British victory in Burma was laid.[3]

The third military engineering enterprise was the Japanese undertaking: the building by the Southern Army railway staff of a line, over 400 kilometres in length, designed to link the railway system of Burma with those of Thailand and Malaya. The essential aim of the undertaking was to obviate the long sea journey around the Malayan peninsula and on to Rangoon for Japan's small, overstretched and increasingly vulnerable merchant marine. Its military benefits were obvious enough and its engineering difficulties, though considerable, by no means insuperable. What made this project so daunting, and its contrast with the other two so stark, was that the Japanese were to attempt it with virtually none of the engineering equipment and resources available to their adversaries, minimal support from a metropolitan base of any kind on which the British and Americans relied, and in a region which was for the most part one of the most disease-ridden and inhospitable of the territories they had conquered. The British had contemplated con-structing such a railway some years earlier, but had rejected it because of

[2] Field-Marshal Sir William Slim, *Defeat into Victory* (London, 1954), p. 171. Slim was com-mander of the British 14th Army. The technical details of these road and rail building efforts are given in R. S. Colquhoun, 'The Design and Construction of the Tamu-Kalewa Road, Burma', and F. J. J. Prior, 'Military Railway Engineering on the Assam Line of Communication, 1942–45', in *The Civil Engineer in War*, i (London, 1948), pp. 292–321, 486–508.

[3] A. Snelling, 'Notes on Some Administrative Aspects of the Campaign of Fourteenth Army, 1943–45', *Army Quarterly*, July 1965.

the engineering problems and the physical conditions involved, as well as changing economic circumstances.

That judgement had been taken during a period of peace and with all the necessary engineering resources readily available. In constructing the railway their Japanese adversaries were to rely very heavily on what they could find in the local theatre of war. Just as the locomotives and wagons were taken from Java, Malaya and Burma, and the bulk of the rails acquired by ripping up the Malayan east coast line and branch lines there and in Burma, so also the labour force was local, drawn from the peoples of the conquered territories and from the very large number of prisoners of war who had fallen into their hands. Throughout the duration of the project speed was of the essence and became increasingly critical as the Japanese logistical situation deteriorated. Consequently, although hardwood was readily available, softwood was preferred for the 688 bridges which had to be built. It was less durable than hardwood, but it was more easily cut, worked and erected. Since there was so much of it available, it could easily be replaced. Similar reasoning appears to have been applied to the labour force. In the Japanese project human muscle was to replace machinery. The engineers would be demanding a great deal of it, but much was available. That Japan should have been reduced to embarking on so hazardous an undertaking so early in the war, and to relying on POWs as a major part of the labour force, illustrates the character of the strategic dilemma with which its high command was wrestling and the extent to which it was prepared to subordinate all other considerations to its military goals. In the complex of cultural, social, legal and military factors which account for the treatment of the POWs assembled in Thailand and Burma, the overriding one was the strategic imperative for the railway to be built and built quickly.

The most significant collective experience of the Allied POWs held by the Japanese during the Second World War was their involvement in the building of the Burma-Thailand railway. The Japanese held prisoners throughout the South-East Asian region, the majority initially in Singapore, but nowhere were they to be concentrated in such great numbers, and used in the service of a single strategic purpose, as they were on that stretch of the Thai-Burmese border country which the railway occupied. The multinational POW labour force used on the railway project totalled about 62,000 men.[4] In addition

---

[4] South East Asia Translation and Interrogation Centre (SEATIC), bulletin 246, 'The Burma-Siam Railway', October 1946, Imperial War Museum (IWM), based on Allied and Japanese records; D. Nelson, *The Story of Changi*, privately published (West Perth, 1974). Nelson helped establish the Bureau of Record and Enquiry at Changi which traced the POW moves to and from that base.

there was a huge force of local labourers, the *romusha* as the Japanese called them, about 270,000 strong, drawn from many parts of the region.[5] To these must be added the numbers of the Japanese themselves, the two railway regiments (the 5th in Burma and the 9th in Thailand) responsible for the technical direction of the project, the Japanese POW administration, initially only 125 strong, supported by a guard force of almost 1300 Korean auxiliaries (*gunzoku*), together with the engineer reinforcements who arrived later to hasten the project's completion. The grand total was well over a third of a million men concentrated in a narrow strip of riverine jungle and plain with, for much of its length, a very sparse indigenous population.

The Allied prisoners were a very heterogeneous group. The largest element was the 30,000 British, many of them from the 18th Division, an East Anglian reservist force, two brigades of which had arrived in Singapore only two weeks before the surrender after a voyage to the Far East of almost three months. Before that some of them had been training in Scotland in six inches of snow. Imprisoned with them were the well-acclimatised regular infantry units which had been in the Far East since long before the war against Japan had begun. Similarly accustomed to the tropics were European members of the local Malayan and Singaporean reserve forces whose knowledge of local languages and conditions was of value throughout their captivity. The many British officers of the Indian army divisions and other locally recruited units, who the Japanese had quickly separated from their Asian soldiers, completed the British group. In addition there were the men of the Australian 8th Division, the bulk of them not regular soldiers, of whom the majority were veterans of the division's brief campaign on the Malayan mainland or in Timor and Java. Others among them were raw and ill-disciplined recruits who had arrived in Singapore in the last days of the campaign with virtually no training behind them. The Australians totalled about 13,000. The Dutch contingent was formed of the captives from the brief fight for Java and numbered about 18,000. They too lacked homogeneity, being composed of Hollanders serving in the East Indies on government or business arrangements, Dutchmen raised and living permanently in the colonies and, finally, the mixed race *indische jongen*. Some had been part of the conventional Dutch forces, others of the local Home Guard. Finally there were the Americans, survivors mainly of the sinking of the battle cruiser *Houston* or else men of the Texan National Guard

---

[5] This is a higher total than some Japanese authorities quote. The source is SEATIC, bulletin no. 246, which uses the records of HQ 4th (Japanese) Railway Corps for Malaya, Java, Siam and FIC recruitment and U Aung Min, Deputy Director of Labour in the Japanese-sponsored Burma Provisional Government, for the Burmese.

artillery regiment which had helped to defend Java. There were almost 700 of them. New Zealanders were also represented among the railway labourers, as were all three fighting services. To their lack of common nationality, great variety of military background and experience of the Far East was added a very varied operational record. Men who had demonstrated extra-ordinary courage in the short campaign for Malaya were held captive alongside others who had deserted the lines during its latter part but had later been captured. Although there was little homogeneity across the national groups, and not a great deal within them, all shared the shock and demoralisation of defeat and the rancour and recrimination to which it gave rise. In the stern test which lay ahead of the POWs, group cohesion was of overwhelming importance in the face of a Japanese military system which, for all its technological sophistication and its superficial similarity to their own, was in the case of all the nationalities involved, in many ways its antithesis.

Two factors were to be of particular importance for the survival of the POWs. The first was the framework of military organisation, with the large officer group at its head, which was preserved for most of the captivity. At an early stage the Japanese separated the relatively small number of officers above the rank of lieutenant-colonel from the rest of the troops and held them elsewhere. Early in 1945 the remaining officers were moved to a separate camp at Nakhon Nayok, but for the critical construction phase of the captivity they remained with their men and the Japanese chose to operate through their captives' military hierarchy for their railway-building and administrative tasks, though generally making their own choice of lieutenant-colonel to be in charge of each group of POWs. This inevitably led to management and command difficulties when junior lieutenant-co-lonels appointed by the Japanese had to get their seniors to accept their command decisions.[6] Nevertheless, the crude framework of order, control and administration which this arrangement made possible served to preserve the social cohesion of prisoner groups when the pressures upon them were intense. The second factor was the large number of medical staff among the prisoners. The Japanese had captured the bulk of the male military personnel of six military hospitals, twenty-two field ambulance units and three casualty clearing stations, as well as field hygiene specialists among the personnel of Malaya Command. Despite the shortage of both med-icines and medical equipment in the railway camps, the expertise and efforts

---

[6] The difficulties which this caused are illustrated in S. J. Flower, 'Captors and Captives on the Burma-Thailand Railway', in B. Moore and K. Fedorovich, eds, *Prisoners of War and their Captors in World War II* (Oxford, 1996), pp. 243–44.

of the medical staff, among whom were officers of outstanding character, proved a great life saver.

In late December 1941 the United States announced its intention to observe the Geneva Convention in regard to Japanese prisoners and requested Japan to do the same concerning Americans. Early in January 1942, Australia, Britain, Canada and New Zealand did likewise. Japan had signed the 1929 Geneva Convention but never ratified it, unlike other members of the Tripartite Pact, Germany and Italy. But Japan had ratified the accompanying convention on the treatment of sick and wounded and the earlier Hague Convention of 1907, whose general principles the Geneva Convention elaborated and extended.[7] On 29 January 1942 Japanese Foreign Minister Togo Shigenori declared that Japan would observe the main Geneva Conventions *mutatis mutandis* subject to reciprocity in the matter of national and racial customs regarding food and clothing.[8] These promises were repeated at the capitulation by the various Japanese commanders,[9] to whom orders for compliance with the Convention had been sent even before the Foreign Minister's communication to the Protecting Powers.[10] For example, as the 5th Division embarked for Malaya it received regulations explaining how POWs should be treated which read: 'The regulations governing the China theatre shall not apply [but instead] in accordance with international law.'[11] In the War Ministry in Tokyo a POW Information Bureau was established in December 1941 in apparent conformity with article 77 of the Convention. Lieutenant-General Mikio Uemura headed both this body and the POW Management Division, set up at the end of March 1942 to handle policy for the unexpectedly large number of prisoners already in Japanese hands.

Responsibility for the construction of the railway was shared between IJHQ in Tokyo and HQ Southern Army. After discussions in April 1942 in which General Tojo Hideki, Prime Minister and Minister for the Army, was himself involved, in June 1942 IJHQ in Tokyo authorised the project, the use of 50,000 POs as the labour force together with the initial contingent

---

[7] International Convention for the Amelioration of the Conditions of the Wounded and Sick in Armies in the Field 1929, ratified in Japan in 1934.

[8] Hisakazu Fujita, 'POWs and International Law'.

[9] For example, General Maruyama confirmed this in writing at the time of the Allied surrender in Java.

[10] Utsumi Aiko, 'Prisoners of War in the Pacific War: Japan's Policy', trans. G. McCormick, in G. McCormick and W. Nelson, eds, *The Burma-Thailand Railway* (St Leonards, New South Wales, 1993), p. 71.

[11] Ikuhito Hata, 'Japanese Military and Popular Perceptions of POWs', in Moore and Fedorovich, *Prisoners of War and Their Captors in World War II*, p. 264.

of 87,000 civilian *romusha* from Burma, set December 1943 as the completion date for the new line and 3000 tons daily in each direction as the freight load which the railway was to deliver.[12] The railway specialists in Southern Army, headed initially by General Shimoda, were responsible for the project's execution. Already on 22 May it had been announced that Korean *gunsoku* would guard the prisoners on this project and elsewhere in the Southern Region. The POW workforce was to be organised in six major groups, two operating at the Burma end and four in Thailand, with a separate engineer regiment directing the work in each country. (See Table 1).

By the time the first group of POWs were being moved north to the railway trace the general pattern of their treatment had been established. The gap between this and the requirements of the Geneva Convention was already very clear. Officers had been forced to remove their badges of rank; Japanese soldiers of whatever rank had to be saluted. Prisoners were executed for trying to escape, and under duress the Allied commanders had signed a declaration that their forces would not attempt to escape. Disciplinary infractions brought immediate physical punishment. For refusing to answer questions of a military nature Lieutenant-General Sir Lewis Heath, the commander of 3rd Indian Corps, had received a beating and Lieutenant-General A. E. Percival, the British GOC, spent sixteen days in solitary confinement, without food for the first two and a half days.[13] The troops were already working on a variety of tasks, some of them war-related, long before they began their journeys to Thailand and Burma. The diet was also proving inadequate; men were losing weight and many were beginning to suffer from a variety of tropical diseases. As early as April 1942, of the 1000 POWs in Pudu Jail, Kuala Lumpur, 300 were suffering from beriberi and the supply of quinine to suppress malaria was irregular and insufficient. The totally unprotected situation of the POWs, so far as international law is concerned, was exemplified by the armband required to be worn by some of the camp administrative staff which bore the inscription, 'One captured in battle is to be beheaded and castrated at the will of the Emperor', and by the remark of Lieutenant Okasaka to a POW officer, 'The Japanese Army does not like to put to death prisoners, but unless you obey our orders you will be put to death'. As one studies the ninety-seven articles of the Geneva Convention, seventy-three of which dealt directly with the treatment of prisoners, it is difficult to find more than one which the Japanese railway

---

[12] Burma-Thailand Railway Construction Order No. 1, dated 7 June 1942; Aiko Utsumi, 'The Korean Guards on the Burma-Thailand Railway', trans. G. McCormick, in McCormick and Nelson, *The Burma-Thailand Railway*, p. 130.

[13] A. E. Percival, *The War in Malaya* (London, 1949).

Table 1

### Burma-Thailand Railway Organisation
### IGHQ Tokyo
### HQ Southern Army
### No. 2 Railway Supervision Section
### Major-Generals Shimoda/Takasaki/Ishida

| Engineer Organisation | POW Administration |
| --- | --- |
| Burma Side | Thai POW Camps |
| 5 Railway Regiment | Burma Side |
| Lieutenant-Colonel Sasaki | No. 3 Group.  Colonel Nagatomo |
|  | (9000 POWs) |
|  |  |
| Thailand Side |  |
| 9 Railway Regiment | No. 5 Group. |
| Lieutenant-Colonel Imai | Captain Mizutani (2000 POWs) |
| Railway Materials Workshop |  |
|  | Thailand Side [1] |
|  | No. 1 Group. Major Chida (7200 POWs) |
| *Romusha* (Forced Labour Administered | No. 2 Group. Colonel Yanagida |
| by railway Regiments) | (9600 POWs) |
| Burma 'Sweat Army' July 1942 to | No. 4 Group. Lieutenant-Colonel Ishii |
| January 1943 87,000[1] | (11,200 POWs) |
|  | No. 6 Group. Major Ebiko (6000 POWs) |
| Reinforcements for Engineer and | Replacements from POW Camps Malaya |
| *Romusha* Organisations |  |
| Special Bridging Unit, March 1943 |  |
| Captain Murahashi | F Force. Colonel Banno |
|  | April 1943 (7000 POWs) |
| 4th (Guards) Engineer Regiment | H Force. Captain Hachizuka |
| Captain Murayama | May 1943 (3700 POWs) |
| Burma Labour Service Corps (*Romusha*), |  |
| March 1943 to August 1944, 91,386 [2] |  |
| Malayan *Romusha* April 1943 to |  |
| September 1943, 70,000 |  |
| Other *Romusha* and technical workers |  |
| August 1943 to August 1945, 21,112 [3] |  |
| K Force (POW Medical Unit) for *Romusha* force, June 1943, 230 POWs | |
| L Force (POW Medical Unit) for *Romusha* force, August 1943, 115 POWs | |

authorities did not at some time flout, many regularly. The exception was article 76, concerning the honourable burial of dead prisoners, which seems to have been permitted in all but the worst camps and the most difficult conditions.

The Japanese plan appears to have been to assemble the resources for their railway during the monsoon of 1942 and begin the serious work on the track once the rains had abated in November. Parties of POWs, in labour gangs of between five and six hundred and with a limited number of officers allowed in each, were moved north to the Thailand and Burma ends of the project from June onwards and in increasing numbers in October and early November 1942, when rice trucks crammed with POWs were leaving Singapore station on an almost daily basis. From the railhead at Ban Pong the workers had to march to their appointed positions along the trace, often build their own bamboo and atap huts and start work on the track. The procedure was simple. The engineers responsible for each section of the track would determine the work schedule for the day and the number of POWs required. The camp authorities would supply the workforce and when the work quota had been completed they would be allowed back to camp. This system worked reasonably well in the easier sections at each end of the line, though with many falling sick. As the trace moved inland the conditions worsened and the work became more arduous, just as the POWs were being debilitated by virtue of their inadequate diet and more of them were seriously ill. There were major bridging tasks to be completed for the crossing of the Mac Khlong river and beyond it huge viaducts to be erected and cuttings to be excavated, all with the most basic of equipment and by the human wave methods later to be associated with Communist China's so-called 'Great Leap Forward'. Before long it was not unusual for the numbers of prisoners sick to exceed those fit to work, and of course prisoners were dying.

In February 1943, in the face of a worsening strategic situation, the Japanese

---

[1] Figures in this section are given for comparative purposes only and do not include roughly 6000 early 1943 POW reinforcements whose distribution between groups is uncertain. Total POW strength on the railway was about 62,000. Figures based on Nelson, *The Story of Changi*, tables 3 and 4: SEATIC, bulletin no. 246; Utsumi, 'The Korean Guards', p. 130.

[2] SEATIC, bulletin no. 246 based on figures supplied by U Aung Min, Deputy Director of Labour in the Japanese-sponsored Burmese government.

[3] SEATIC, bulletin no. 246 based on records of the Labour Department HQ 4th (Japanese) Railway Corps.

made plans to shorten the construction period by four months.[14] Large numbers of additional *romusha* were procured in Burma, Malaya and Java; thousands of additional prisoners were brought up to the railway and further engineer troops were allocated to the project. The period of rushed construction, known locally as the 'speedo', which saw twenty-four hour working in shifts at some of the sites at the height of the monsoon, caused the death rate to rise alarmingly, particularly when cholera broke out in many of the camps. Huge numbers were sick: in Songkurai Camp in late July 1943 the figure was 1050 out of a camp strength of 1300. But the workers were driven relentlessly by the guards and increasingly by the engineers. Ultimately the line was completed on 17 October 1943. The human cost was very great: over 12,000 of the railway prisoners died,[15] and a much larger number of civilian labourers, perhaps as many as 90,000.[16] The worst death rates among the prisoners were suffered by the final reinforcements, F and H Forces, which left Singapore in April and May 1943, F Force being destined for the worst section of the line near the Burma border. These forces, which were administered separately from the remainder, were the only ones for which detailed medical statistics are available. F Force left Changi 7000 strong; by the end of August 25 per cent were dead and 90 per cent of the remainder sick. By December 40 per cent were dead. In April of the following year, when the remains of the force were back in Singapore, the death total had reached over 44 per cent. The survivors were in such a state of sickness and total debilitation as profoundly to shock the prisoners who remained in Changi. Many of the POWs suffered psychological damage which endured long after their physical sickness had been treated and they had been restored to apparent health.

Before an attempt is made to account for this human tragedy and the fundamental breach of the international conventions which it represented,

---

[14] IGHQ Tokyo had wanted an even earlier completion date, May 1943, but the railway authorities argued against it and the end of August 1943 became the target date. Yoshihiko Futonatsu, *Across the Three Pagodas Pass* (Tokyo,1985), trans. C. E. Escritt, IWM, p. 226.

[15] The breakdown of deaths among the national contingents was as follows: British 6318, Australian 2816, Dutch 2490, US 337 with a further 559 'unknown'. The final total may have been greater.

[16] This could well be an underestimate; one source speaks of one lakh (100,000) Malayan Indian deaths alone. See C. S. R. Sastri, *To Malaya* (Tenali, 1947). The *romusha* were buried in mass graves and during the cholera epidemic their bodies were burned. A mass grave was discovered as recently as 1990. The families of many Tamil *romusha*, who travelled with them to the railway, also died, but are probably not recorded. Death rates among children were very high. Captain W. B. Young, RAMC, 'Report to the Colonial Office', Benson Papers, IWM, p. 1. See also C. Kinvig, *River Kwai Railway* (London, 1992), pp. 199–202.

it needs first to be put into context. The treatment of prisoners on the railway was neither the worst nor the least severe in the POW camps in South-East Asia. Indeed, despite the railway episode's subsequent notoriety, its prisoner death rate at roughly 20 per cent was less than that in Japanese camps overall, where it averaged 27 per cent.[17] Its worst statistic, the 60 per cent death rate in the British contingent of F Force, was put in the shade by the fate of 2500 British and Australians imprisoned in the Sandakan area of North Borneo in late 1944 of whom only six survived, and that of Gull Force, a battalion group captured on Ambon in late 1942, whose members were starved and ill-treated to a degree experienced by few elsewhere: their death rate was 77 per cent.[18] On the other hand the 1000 men held captive on Blakang Mati island off the southern coast of Singapore, suffered only four deaths in their entire captivity. By contrast with these statistics from the Far Eastern Theatre, the Australian, American and British death rates as prisoners of the Germans in this war were 2, 3 and 5 percent respectively. What gave the railway experience its particularly gruesome place in western POW annals was that the scale of death and suffering was shared with so many thousands of *romusha*.

In failing to ratify the Geneva Convention after its signature in 1929, and then declaring in 1942 that it would observe its forms *mutatis mutandis*, it is clear that Japan had some difficulties of principle with its application. Perhaps the first concerned the unilateral advantage which the Convention tended to confer on its opponents. In the earlier wars against China and Russia the ratio of enemy to Japanese prisoners had been fifteen to one and forty to one respectively and the 80,000 Russian prisoners from the latter conflict had been treated particularly humanely. But, as General Uemura was later to explain, 'we gave them excellent treatment in order to gain recognition as a civilised country'. This purpose no longer applied in the changed circumstances of 1942.[19] Prime Minister and Minister for the Army Tojo confirmed this (and his customary hard line on the subject) in declaring, 'Where the Japanese troops are facing hardships ... there is no need to pamper [the] POWs'. Consequently Uemura laid down two simple principles: within the limits prescribed by humanity enemy POWs must be treated severely and they must be used to expand production. For the Japanese Ministry of the Army *mutatis mutandis* was interpreted not

[17] The national death percentages overall were: Australia 34 per cent, Canada 16 per cent, UK 25 per cent, New Zealand 26 per cent, USA 33 per cent, Dutch 23 per cent. R. J. Pritchard and S. Zaide eds, *The Tokyo War Crimes Trials* (London, 1981), xvi, pp. 40, 537.

[18] L. Wigmore, *The Japanese Thrust*, Australian War Memorial (Canberra, 1957), pp. 604, 608.

[19] Ikuhiko Hata, 'Japanese Military and Popular Perceptions of POWs', pp. 263–66.

as western jurists would understand the term but to the effect that 'we shall apply it with any necessary amendments: not that we shall apply it strictly'.[20]

This determination was reinforced both centrally in Tokyo and locally in Burma and Thailand by powerful customary attitudes among the Japanese military towards the notion of surrender which could not but encourage a harsh interpretation of Uemura's instructions. Contrasting with the treatment of the Russian POWs taken by the Japanese during the Russo-Japanese War had been the very mixed reception accorded to the 2000 Japanese POWs who returned at its conclusion. Official courts of enquiry were held and punishments imposed over a wide spectrum. By the Nomonhan Incident of 1939 attitudes had hardened to the point where all the Japanese officers who had been returned after capture were forced to commit suicide. The other ranks received punishments according to the circumstances of their capture and, having served their sentences, were made to reside outside Japan. By the outbreak of the Pacific War these attitudes had strengthened further and found expression in the *Senjinkun* or Field Army Service Code of January 1941: 'You shall not undergo the shame of being taken alive. You shall not bequeath a sullied name'. It was death rather than surrender which should be faced when the Japanese soldier's fighting efforts were exhausted: 'After exerting all your powers, spiritually and physically, calmly face death rejoicing in the eternal cause for which you strive'.[21] The 'no surrender' provision was never extended to the navy, nor was it ever clearly embodied in the Army Criminal Code, but its influence was powerful and pervasive. Although roughly 150,000 Japanese were to be killed in Burma, only 1700 were taken prisoner, of whom only 400 could be described as physically fit. No regular officer was captured and none above the rank of major. For the first week of captivity all tried to commit suicide.[22] Yoshihiko Futamatsu, a civilian engineer *gunzoku* attached to Colonel Imai's 9th Railway regiment, recognised that, 'all soldiers believe that to become a prisoner of war is a most shameful thing, and so in the opinion of Japanese generally the real truth is that to be a prisoner of war is to put oneself beyond the pale'.[23] Many Japanese civilians in the 'Southern Regions' considered themselves bound by this

---

[20] Ibid.

[21] The Field Army Service Code was reprinted in the *Tokyo Gazette* in April 1941.

[22] General Slim at the RIIA discussion group in September 1948, cited in L. Allen, *Burma: The Longest War* (London, 1984), p. 611.

[23] Yoshihiko Futamatsu, *Account of the Construction of the Thai-Burma Railway* (1954) trans. C. E. Escritt, IWM, p. 2.

code, as the mass suicides at Saipan bear witness. The contradiction in attempting to apply quite different norms to enemy captives was profound.

If these powerful factors affecting the treatment of the prisoners are put in the context of the importance of the railway project for Japan's strategic ambitions, it becomes clear that the project would be driven to a conclusion whatever its cost to the military labour force. The fate of many prisoners was thus effectively determined in advance. As one senior staff officer explained it to Colonel Shoichi Yanagida, commanding Number Two Group, so long as the railway was completed 'it does not matter if all the prisoners collapse in the process'.[24] Racial attitudes, strong on both sides during the Pacific War, reinforced this likelihood. The Allies regarded themselves and their civilisation as superior to the Asian races and theirs. Western propaganda saw the Allies as fighting not a Japanese equivalent of Hitler and his Nazi Party but the entire Japanese race. It was a recrudescence of the Yellow Peril scare of the end of the previous century. There is strong evidence that even President Roosevelt seriously entertained the bizarre notion that Japanese 'nefariousness' sprang from a skull pattern that was less developed than that of the Caucasians.[25] For their part, the Japanese were stung by such slights as the US anti-immigration laws and the rejection of the racial equality clause in the League of Nations Covenant. The new conflict offered an opportunity to put matters to rights. 'The present war is a struggle between races', a Japanese military orientation pamphlet declared, 'and we must achieve the satisfaction of our just demands with no thought of leniency to Europeans.'[26] There was consequently a deliberate policy of humiliating the Europeans, of using them 'for an intellectual propaganda exercise aimed at stamping out the respect for the Europeans and Americans' which had been widespread in the territories which the Japanese had now conquered.[27] 'We shall use the POWs to make the native peoples realise the superiority of the Japanese Race', General Uemura announced at a conference in June 1942.[28] One Japanese academic, who had himself tasted British captivity after Japan's formal surrender in 1945, writing seventeen

[24] Shoichi Yanagida, 'Taimen tetsudo kensetu no jisso to senpan saiban', mimeograph 1954, quoted in Ursumi, 'Prisoners of War', in McCormick and Nelson, *The Burma-Thailand Railway*, p. 81.

[25] He appears to have been encouraged in this belief by none less than the Curator of the Division of Physical Anthropology of the Simthsonian Institute. C. Thorne, *Racial Aspects of the Far Eastern War of 1941–45* (London, 1980).

[26] Masanobu Tsuji, *Singapore: The Japanese Version* (London, 1966), p. 246.

[27] 'Kyokuto Gunji Saiban Sokkiroku', no. 146, quoted in Utsumi, 'Prisoners of War', p. 73.

[28] Ikuhiko Hata, 'Japanese Military and Popular Perceptions of POWs', p. 266.

years after the war's end, added an opinion which was as bizarre in its way as Roosevelt's when he advanced the view that it was the Japanese lack of experience with large-scale animal husbandry which accounted for their managing their POWs so badly.[29] Against such a background of racial attitudes, military culture and strategic policy, the obligations of the Geneva Convention had little chance of prevailing, even to the extent that Tokyo proposed to meet them.

There were also strong local features which exacerbated the inevitable human disaster, the generally poor quality of the Japanese POW adminis- tration being prominent among them. Armies seldom allocate their best people to this sort of work and, given the manpower difficulties Japan was already experiencing, it is not surprising that the railway prisoners found themselves controlled by what one of their senior officers called the 'dregs of the army system'. There were notable exceptions among both the Japanese administrators and the Korean *gunzoku* and, of course, individual person- ality, experience and situation moderated the way in which these general influences applied.[30] General Slim's characterisation of the Japanese as the 'most formidable fighting insect in history',[31] implying that each individual soldier was activated, as it were, solely by the same imperial pheromone, was an unfortunate dehumanising analogy. Such racial stereotypes of the Japanese applied even less to the rear areas away from the battlefield, but the general factors noted above no doubt had a powerful effect.

Among the Japanese Group Commanders were men too old to manage affairs competently, too weak to cope with the rigours of the local situation or to dominate strong subordinates and only intermittently engaged about the welfare of their prisoner charges. They occasionally intervened to remedy the worst excesses, but when they inspected the POW camps the guards were often able to conceal the worst conditions and the true situation. Colonel Banno, the commander of F Force, which suffered the greatest trials of the railway experience, was a particular example, failing to restrain not only the excesses but the sheer incompetence of his subordinates. One POW commander quotes the case of a Japanese cadet officer (subsequently promoted), the subject of repeated complaints, 'who appeared to us to be mentally deficient', but whom Banno did nothing to restrain.[32] However, it was the individual camp commanders, the Japanese junior officers and

[29] Yuji Aida, *Prisoner of the British* (London, 1966), pp. 45–46.

[30] See S. J. Flower, 'Captor and Captives on the Burma-Thailand Railway', pp. 236–38, for some character sketches.

[31] Slim, *Defeat into Victory*, p. 381.

[32] S. W. Harris, 'History of F Force', IWM, p. 54.

NCOs with whom the POWs' senior officers had to deal on a daily basis. These were men whose military attitudes had, in many cases, been formed in the brutal and often irregular anti-guerrilla campaigning in the China War. Experiences there were more likely to have influenced their behaviour than any consideration of international law about which, like their subordinates, they had received no training. Within the limits of their discretion some camp commanders behaved with humanity and restraint: Sergeant-Major Saito at Tamarkan Camp was hard but fair; the middle-aged, Englishspeaking Lieutenant Hattori of Wampo was sympathetic, helpful and in control of his subordinates; even in the appallingly treated F Force its POW commander was able to speak well of Lieutenant Wakabayashi, who listened to the POWs' grievances and did his best to improve their conditions.[33] His approach contrasted with the brutal and toilsome regime of Lieutenant Fukuda in a neighbouring border camp. Other guards were as corrupt and venal as they were harsh.

The force of Korean *gunzoku* was the group with which the POWs had most regular daily contact and its members were generally feared and detested by them. The Koreans were technically volunteers but often chose this work, for which there was in any case a district quota, in order to avoid other forms of military service. They had been given only a short period of military training in which corporal punishment played its authorised and regular part, but no specific instruction for their actual task of guarding and supervising prisoners. 'Every day we were beaten a few times, and after two months' training we were sent to South-East Asia', was how one summarised his preparation.[34] The Koreans were little respected by the Japanese and appeared not unwilling to displace their own frustration and sense of inferiority on the hapless prisoners. There were those among them who attempted to help and even befriend the prisoners (a practice which became notably more common when the war had turned against the Japanese), but the evidence of their cruelty is too widespread for their reputation as the POWs' worst tormentors to be redeemed. In the relatively isolated circumstances of the railway camps, where they had total power over their captives with little supervision, they were easy prey to the corruption which proverbially results. One POW commander reported that the Korean guards 'received written instructions, which were posted in their Guard Rooms that they had supreme powers while they were on duty and

[33] Ibid.
[34] Yi Hak-Nae, ' The Man Between: A Korean Guard Looks Back', in McCormack and Nelson, *The Burma-Thailand Railway*, p. 121; Saburo Ienaga, *Japan's Last War* (Oxford, 1979), pp. 156–59.

were entitled to kill us without reference to anyone else'.[35] Throughout the guard force great responsibility was exercised at very low levels. Simple administrative decisions taken by very junior ranks could have life-and-death consequences for the labourers. A POW group several thousand strong would be dispersed over a series of isolated camps, some without even an officer in charge. At one stage in No. 2 Group, one Japanese NCO and four or five Korean guards had the task of moving 1200 men through the jungle to their next camp. Eminently sensible suggestions made by experienced officers or doctors among the prisoners would be brushed aside for no better reason than that the POWs had made them. The guards' self-esteem and their wish not to lose 'face' inevitably played their part.

The Japanese engineers were a separate, professional group and had little in common with the guard force. Having two organisations concerned with the same project was a recipe for trouble. Disputes between guards and engineers broke out increasingly as the debilitation of the POWs coincided with the growing importance of the project's speedy completion and the difficulties of the monsoon. Engineers would believe that the camp staff were taking the side of the POWs in disputes over the number of labourers who could be supplied, conduct their own inspections of the sick and administer their own punishments. F Force was particularly prey to their intervention as it marched north to the border camps. Groups would be summarily detached by the engineers along the way to help with sections of the line where the work had fallen behind schedule or where it was proving particularly difficult. Some prisoners averred that they were treated worse by the engineers, for all their superior education and training, during the 'speedo' phase than by their own guards. Nor was it only the junior engineers about whom this opinion was held. At one point the lieutenant-colonel commanding the engineer regiment at Songkrai threatened to turn all the prisoners, sick and fit, out into the jungle to fend for themselves, making way for fit *romusha*, unless the work-force was doubled. This was at the height of the monsoon. One group of twenty POWs were taken off the line of march by engineers and set to pile-driving in a river from first light until 10 p.m., up to their armpits in water. They did this for a fortnight before representations finally put an end to the work. All subsequently died.[36]

Two further factors made the position of the railway prisoners infinitely worse. First was the obsessive secrecy of the Japanese about the destination

[35] Report by Lieutenant-Colonel P. J. D. Toosey, appendix D, 'Behaviour of Japanese Guards', p. 1, IWM.
[36] Harris, 'History of F Force', pp. 49 and 56.

of the POW parties which left Singapore for the railway. Perhaps this was because of the line's strategic importance for them, and of their sensitivity over the extent to which international obligations were being flouted by the use of POWs to build it. It may have been merely to facilitate the compliance of their charges. All the POWs were told something to the effect that they were being moved to an area where food was more plentiful and the climate healthier than in Singapore. The consequences were deleterious for all groups but for none more than F Force, whose leaders were told that sick men might be included in the party: over two thousand were. This misinformation virtually guaranteed the death of many of them and of course did little to speed the railway's construction.

Despite the first-class fighting characteristics of the individual Japanese soldier, the Japanese army as a whole was judged to be 'fifth class in its administration', and different elements of their forces, on the battlefield and off it, seemed very poor at cooperating with each other.[37] This exacerbated the problems for F and H Forces since they remained under the control of the Malayan POW authorities rather than the Thai authorities who controlled the up-country areas for which they were bound. The arrangements for their move were particularly poor and reminiscent in their effects of those on the Bataan march to Camp O'Donnell. In the view of its British commander, the Japanese administration of F Force 'attained a standard of inefficiency which is almost beyond description'. He wrote of the evacuation of 1700 sick men to a Burma hospital as following 'the normal Japanese administrative mess'.[38] Similar administrative failings were reported by H Force. Other misinformation retailed to the POWs seems at first quite inexplicable, but may perhaps be accounted for by this lack of cooperation between different elements and the lack of awareness by the Singapore authorities of the true situation of the up-river camps. K and L Forces were two emergency medical teams of prisoners put together by the Japanese authorities to bring some relief to the Asian *romusha* who were dying in their hundreds. They were told not to take medical equipment with them since they would find well-equipped hospitals at their destinations. Of course there were none and many medical staff found themselves

---

[37] The view is Slim's, but most railway POWs would have agreed. Slim's full evaluation reads as follows: 'The Japanese Army was in many ways a second class army. It was second class in the mental capacity of its leaders and its staff work; fifth class in its administration, and second class again in a great deal of its equipment. In fact but for one thing, the Japanese Army would have been a completely second class army, somewhere below the Italians. But that one thing made all the difference — it was the individual Japanese soldier'. Address to the Royal Empire Society, 6 February 1946.

[38] Harris, 'History of F Force', pp. 54–55.

frequently occupied not in treating patients but in basic labouring tasks. They too were under the Malayan rather than the Thai IJA administration. As one of their commanders recorded, 'there was no liaison between them, and the one would give the other no help in any way'.

Concerning the prisoners' food and medical supplies, the point is often made that in the monsoon conditions supplies could not be got forward to the distant camps near the Burma-Thai border. This was perhaps true for one short period at the height of the monsoon, but for the rest of the time it was not. The Japanese themselves seldom went short and the prisoners' rice ration in the worst phase was one fifth of the Japanese. The under-nourishment was made worse by the practice of putting sick men who were unfit to work on half rations and without pay, as a means, one supposes, of encouraging them back to health. That sickness signified mental frailty seemed a prevalent Japanese military belief. 'There is nothing to be more regretted than to fall victim to disease in the field', declared the Service Code. Not to do so, however, in this notoriously unhealthy region was difficult. Writing of the Burma theatre as a whole, the British campaign medical history declared that 'there were very few other theatres on earth in which an army would encounter so many and such violent hazards. In Burma all the dread agents of fell disease and foul death lay in wait'.[39] In the same year as the railway was completed, 14th Army in Burma suffered 120 soldiers evacuated sick for each man evacuated with wounds.

By normal standards the prisoners' camps were well supplied with medical officers, but these faced a Herculean task. They often found their professional advice on the most routine health and medical matters countermanded by junior Japanese guards. The doctors were chronically short of medicines and medical equipment, although the Japanese dispensaries seemed to be reasonably stocked with the former. One explanation, though hardly a sufficient one, is that in some camps the guards were trading in medicines, as they were in the canteen items which the prisoners were able to purchase to supplement their diet. Quinine in particular, of which the Japanese had captured the major world supply, proved a very tradeable commodity.[40] When the surrender finally came, large stocks of medicines and Red Cross parcels previously withheld suddenly became available to the prisoners: 'any amount of atebrin, iron, vitamins, in fact everything we need. Why on earth could they not have let us have them at once?', wrote one exasperated

[39] F. A. E. Crew, *History of the Second World War: The Army Medical Services Campaigns* (London, 1966), v, p. 22.

[40] Siamese prostitutes were often paid for their services in quinine rather than cash. Young, 'Report to the Colonial Office', p. 7.

medical officer at Tamuang, where 35,000 ticals of withheld Red Cross money were handed over.[41]

The prisoners' commanding officers, besides managing the organisational structure which sustained the camps, provided two other services for their men. They stood between them and the demands of the Japanese and the methods by which these were enforced, treading the narrow path between cooperation and collaboration, and suffering endless humiliations in the process as they attempted to protect the sick and defend the workers against brutality. Lieutenant-Colonel Toosey at Tamarkan adopted a policy of complaining formally to the Japanese authorities at every beating that took place and believed that this tactic finally reduced the occurrence of such incidents. Many became expert at negotiation; others tried a range of different approaches, 'varying from a "firm stand" to trading one's cigarette case or fountain pen, or giving English lessons to Korean guards – all with the same end in view and with regrettably little result'. Quoting the international conventions to the Japanese authorities often brought the response that, since Japan would win the war, the conventions did not matter.[42]

The troops also benefited from the fact that, after a delay of several months, officer POWs were paid by the Japanese in apparent conformity with the Geneva Convention,[43] while the other ranks were paid only if they worked and then at a mere pittance. The agreement that officers should subscribe part of their pay to supplement the other ranks' messing and purchase of medical supplies was a genuine life saver. Some officers thought the subscription was 'a rather niggardly contribution' and wished to see it raised, others objected to paying it at all; but, although the pattern and level of payment varied between groups and individual camps, there was fairly general agreement on these contributions. Given the large numbers of officers involved and the additional beneficial canteen-running possibilities which bulk-buying created, the system made an important contribution to the survival of the labour force.

Some, though relatively few, of the railway prisoners were killed directly by the Japanese, summarily executed or beaten to death. Quite a number were tortured by the *Kempeitai* and some were so severely physically punished

---

[41]  R. Hardie, *The Burma-Siam Railway,* IWM (London, 1983), p. 176.

[42]  Toosey, 'Behaviour of Japanese Guards' p. 1; Harris, 'History of F Force', p. 54; 'Report by Captain T. Wilson RAMC', Benson papers, IWM.

[43]  Article 23 requiring such payment, stipulated that 'no deductions therefrom shall be made for expenditure devolving upon the detaining power'. But the Japanese authorities made deductions for food, accommodation and clothing and banked a separate amount for repayment after the war. Thus the officers received only a small proportion of their entitlement.

that their deaths were inevitably hastened. The railway was also the setting for some despicable atrocities perpetrated on the *romusha*: death by lethal injection or the deliberate withholding of water (both in a hospital setting), torture and mutilation.[44] Most POWs died from tropical discases: dysentery, cholera, beriberi, tropical ulcers and malaria, often from a combination of them. They died because they were already weakened by serious under-nourishment and because they were forced to work in this debilitated condition and while sick. They died because they were denied the drugs which might easily have kept them alive. Despite its fearsome reputation, cholera is relatively easy to treat providing it is caught early and reasonable facilities are available. Disease, undernourishment and sickness were all factors over which the Japanese authorities had a large measure of control and for the consequences of them they must bear the responsibility. What characterised their attitude most of all, aside from the unwavering determin-ation to ensure that the railway was completed, was sheer neglect and passive cruelty.

The largely military-cultural explanation sketched out above for the neglect and ill-treatment of the railway labour force applied, of course, only to the military prisoners. It is not a purpose of this essay to attempt to offer any explanation for the Japanese military authorities' treatment of the *romusha*. They seemed simply caught up in the vortex of military extremism which not only belied completely another injunction of the *Senjinkun*: 'Be gentle to and protect innocent inhabitants in a spirit of benevolence in accordance with the true ideal of the Imperial Army', but also negated Japan's larger political purposes for its Greater East Asia Co-Prosperity Sphere. The treatment of both groups served ultimately to vitiate the main purpose of their employment, the building of the rail-way itself. Although the Japanese engineers were very proud of their achievement (and a remarkable achievement it was), which their surviving veterans still celebrate today, the fact remains that the line was not com-pleted until after Tokyo's deadline had expired, that at no stage did it carry the planned tonnage, neither the initial 3000 tons nor the later reduction to 1000 tons.[45] Journeys along the railway were generally slow and the early ones in particular were marked by derailments and embankment collapses. By the time of its completion the Allied air forces were in a position to bomb both the new line itself and the more distant systems

[44] Young, 'Report to the Colonial Office', p. 2. J. F. N. Clarkson, 'Atrocities', p. 2, Benson Papers, IWM.

[45] The tonnage figures as compiled by 9 Railway regiment are given in SEATIC, Bulletin no. 246 appendix G, table 2.

which it was designed to connect. As Colonel Kurahashi, the logistics officer of Burma Area Army noted, 'Shipment over the Burma-Thailand Railroad did not meet with any degree of success'.[46] It was unable to deliver the one-third of the combat supplies for the Burma Area Army's 1944 offensive that had been assigned to it. According to Lieutenant-General Takaze Numata, Chief of Staff to Southern Army, this failure was attributable not so much to Allied bombing as to the condition of the new railway, 'the efficiency of which was marred by the defect in the hurried original construction'.[47] In Burma, the war theatre which the railway was designed to supply, the Japanese suffered their greatest defeats on land of the entire war.

What has proved most enduring about the Burma-Thailand Railway is not the structure itself, and the achievement which it represented, but rather the facts of the human cost which it entailed. These are etched on the memory of the dwindling band of surviving prisoners and preserved for posterity in the written record in one of the most substantial, if not perhaps the most scholarly, bodies of literature to record war experience. Books about the railway, generally personal reminiscences, have appeared in English regularly every year since 1946 and there has been little tailing off in the publication rate as the years have gone by. Twenty-four books about the railway were published in Australia, for example, between 1980 and 1989, five in 1988 alone. As recently as 1995 one personal memoir became a British best-seller.[48] Numerous documentary films have supplemented the written record which has also formed the basis on which popular imaginative writing of which Pierre Boulle's *The British on the River Kwai*, however misleading its interpretation, is probably the most celebrated. It seems clear that the human tragedy of the railway experience will not fade away; indeed it is an aspect of Japan's 'dark valley' which deserves to be more widely acknowledged, researched and explained.

---

[46] Kurahashi Takeo, 'Burma Operations Record: Outline of Burma Area Line of Communications' (Japanese Monograph, no. 133), HQ Armed Forces Far East February 1952, p. 15.

[47] SEATIC, historical bulletin 242 (Singapore, 1946), p. 33, IWM.

[48] E. Lomax, *The Railway Man* (London, 1995).

# 4

## *Understanding the Enemy: Military Intelligence, Political Warfare and Japanese Prisoners of War in Australia, 1942–45*

### Kent Fedorowich

Japanese soldiers appear to be taught that to be taken prisoner is an everlasting disgrace. This is borne out by the fact that prisoners do not desire to write home as they say their families would be disgraced if it became known that members of them were prisoners of war. More than that several have stated that they can never return to Japan.[1]

The onset of the Pacific War in December 1941, and the subsequent collapse of European and American imperial authority in East Asia and the western Pacific, forced the Allied nations to reassess dramatically the fighting capabilities of their Japanese opponents. Racial bigotry and the cultural stereotyping of Asians by Europeans, which had been prevalent for several centuries, acquired a ferocity with the spread of Social Darwinist thought and Anglo-Saxon race patriotism between 1860 and 1914. In spite of the enormous strides to modernise and industrialise made by Japan under Emperor Meiji (1868–1912), and the impressive feats demonstrated by Japanese military forces during the relief of Peking in 1900 and more convincingly against the Russians during the Russo-Japanese war of 1904–5, increasingly discriminatory and restrictive immigration policies were enacted by many western governments, especially those of the British dominions. These exclusionist policies, aimed as they were to preserve the Anglo-Saxon character of these white settler societies, were a constant irritant in the

[1] New Zealand National Archives (hereafter NANZ), Navy Department 1, 8/7, Lieutenant-General Sir Edward Puttick, Chief of General Staff and General Officer Commanding New Zealand Military Forces, to the Naval Secretary, Wellington, 21 October 1942. I would like to thank the Australian Army and the Faculty of Humanities Research Committee at the University of the West of England for grants-in-aid of research which facilitated work on this project in 1997. Versions of this essay were given at conferences and seminars held at the Universities of Cambridge, Auckland and London. My thanks to Bob Moore of Manchester Metropolitan University and Martin Thomas, UWE, for reading earlier drafts.

external relations between Britain and Japan prior to the First World War.[2] Attitudes and policies did not change with the onset of war in 1914 or immediately after the Armistice in 1918, even though Japan had been a trusted ally. Rather, Anglo-Saxon race prejudice intensified during the inter-war period as the western powers became more fearful of Japan's increasingly restive military power and inexorable national ambitions.

This was particularly evident in Australia, where politicians repeatedly exploited deep-seated fears concerning the 'Yellow Peril'. Japan's quest for equal status amongst the western nations alarmed many Australians who firmly believed that, if left unchecked, Japanese expansion would eventually subsume the white enclaves in Australasia. Japan's mushrooming population, and its demand for greater access to world markets and raw materials, posed a serious threat to the future well-being of the dominion, argued leading xenophobes such as Australia's wartime Prime Minister, W. M. Hughes. As a result, these long-standing fears – which had already been translated into a series of racially discriminatory immigration laws, better known as the 'White Australia' policy – became important stimulants in Australia's desire to safeguard her Anglo-Saxon heritage.[3] Indeed, the pursuit of such a racially blinkered policy meant Australian (and western) perceptions of Japan's ability to wage a war against a materially and technologically superior opponent were dangerously clouded by bigotry and cultural stereotyping.[4]

The swiftness of the Japanese advance in Malaya, Burma and the Dutch East Indies, coupled with Japan's proficient consolidation of power in the south and central Pacific during the first six months of 1942, stung the western Allies into action. One essential task which they had to tackle

---

[2] Robert A. Huttenback, *Racism and Empire: White Settlers and Coloured Immigrants in the British Self-Governing Colonies, 1830–1910* (Ithaca, 1976); Avner Offer, *The First World War: An Agrarian Interpretation* (Oxford, 1989), pp. 164–214.

[3] Henry P. Frei, *Japan's Southward Advance and Australia* (Honolulu, 1991), pp. 65–128; Neville Meaney, *Fears and Phobias: E. L. Piesse and the Problem of Japan, 1909–39* (Canberra, 1996); Sean Brawley, *The White Peril: Foreign Relations and Asian Immigration to Australasia and North America, 1919–78* (Sydney, 1995).

[4] John Ferris, 'Worthy of Some Better Enemy? The British Estimate of the Imperial Japanese Army, 1919–1941, and the Fall of Singapore', *Canadian Journal of History*, 28 (1993), pp. 223–56; Antony Best, 'Constructing an Image: British Intelligence and Whitehall's Perception of Japan, 1931–1939', *Intelligence and National Security*, 11 (1996), pp. 403–23; idem, '"This Probably Over-Valued Military Power": British Intelligence and Whitehall's Perception of Japan, 1939–1941', *Intelligence and National Security*, 12 (1997), pp. 67–94; Richard J. Aldrich, 'Britain's Secret Intelligence Service in Asia during the Second World War', *Modern Asian Studies*, 32 (1998), pp. 179–217.

immediately was to reassess Japanese military prowess. In particular, this demanded a balanced evaluation of the qualities, abilities, motivation and mind-set of Japanese servicemen. As the Pacific war progressed, the formulation of cultural, social, political and psychological profiles of their Asian enemy became important tools for Allied military strategists and field commanders confronted by a determined foe. The same was true of Australian political analysts and propagandists who, under the auspices of the Allied Political Warfare Committee (established in January 1943), conducted their own campaign against Japanese civilians in the Home Islands. But how was this information gathered, processed and acted upon? One key source was information extracted from the 19,500 Japanese servicemen captured by Australian and United States forces in the South-West Pacific Area (SWPA) between 1942 and 1945.[5]

This essay focuses on the all-important work of the Australian branch of the Allied Translator and Interpreter Section (ATIS), which was established in mid September 1942. It examines the interrogation methods used by Allied intelligence officers; and the type and quality of information derived from the Japanese prisoners of war (POWs). What, for instance, did the Australians discover about the Japanese soldier? What bearing did this information have on the future conduct of Australian propaganda and psychological warfare operations; and how was this information shared, disseminated and employed by the Allies between 1942 and 1945 at both military and political levels?

Of crucial significance during the initial stages of the Pacific War was the widely held belief amongst Allied troops and many of their commanders that the Japanese soldier, deeply imbued with the Samurai tradition, never surrendered. Death was a noble fate; to be captured was to dishonour oneself and bring shame to one's family and ancestors. The suicidal break-outs attempted by Japanese POWs at Featherston, New Zealand, in February 1943 and Cowra, New South Wales, in August 1944 seemed, on the surface, to reinforce these widely held views that Japanese soldiers, even in captivity, were fanatics who preferred to kill or be killed. But, as Allied interrogators were already aware, this was far too simple an explanation because not all

[5] Allison B. Gilmore, *You Can't Fight Tanks with Bayonets: Psychological Warfare against the Japanese Army in the Southwest Pacific* (Lincoln, 1998), p. 2. Estimates vary as to how many Japanese were captured by the Allies. One Japanese historian claims that as many as 50,000 were taken before Japan surrendered in August 1945. Ikuhiko Hata, 'From Consideration to Contempt: The Changing Nature of Japanese Military and Popular Perceptions of Prisoners of War through the Ages', in Bob Moore and Kent Fedorowich, eds, *Prisoners of War and their Captors during World War II* (Oxford, 1996), p. 263.

those incarcerated were bent on committing suicide.[6] The remit for ATIS was therefore to provide more sophisticated analyses of the Japanese soldier, his culture and society. Reasoned arguments had to replace emotion and racial bias if a realistic and comprehensive profile of the enemy was to be provided to Allied intelligence and political warfare agencies operating in the Far East. Of fundamental importance was the proper utilisation of information gleaned from captured Japanese POWs.

After six months of war with Japan, the Australian Department of External Affairs decided in May-June 1942 to evaluate the cache of Japanese POWs incarcerated in the dominion. At that time, the total captured by Australian forces had been the 'deplorably small' number of twenty. According to External Affairs, the dearth in numbers was, in part, due to the defensive trend of Allied campaigns in the Far Eastern theatre of operations. 'Almost continuous withdrawals have not favoured the capture of Prisoners of War.'[7] But there was another potent reason for the Allied failure to take substantial numbers of Japanese POWs.

> Such a contingency as capture by the enemy is not recognised by the Japanese military authorities. It is carefully inculcated into the Japanese soldier that to allow himself to be captured is a disgrace worse than death. Indeed, to some extent, he even welcomes the chance to die for his country ... The Japanese is therefore a difficult fish to catch. He will resist to the last, and under the circumstances our forces can scarcely be blamed for helping him to achieve his ambition to die for his country.[8]

Running in parallel with the Department of External Affairs' preliminary analyses of its Asian enemy, was an investigation by Australia's internal security agencies of the German, Italian and Japanese civilians who had been interned on the outbreak of the European and Pacific wars respectively. S. C. Taylor, Deputy Director of Security for New South Wales, reported to his superior in Canberra that for the last eighteen months Lieutenant J. W. Louwisch had been in regular contact with internees from all of the above nationalities. A rabbi, Louwisch had worked in the United States

---

[6] John W. Dower, *War Without Mercy: Race and Power in the Pacific War* (London, 1986); idem, *Japan in War and Peace* (New York:, 1993), pp. 257–85; Hata, 'From Consideration to Contempt', pp. 253–76; Nancy Brcak and John R. Pavia, 'Racism in Japanese and US Wartime Propaganda', *The Historian*, 56 (1994), pp. 671–84; Clayton D. Laurie, 'The Ultimate Dilemma of Psychological Warfare in the Pacific: Enemies Who Don't Surrender, and GIs Who Don't Take Prisoners', *War and Society*, 14 (1996), pp. 99–120.

[7] Australian Archives, Canberra (hereafter AA), Commonwealth Record Series (hereafter CRS), CRS A1067/1, item PI46/2/1/7, secret report, 'Characteristics of Japanese Prisoners of War', *c.* May-June 1942.

[8] Ibid.

prior to the war and for some years had lectured at the synagogue in Sydney. Fluent in Russian, German, Italian and Javanese, he was equally proficient in Japanese. His investigative work was not confined to enemy aliens, however, for it was revealed that he had also participated in a number of POW debriefings, including those of several recently captured Japanese. In his report, submitted to senior internal security officers at the Department of Defence in December 1942, some absorbing discoveries were made concerning these Japanese POWs.

According to Louwisch, the Japanese soldier demonstrated in battle a complete contempt for life. One was apt to ascribe this as recognition of the Japanese soldier's devotion to 'duty, patriotism and loyalty'. However, Louwisch attributed such contempt for one's own life as being driven simply by the instinct of fear. The Japanese soldier was afraid of life and therefore sought death in battle. The most arresting observation, however, concerned the shame associated with capture, and the personal and family dishonour attached to it. The allusion here was to the legacy and myths surrounding the Samurai warrior, many of which had been refashioned after the First World War to serve a number of Japanese interest groups, especially the military elites. The belief that to be taken prisoner was a dishonour disguised the contradictions which existed within Japanese society itself over this issue. Nevertheless, the reinvention of some aspects of the Samurai tradition in the 1920s, and in particular, the 'death before dishonour' dictum which was feverishly inculcated into every Japanese servicemen, were, argued Louwisch, factors which could be exploited handsomely by Allied propaganda.[9]

In addition, it was perceived that Japanese soldiers were given very little security training. This was confirmed by a long-serving member of British Naval Intelligence, Lieutenant-Colonel B. F. Trench, Royal Marines, during a tour of the Antipodes in mid 1942. In his experience, when captured, the Japanese POWs felt 'completely isolated and lost'.[10] This, in combination with the 'peculiar' Japanese attitude that upon capture the individual was for all intents and purposes dead made these prisoners, according to Louwisch, highly susceptible to Allied propaganda. If cultivated properly these POWs

[9] AA, CRS A373/1, item 3022, report by Louwisch forwarded by Taylor to Canberra, 22 December 1942. For an insight into the internal workings of the Japanese military in the inter-war period see Leonard A. Humphreys, *The Way of the Heavenly Sword: The Japanese Army in the 1920s* (Stanford, California, 1995); Edward J. Drea, 'In the Army Barracks of Imperial Japan', *Armed Forces and Society*, 15 (1989), pp. 329–48; Hata, 'From Consideration to Contempt', pp. 261–63; Gilmore, *You Can't Fight Tanks with Bayonets*, pp. 36–70. Also see Meirion and Susie Harries, *Soldiers of the Sun: The Rise and Fall of the Imperial Japanese Army* (New York, 1991).

[10] NANZ, Navy Department 1, 8/7, Puttick to Navy Secretary, 21 October 1942.

might, therefore, become a useful means to undermine the morale of the
Imperial Japanese Army. 'From my conversations with a few prisoners',
continued Louwisch:

> there is a complete lack of the 'cobber' spirit in the Japanese Army. Their
> mentality as well as their tactics is not an open fight but sneaking infiltration.
> Therefore, by well-organised propaganda, it is my conviction, we could set them
> against each other and make the Army a house divided against itself ... In other
> words the disruption of the Japanese Army would be easy merely by following
> the true facts. The Army consists of two classes; there is no democracy, neither
> in its form nor in its substance. Wherever there are classes, one could easily set
> up one class against the other. That the Japanese soldier feels his subservience
> to the upper class there can be no doubt.[11]

This shows that Louwisch's initial impressions may have been coloured by
his own prejudices towards the Japanese; no doubt a serious problem for
the Allies during the first year of the Pacific War.[12] For instance, note the
phrase 'sneaking infiltration' (which, as a tactic, the Allies used themselves to great effect during the war). Nevertheless, potential weaknesses
had been identified which Louwisch's superiors in the Department of
Defence and their colleagues at External Affairs were eager to exploit. It
was now a matter of finding out how best to capitalise upon these initial
assessments.

Two of the cardinal principles underpinning all Allied propaganda was
that it had to be factual and tell the truth. To lie, thereby following the
path taken by Axis propaganda, would undermine completely the moral
legitimacy of the Allied cause. Furthermore, racial bigotry and cultural
stereotyping had to be expunged from propaganda directed at Japanese
troops and civilians. To dehumanise the Japanese and portray them as
ape-like and sub-human – themes which dominated Australian and American popular images of the Japanese during the early stages of the Pacific
War and which were exploited for domestic consumption – were counter-
productive when directed at enemy-occupied territory.[13] Another maxim

---

[11] Ibid., minute by Lieutenant-Commander F. M. Beasley, RN, Director of New Zealand
Naval Intelligence, 23 October 1942; AA, CRS A373/1, item 3022, report by Louwisch, 22
December 1942.

[12] For an exemplary examination of Australian internment policy see Margaret Bevege, *Behind
Barbed Wire: Internment in Australia during World War II* (St Lucia, Queensland, 1993),
especially chap. 6 on Japanese civilians interned in Australia; Yuriko Nagata, *Unwanted Aliens:
Japanese Internment in Australia* (St Lucia, Queensland, 1996).

[13] Charles Cruickshank, *The Fourth Arm: Psychological Warfare 1938–1945* (London, 1977).
For Australian policy see Kay Saunders, '"An Instrument of Strategy": Propaganda, Public
Policy and the Media in Australia During the Second World War', *War and Society*, 15

was that the Allies had to refrain from criticising Emperor Hirohito. 'No people in the world have a greater sense of loyalty than have the Japanese and they follow orders blindly. The strongest attachment is loyalty to the Emperor. We must never attack these characteristics', exorted one British Foreign Office briefing paper, but rather 'use them for our own ends'.[14]

The validity of this strategy was confirmed by a New Zealander and former member of the Australian branch of ATIS, Lieutenant E. H. Thomson. A veteran of at least thirty POW interrogations, Thomson confirmed that the Allies, in his opinion, had indeed pursued the correct strategy. It had been essential for Allied propaganda to isolate the military elites from the rest of Japanese society and stress how they had misled the Emperor and the ordinary Japanese citizen. The truthful nature and reliability of Allied war news was fundamental to this war for hearts and minds, a key ingredient of which was to play on the loyalty factor. To reiterate this point, Thomson pointed to his debriefing of a battalion commander, Lieutenant-Colonel Masaharu Takenaga, in July 1945. Anxious to know if the Imperial Palace had been hit by Allied bombers, Takenaga stated that if the Emperor were killed, 'the whole Japanese nation would fight to the very end'. However, if the Japanese government made peace and its armies were ordered by the Emperor to cease fighting, there was no doubt in Takenaga's mind that they would do so. Therefore the Allies would not have to fear continued action by independent armies after the surrender.[15]

That the Japanese military lacked any kind of security training was indeed

---

(1997), pp. 75–90; Lynette Finch, 'Knowing the Enemy: Australian Psychological Warfare and the Business of Influencing Minds in the Second World War', *War and Society*, 16 (1998), pp. 71–91.

[14] Public Record Office, London (hereafter PRO), Foreign Office Papers (hereafter FO), FO 898/267, 'Outline Plan for Joint Political Warfare Action for the Far East', February-March 1941.

[15] Thomson was seconded in January 1944 to Central Bureau, the combined Allied signals and intelligence facility which was initially established in Melbourne as part of Commander-in-Chief, General Douglas MacArthur's Southwest Pacific Area headquarters in April 1942. Competent in Japanese, Thomson had previously served at the Featherston POW camp and with the New Zealand forces at Vella Lavella in the Solomon Islands before his transfer to Australia. After serving between three to four months in Brisbane with the Central Bureau (which had moved with MacArthur to Queensland in September 1942), Thomson was deployed to Rabaul on New Britain before spending the last three months of the Pacific war in Lae, New Guinea, interrogating Japanese POWs at the First Australian Army ATIS Advanced Echelon. Interview with Eric Thomson in Auckland, New Zealand, 22 September 1998. I am indebted to him for the information he gave me including a copy of the Takenaga report which can be found in the Australian War Memorial (hereafter AWM), AWM 54, item 422/7/8, part 1, Takenaga preliminary interrogation report, 7 July 1945.

a startling revelation to Allied interrogators. Combined with the fact that saving face was of fundamental importance in Japanese culture, and that shame, or more accurately its avoidance, played a key role in Japanese society, these considerations were integral to first understanding and then unlocking the secrets held by the enemy. Experience gained during 1942 demonstrated that, because of the Japanese willingness to talk during an interrogation, it was not necessary to invest in large quantities of more specialised and expensive equipment such as hidden microphones and recording equipment. Nor was it necessary to cultivate an extensive system of stool pigeons to undertake clandestine work in the POW camps. While these methods had proved extremely rewarding in the European and North African theatres, it must be emphasised that they had to be used because Axis forces, especially the Germans, were much more security conscious. Culture and differences in military indoctrination and training in some respects made it easier to prise information from the Japanese. However, the success achieved using direct interrogation methods made the use of hidden microphones and stool pigeons almost redundant. This is not to say that such techniques were never deployed in SWPA. Indeed, excellent results were obtained from mid 1943 onwards using the one Japanese stool pigeon who had eagerly volunteered his services to the Allies – but he was the exception to the rule. The perceived norm, as one US air intelligence officer said of captive Japanese he had encountered in SWPA, they 'grind information out like talking machines. They tell everything they know ... There is no shutting them up'.[16]

What were the techniques and procedures employed by Australian interrogators? The guidelines for officers conducting POW examinations were relatively simple and straightforward, relying on common sense and experience rather than any hard and fast set of rules. This was spelt out in no uncertain terms in mid 1942: 'For all further information beyond name and rank, the interrogator is dependent on his own skill and resource, qualities which are largely innate, but can be acquired or developed to a

---

[16] AWM 54, item 779/3/31, 'Report on the Methods Followed in the Interrogation of Japanese Prisoners', 30 May 1944; *Sydney Morning Herald*, 26 July 1944. For Japanese misperceptions of enemy capabilities and the low priority attached to systematic intelligence gathering see Alvin D. Coox, 'Flawed Perception and its Effect upon Operational Thinking: The Case of the Japanese Army, 1937–41', *Intelligence and National Security*, 5 (1990), pp. 239–54; Louis Allen, 'Japanese Intelligence Systems', *Journal of Contemporary History*, 22 (1987), pp. 547–62; J. W. M. Chapman, 'Japanese Intelligence 1919–1945: A Suitable Case for Treatment', in Christopher Andrew and Jeremy Noakes, eds, *Intelligence and International Relations, 1900–1945* (Exeter, 1987), pp. 145–89.

considerable extent by training and practice'.[17] Obviously, an intimate knowledge of the enemy's language was fundamental. Equally valuable were insights into his national psychology, literature, history, government structures and, above all, military establishments. Another essential characteristic of a good examiner was a thorough familiarity with the battle front and with the particular subject matter about which he desired to obtain information. 'It may be laid down as an axiom that the secret of successful interrogation lies in the extent of the examiner's knowledge. Furthermore, before beginning an interrogation, the examiner must be quite clear in his own mind as to what he wants to ask.'[18] As a result, it was vital for staff officers to inform the interrogating officer of any specific points they wanted explored and to supply him with the latest maps and aerial photographs for both verification and assisting in jogging the memory of the prisoner.

Interrogations had to be held in secret and on a one-to-one basis. 'The Japanese soldier finds strength in company', claimed one confidential ATIS report. 'While a member of an organised body he is generally fearless, loyal and well disciplined. If he is suddenly wrested away from his fellows and forced to stand alone he is bewildered because he has no rules to go by.'[19] Prisoners also had to be made to feel at ease during the examination. In addition, solitary interviews prevented POWs from contriving a story with other prisoners either in the room or within earshot. In addition, one-to-one interviews helped protect the prisoner's identity from fellow comrades seeking retribution from those who imparted information. As a precaution, it was also vital to segregate prisoners who had been debriefed from those who were awaiting processing. For on previous occasions when this procedure had not been adhered to it was soon discovered that one shrewd prisoner could easily influence what was subsequently revealed by those of his companions who followed afterwards. Moreover, no rules could be laid down as to the manner to be assumed towards prisoners, for 'in each case the examiner must discover for himself the method best suited to the individual'. Finally:

> Knowledge of human nature … power to inspire confidence, tact and patience are all-important qualities in interrogators. It is usually best for the latter to begin by adopting a perfectly natural and conversational attitude and by putting

[17] NANZ, Air Department 120/5/29, 'The Examination of Prisoners of War: Notes for the Guidance of Officer Conducting Examinations', Australian copy supplied to New Zealand Military Forces, n.d. (probably July-August 1942).

[18] Ibid.

[19] AWM 54, item 779/3/31, 'Report on the Methods Followed in the Interrogation of Japanese Prisoners', 30 May 1944.

the prisoner at his ease. In many cases a comfortable chair, warmth, food, drink, and a cigarette will do more to loosen the tongue of an exhausted man than any display of harshness. The examiner, should talk quietly and persuasively, though with firmness and authority. There will be ample time later on to adopt a more forcible attitude and should this become necessary it will be far more effective if it follows a period of quiet reasoning.[20]

In other words, an examiner had to be the consummate actor. He also had to refrain from asking leading questions, as they usually led to doubtful and inaccurate information. Moreover, an examiner had to avoid being over anxious. Any betrayal of eagerness on his part would likely make the prisoner reticent or induce him to lie. Above all, it was vital for the examiner to retain complete control of the situation at all times. It was also deemed essential that prisoners be debriefed in their native tongue, as this prevented the prisoner from disguising his manner, thus allowing the interrogator a better opportunity to detect fabrications. Finally, information gleaned from POWs and captured documents had to be processed as quickly as possible so that combat commanders could digest and deploy this information in the field.

Processing POWs was a step-by-step strategy determined by the potential usefulness of the information it was believed prisoners possessed. Preliminary interrogations were undertaken in the field. At this stage, the priority for battalion intelligence officers was to obtain as much combat and operational information as possible. Questions centred upon the enemy's order of battle, unit strength, organisation, deployment, tactics and morale. Provided that they could be persuaded to talk, the most valuable prisoners from an intelligence point of view were officers and the better-educated non-commissioned officers. One thing was for certain: 'All dead Japs are not good ones!' Field intelligence officers were reminded that it was their duty to impress upon all ranks and whenever possible on members of other services, 'the extremely high intelligence value of Japanese POWs and the necessity for taking every precaution to deliver them safely, quickly, and in the right frame of mind to the proper authorities'. Failure to follow these simple procedures could mean the difference between a 'concocted tissue of lies' and reliable information.[21]

Once identified, these prisoners were sent to divisional and corps commands where more in-depth questioning concerning enemy plans, logistics, reinforcements and strategy was carried out. Of vital importance at this stage was their segregation from the rest of the inmate population. Responsibility

[20] NANZ, Air Department 120/5/29, 'Notes for the Guidance of Officers', 1942.
[21] AWM 54, item 423/2/11, procedural file for processing Japanese POWs, c. 1944.

for the interrogation of prisoners in transit camps and casualty clearing stations was not overlooked either. Pro formas for both preliminary and detailed interrogations were constructed so that information could be systematically catalogued for future reference. For captives attached to elite combat units, or specialist formations requiring knowledge of a highly technical nature such as engineering, anti-tank or anti-aircraft units, special questionnaires were provided to assist the interrogating officer. By 1944 the range and sophistication of these questionnaires was remarkable. Topics varied from the essentials concerning manpower, tactics and strategy, logistics, recruitment, mobilisation, administration and organisation to questions relating to weapon development (including chemical and biological weapons), fortifications, propaganda, morale, relations with puppet regimes and the use of satellite troops.[22]

Right from the beginning, Australian interrogators were requested to gauge POW morale and probe for material which could be utilised for psychological and political warfare purposes. Although this type of information was extracted from preliminary interrogations conducted in the field, much of the painstaking and detailed profile work was undertaken by officers in the rear echelons and in the POW camps themselves. Before an analysis of the material obtained from POW interrogations can be attempted, it is imperative to outline the machinery established to process this information, and the agencies which formulated the propaganda strategies framed in Australia. Only then can the role played by Japanese POWs in Allied intelligence, propaganda and political warfare be properly examined.

In April 1942 the British and Americans began to discuss the need for a coordinated political warfare strategy against Japan. The same month, London cabled Canberra outlining the parameters for a political warfare campaign against Japan. This was followed shortly afterwards by another request that any Australian ideas and plans be forwarded to London and the newly established Political Warfare (Japan) Committee. Clearly, Australia's geographic proximity to Japan and her obvious strategic interests in the

---

[22] AWM 54, item 779/2/15, ATIS briefing paper which contains samples of CSDIC (Middle East) questionnaires, 8 February 1943; list of question topics suggested by Australian military intelligence services for Japanese POWs, August 1944. For questions on Japanese civilian defence and protection against chemical attack see AWM 54, item 179/1/17, interrogation report no. 550, ATIS serial 704, 28 November 1944. Information revealed on biological warfare by Japanese POWs and captured documents is discussed in Yuki Tanaka, *Hidden Horrors: Japanese War Crimes in World War II* (Boulder, Colorado, 1996), pp. 135–65.

South-West Pacific made it politically desirable for the dominion to play an active part in the campaign being planned against Japan.[23]

On 11 June 1942 a conference was convened in Melbourne to consider the British proposals and the nature of Australia's participation. Representatives from the departments of Defence, Navy, Army, Air, Information and External Affairs met General MacArthur to discuss a draft cabinet agendum which had been prepared by the Department of External Affairs as a basis for discussion at the conference. The recommendations, which were submitted and approved by the Australian War Cabinet a week later, emphasised two important objectives. First, it was essential that there should be immediate consultation between the Allies to 'define reasonable and practicable objectives'. To facilitate this, the Australians announced plans for the creation of their own political warfare agency which would work closely with similar organisations already established, such as the British Ministry of Information and the United States Office of War Information (OWI). Secondly, Canberra urged the closest cooperation between these national organisations and, if it was desirable, the establishment of an inter-Allied body in Australia which would coordinate these political warfare stratagems against Japan. Above all, it was stressed that matters of policy should be the subject of consultation between the Allied governments concerned.[24] London agreed and suggested that effective coordination between the partner nations could best be effected by the presence in all the main centres (London, Washington, Melbourne, New Delhi and Chungking) of responsible liaison officers who would be in close contact with the governmental organisations responsible for political warfare in each centre.

In accordance with the Australian War Cabinet decision to set up a Political Warfare (Advisory) Committee, an inaugural conference was called by the Minister for External Affairs, Dr H. V. Evatt, on 16 July 1942. The conduct of political warfare was put under the control of the Minister for External Affairs, assisted by the committee. The Australian organisation was to be essentially a pragmatic one, 'not too ambitious for the start and shaped to do the tasks which may be begun at once'. Nevertheless, its overall structure would be such as to give the new organisation the flexibility to meet the demands for expansion, to undertake its share in any inter-Allied activity and make a major contribution if and when it was decided to create an inter-Allied bureau in Australia. The consensus reached at the meeting about the role of the Political Warfare (Advisory) Committee was that it

---

[23] AA, CRS A1066/4, item PI45/1/1/5, most secret report on the establishment of Australia's Political Warfare Organisation, 27 August 1942.
[24] Ibid.

should facilitate consultation between departments and provide a pool of knowledge and ideas. Using the collected experiences and information of the committee's membership, general guidelines for a political warfare campaign could then be formulated. Once clear lines of communication had been established, it was essential to investigate the available resources and verify what activities could be initiated immediately. Suggestions included the erection of stronger short-wave transmitters to beam propaganda into larger areas of Japanese-occupied territory, qualified translators, native announcers in Asiatic languages, typographical resources for printing in these languages, coordination in leaflet distribution, recruitment of under-cover agents and the establishment of an intelligence network in enemy-occupied territory.[25]

Once the Australian Political Warfare (Advisory) Committee had been established and its membership constituted, a secretariat was needed. The lack of an effective bureaucracy had initially hampered Australian efforts, but this was quickly rectified in July 1942 when a Political Warfare Division was created at the Department of External Affairs. H. A. Stokes was appointed as head of the secretariat and sometimes sat as Evatt's proxy on the Advisory Committee when the minister himself was not in attendance. Apart from External Affairs, membership included representatives from the three armed services, the departments of Defence and Information, and W. Macmahon Ball, head of the Short-Wave Broadcasting Division of the Australian Broadcasting Commission. The first meeting was held on 30 July 1942.

Working closely with the Advisory Committee was the Far Eastern Liaison Office (FELO) which was founded on 19 June 1942. As Section 'D' of the Australian Intelligence Bureau (AIB), FELO originated under the control of General Headquarters, SWPA. Later transferred to the control of the three Australian Chiefs of Staff and the senior officer of the Netherlands Forces, it subsequently became the exclusive responsibility of the Commander-in-Chief, Australian Land Forces, Lieutenant-General Sir Thomas Blamey.[26] FELO's chief responsibility was combat propaganda, as distinct from psychological or political propaganda in the broader sense. Apart from front line radio broadcasts, its primary weapon in this war of words were the millions of leaflets dropped by air behind or on enemy lines. Until June 1944, when the Americans established the Psychological Warfare Bureau (PWB) in preparation for their return to the Philippines, FELO was allowed by MacArthur to dominate the dissemination of Allied combat propaganda.

---

[25] Ibid.
[26] For Blamey's role in reorganising Australia's intelligence agencies see David Horner, *Blamey: The Commander in Chief* (Sydney, 1998), 310–15.

With the creation of PWB, FELO's activities were then confined to operational zones involving Australian, British and Dutch forces. Nevertheless, FELO had provided the Americans with invaluable experience, even if some senior US commanders saw it as a cover agency for reestablishing British imperialism in the Far East.[27]

Combat or military propaganda was defined as 'all propaganda directed against enemy forces in the field, or to native populations within the combat zone, or zones likely to become theatres of operations'.[28] Its objectives were threefold: to lower enemy morale and thus impair fighting efficiency; to mislead the enemy regarding Allied military intentions; and to influence subject populations in enemy-occupied territory to mar further the enemy's ability to fight. When small parties and agents operated behind enemy lines, another vital task was to collect intelligence and forward it to Allied forces. To assist in this work, offices were situated in forward areas, with Port Moresby in New Guinea being established as the first forward office in November 1942. The number of forward offices and the personnel assigned to them increased as the strategic advantage in SWPA swung in favour of the Allies. From its humble beginnings in June 1942 only five personnel, commanded by Commander J. C. R. Proud, Royal Australian Naval Volunteer Reserve, were attached to this fledgling unit. By August 1945 personnel had increased to 474, comprised of thirty-one Royal Australian Navy (RAN), 285 Australian Military Forces (AMF), nineteen Royal Australian Air Force (RAAF), twenty-one Dutch, eight civilians, 105 New Guinea natives and five Japanese POWs.[29]

The mobilisation of Australian resources for the prosecution of political and psychological warfare against Japan coincided with a similar restructuring and expansion of Allied intelligence agencies in SWPA. Early in 1941 the AMF created a Japanese language intelligence section at Eastern Command Headquarters, Sydney. One of its chief functions was to interview people returning from Japan and enlist them in the AMF. However, there was a paucity of competent linguists (a problem which plagued Allied operations throughout the war). In fact, the shortage was so acute that the RAN obtained only one qualified civil servant for its purposes. The RAAF did not have much success finding linguists either, when, in January 1942, it established a prisoner of war section in Melbourne. That same month, pressures to find qualified linguists and translators increased as

[27] Gilmore, *You Can't Fight Tanks with Bayonets*, pp. 21–35; Laurie, 'Ultimate Dilemma', p. 104.
[28] AA, CRS A1066/4, item PI45/1/1/22, Report on Activities of Far Eastern Liaison Office for period June 1942 to September 1945.
[29] Ibid.

Australian Army Headquarters established its document translation centres in Melbourne, and later in Brisbane, at the Australian Advanced Land Headquarters.[30]

As the armed services grappled with the demands of organising intelligence work within Australia, two officers – one from the RAAF and the other from the Australian Imperial Force (AIF) based in Cairo – had been selected for training at the Combined Services Detailed Interrogation Centre (Middle East). In July, it was decided to create an Australian arm of this bureau which was further bolstered by the inclusion of a naval representative. 'Experience overseas has shown the necessity for the most complete and detailed examination of prisoners of war', proclaimed one report. 'It is estimated that at least 40 per cent of our intelligence has been obtained in this way while most essential confirmation of that obtained from other sources has also been obtained from prisoners of war.'[31] In August a site was located in Brisbane at Indooroopilly for the detailed interrogation of Japanese POWs. By mid September technicians from the Royal Corps of Signals, Middle East Command, and some of the language personnel from the various Australian intelligence agencies, had been relocated and merged into CSDIC (Australia). Shortly after this, on 19 September 1942, a directive was implemented establishing the Allied Translator and Interpreter Section. The personnel and activities of CSDIC (Australia) were gradually absorbed into this new unit by the end of the year.[32]

In its first month of operations, the small staff of twenty-five officers (of whom only fifteen were qualified linguists), and its complement of ten enlisted men, had processed more than a thousand captured documents and completed seven POW interrogations. At its peak in 1945, ATIS had expanded to no less than 250 officers and 1700 enlisted men and women, including an indispensable number of second-generation Japanese Americans or *Nisei* from Hawaii and California. With the end of the Pacific War in August 1945, the breadth and multiplicity of ATIS operations throughout

[30] AA, CRS A3269/1, item 011, General Headquarters, Far Eastern Command, Military Intelligence Section, General Staff, *Operations of the Allied Translator and Interpreter Section GHQ, SWPA*, v, *Intelligence Series*, 3.

[31] NANZ, Navy Department 1, 8/7, New Zealand Intelligence Chiefs to Chief of Naval Staff, 22 June 1942. For British procedures and early successes in the use of POWs for intelligence purposes see Kent Fedorowich, 'Name, Rank and Number: Prisoners of War as Sources for British Military Intelligence, 1939–1942', *Intelligence and National Security* (forthcoming).

[32] Ibid. Recent scholarship on Australian intelligence and code breaking include Alan Powell, *War by Stealth: Australians and the Allied Intelligence Bureau, 1942–1945* (Melbourne, 1996); Edward J. Drea, *MacArthur's ULTRA: Codebreaking and the War against Japan, 1942–1945* (Lawrence, Kansas, 1992).

MacArthur's SWPA command were indeed staggering. Over 350,000 captured documents had been catalogued and collated. Of these, 18,000 were
translated and 16,000 printed. Equally impressive was the compilation and
publication of 779 interrogation reports which were based upon information
gleaned from more than 10,000 POWs who had been screened or examined
by ATIS personnel. These publications were disseminated widely to all
intelligence agencies throughout South-East Asia and the Pacific theatres.
In its own words, the published information circulated by South-West
Pacific Area's ATIS services 'contributed materially to the success of [Allied]
operations'.[33]

By the end of 1942 a profile of the enemy's attitudes and fighting qualities
began to emerge from the material processed by ATIS and its antecedents
over the past year. Some of the first Japanese prisoners to be captured and
interrogated by the Australians were Japanese Army Air Service personnel
who had crashed near or had been shot down over Darwin, and naval
ratings from ships sunk by Allied submarines operating in waters between
Australia and the Dutch East Indies. For instance, on 19 February 1942, nine
Japanese aircraft based in Ambon were ordered to bomb the aerodrome at
Darwin. One machine caught fire en route. The crew were forced to bail
out and the air gunner, Sergeant Tadao Minami, swam ashore on nearby
Bathurst Island, located north of Port Darwin. After wandering about for
three days he was discovered by an aboriginal, taken to the aerodrome he
was to have attacked, and made prisoner. He was interrogated by the RAAF
and RAN before being sent to Melbourne for further questioning by military
intelligence. The preliminary interrogation report stated that the prisoner
'talked easily, was unselfconscious, and gave the impression of speaking the
truth so far as he knew it. His knowledge of his own job was adequate; his
knowledge of, and, apparently interest in extraneous matters [was] practically nil. This is considered to be consistent with his type – a peasant
farmer'.[34]

During the interrogation carried out by the RAAF, Minomi revealed that
he did not want to be sent back to Japan. The shame of being captured
was too much for him. 'He thought', recorded the interrogating officer,
'that his friends would not want to have anything to do with him because

[33] AA, CRS A 3269/1, item 011, General Headquarters, Far Eastern Command, Military
Intelligence Section, General Staff, *Operations of the Allied Translator and Interpreter Section
GHQ, SWPA*, vol. 5, *Intelligence Series*. See Gilmore, *You Can't Fight Tanks with Bayonets*, for
examples of ATIS's role in using POWs to fine-tune Allied propaganda, pp. 125–45.
[34] AWM 54, item 779/3/75, Japanese Prisoner of War No. 1, Army Interrogation Report,
Sergeant Air Gunner Tadao Minami, 1 March 1942.

he had been taken prisoner, and that he would not be regarded as a good character, and would not be able to get back into the Army. He prefers to stay in Australia.'[35] This refrain would often echo throughout subsequent debriefings of Japanese POWs conducted by Allied intelligence. In fact, according to Allison Gilmore, 88 per cent of all Japanese POWs questioned by ATIS about their prospect of returning home claimed that they had absolutely no ambition to do so.[36] Equally significant was the ease which many Japanese prisoners displayed when talking to their interrogators and the willingness with which they divulged information. Nevertheless, Allied interrogators had to be on their guard at all times to prevent complacency, for there were those who, motivated not by a profound sense of duty but rather by the ignominy of being taken prisoner, often sought to deceive their interrogators by providing false names and information.

For example, in mid September 1942 a Japanese marine, captured the previous month by Australian forces at Milne Bay, on the south-east tip of New Guinea, was interrogated at Gaythorne internment camp, Queensland, by Captain G. C. Batchelor. A former bank clerk and shop assistant, the thirty-seven-year-old Minoru Sakaki had been attached to a rifle section of the Hayashi unit. Although willing to talk about his unit's command struc-ture, training, logistics and armament, inquiries revealed that the POW's military knowledge was limited and confined to the workings of his own platoon. His captors dismissed most of his statements as unreliable because most of the dates, times and numbers were 'conveniently forgotten'. Never-theless, there was no indication of deception on his part. In this case, ignorance rather than subterfuge was the chief problem. This was corrobor-ated by translations of documents taken during his capture. They revealed that, although he had been vague about most things, some of the information Sakaki had divulged was in fact accurate. As the report stated, the POW 'appeared to be doing his best to give truthful answers'.[37]

A similar conclusion was reached after the interrogation of a captured tail gunner, Mitsumasa Tanabe, shot down during operations in SWPA in August 1943. A farmer in peacetime, the prisoner was deemed not very observant, in part because he had little active air force experience. 'He was

[35] Ibid., Air Interrogation Report, 4 March 1942.

[36] Allison B. Gilmore, '"We Have Been Reborn": Japanese Prisoners and the Allied Propa-ganda War in the Southwest Pacific', *Pacific Historical Review*, 64 (1995), p. 201. Also see Arnold Krammer, 'Japanese Prisoners of War in America', *Pacific Historical Review*, 52 (1983), pp. 67–91.

[37] AWM 54, item 779/3/75, POW Interrogation Report no. 2, 1st Class Seamen Minoru Sakaki, 13 September 1942.

not security conscious', noted his interrogator, 'and made no effort to evade answering questions. He was inclined to get flustered and bewildered during interrogations. On one occasion when it was pointed out to him that his account was obviously incorrect, [he] burst into tears, stating he was re-counting all he knew to the best of his recollection.' The interrogating officer concluded that the POW's actions were sincere and that he had done his best to 'answer truthfully'.[38]

The shame attached to becoming a POW was unacceptable for most Japanese soldiers. Hence their determination to commit suicide and, failing that, their insistence not to be returned to Japan after the war. This was reaffirmed by Dr Leon Bossard, the Swiss delegate for the International Committee of the Red Cross (ICRC) in New Zealand. He noted that most of the men incarcerated at Featherston had been taken prisoner 'against their will and would rather have chosen death in preference to a fate which they considered dishonourable, according to the teaching imbued into them'. He elaborated further:

> by becoming prisoners of war they were dead men as far as their nation was concerned, and should they by some accident ever be returned to Japan, they would on arrival be shot, a fate, which they said, had befallen the prisoners of war who had been returned from the Russian-Japanese war. Consequently, they argued, they might just as well do the only honourable thing left to them, i.e. either individual or mass suicide. They explained to me that this was a way in which an apology could be made to their nation for their crime for having allowed themselves to be taken prisoners of war. They were, however, always careful to mention that their capture [was] against their will, as they were either too exhausted to offer any resistance or in a delirious condition, and thus unable to induce the enemy to kill them …[39]

Conversely, many of those taken during the early campaigns in New Guinea recorded their surprise at not being shot by Allied troops after capture.[40] There were, in fact, examples of such behaviour, especially during the fierce fighting on Guadalcanal in the Solomon Islands.[41] Once the initial shock of having been captured had worn off, with constant reassurance that these

---

[38] NANZ, Navy Department 2, 16a, ATIS report, no. 142, SWPA, Mitsumasa Tanabe, 12 August 1943.

[39] NANZ, External Affairs Department 1, 89/4/7, Bossard's report on the characteristics of Japanese POWs at Featherston, 17 January 1946. Also see PRO, FO 916/790, Foreign Office summary of Bossard's Featherston report, 20 November 1943.

[40] For details see batch of POW interrogations taken by Australian intelligence officers attached to Headquarters, New Guinea Force in AWM 54, item 779/3/11, December 1942.

[41] James J. Weingartner, 'Trophies of War: US Troops and the Mutilation of Japanese War Dead, 1941–1945', *Pacific Historical Review*, 61 (1992), pp. 53–67.

men would be treated fairly and humanely, Allied intelligence and propaganda experts realised that they had the potential to forge an important weapon which they could direct against Japanese morale.

In March 1943, the Allied Political Warfare Committee was briefed by Commander Proud on results achieved by FELO in its psychological warfare campaign in New Guinea. A small number of Japanese soldiers, perhaps as many as twenty, had given themselves up by waving the surrender passes which were attached to propaganda pamphlets dropped on or behind enemy lines. POW interrogations also revealed that over 50 per cent of the POWs had seen the leaflets; and pamphlets were discovered among the diaries and documents found on Japanese dead. Even more encouraging were indications that these leaflets were causing the Japanese authorities considerable concern. A captured Japanese Army order revealed that officers were to guard against the encroachment of this propaganda on their troops, and to report on a special form those that they thought might be affected by it. Heartened by these initial findings, of equal significance to the Allied Political Warfare Committee was that some soldiers' diaries criticised their officers, in particular naval officers. Evidently, cracks in Japanese discipline and morale were becoming a problem. As a result, Dr Evatt suggested that selected extracts might prove useful for propaganda purposes so that the tension which existed between some officers and their men could be exploited further.[42]

Private thoughts were one thing. The challenge for Allied propagandists was to mobilise personal discontent to such a degree that mass surrenders would result. That took time, patience and the right approach. Techniques developed against the Germans and Italians were of little merit when used against the Japanese, whose 'mentality and temperament [were] wholly different'.[43] This was made abundantly clear by some Japanese captured in

[42] AWM, Lieutenant-General Sir Thomas Blamey Papers, 3DRL 6643, 2/56.5, Proud to Director of Australian Military Intelligence, Brigadier John Rogers, 4 December 1943; AA, CRS A989/1, item 43/721/1, minutes of the third meeting of the APWC, 20 March 1943. Apart from Australian, British, Chinese, Dutch and US representatives, a Canadian official from the High Commission in Canberra sat in on the inaugural meeting. Several months later, the Canadian High Commissioner attended these meetings. In March 1943, membership was extended to the outspoken New Zealand High Commissioner, Carl Berendsen, who duly accepted the invitation. With Australia's recognition of the French provisional government in November 1944, a French representative, Monsieur Monmayou, joined the committee the following month. Ibid.; NANZ, External Affairs Department 1, 84/6/1, part 1, A. D. McIntosh, Secretary of New Zealand Department of External Affairs, to Sir Harry Batterbee, United Kingdom High Commissioner to New Zealand, 4 May 1943; AA, CRS 10322, item 20/1944, agenda for APWC meeting, 19 December 1944.

[43] AWM 54, item 795/3/5, RAAF intelligence report entitled, 'Japanese Prisoners for Propaganda', 22 September 1942.

New Guinea in December 1942. One Japanese corporal was emphatic that the surrender leaflets were entirely useless, because the *bushido* code forbade a Japanese soldier to surrender. A seasoned veteran of the Sino-Japanese War (1937–41), he had seen them used in China. Dismissing leaflets as harmless amusement, he stated that they had the opposite effect and made Japanese troops more determined. This claim was substantiated by a fellow private who added that the Allies had an erroneous conception of the Japanese soldier if they thought that he could be influenced using such means.[44]

A third prisoner, however, who was shown several leaflet specimens during his interrogation, stated that with troops who were stranded and without food and ammunition these might have some effect. He reminded his captors that surrender was impossible when Japanese officers were present.[45] This was confirmed by another captured private who had been a pickle dealer before the war. Attached to a transport section, Private Tsukamoto Kanematsu, who was captured in a field hospital suffering from malaria and beriberi, related that many of his comrades – after reading the pamphlets and hearing the news that the coastal strong points of Gona and Buna in New Guinea had fallen to the Allies – 'wished to get into our lines and surrender'. But, according to the captive, they had been closely watched by some of the regular soldiers and therefore were prevented from deserting before being struck down by ill-health. During the interrogation it was noted that bitter feelings existed between the POWs from labour units and those in front-line units, as the latter received better food rations. This apparent hostility between such units provided another potential area to exploit. For, as the senior Dutch representative on the Allied Political Warfare Committee, Charles van der Plas, remarked, many of those enrolled in these construction units were soldiers 'who had been tried and found wanting in China'.[46]

One of the key strategies formulated by political warfare officers early on in the Pacific war was the inducement-to-surrender campaign. If, through propaganda, it could be shown that Japanese service personnel were willing to surrender, that they were well treated when they did surrender, and that

[44] AWM 54, item 779/3/11, preliminary interrogation reports of Japanese POWs, Maroubra Force, conducted at Headquarters, New Guinea Force: Corporal Yoshiyuki Yabuguchi, 23 December 1942; Superior Private Kazuo Matsuoka, 20 December 1942.

[45] Ibid., preliminary interrogation reports of Japanese POWs, Maroubra Force, conducted at Headquarters, New Guinea Force: Superior Private Tatsumi Yamamoto, 18 December 1942.

[46] AA, CRS A989/1, item 43/721/1, minutes of third meeting of the APWC, 20 March 1943. Van der Plas, the former governor of East Java, was also president of the Netherlands Indies Commission for Australia. On van der Plas's career see Louis de Jong, *Het Koninkrijk der Nederlanden in de Tweede Wereldoorlog*, ix, part 1 (The Hague, 1985), p. 245.

they should not hesitate in giving themselves up, then a significant victory would be achieved. Equally important, Japanese soldiers had to be reassured that statements made by their civilian and military authorities – that the Allies tortured POWs upon capture – were absolute nonsense.[47] Running in parallel with this campaign was the Allied belief that if the Japanese could be persuaded that upon capture they would be well treated, and that if propaganda broadcasts made by Japanese POWs were used to reiterate this point, it might secure better treatment for Allied troops in Japanese hands.[48] Unfortunately, this latter point would prove to be a rather forlorn hope.

The mutiny of POWs at Featherston, New Zealand, on 25 February 1943 threatened to slow down the Allies' inducement-to-surrender campaign. The details surrounding the attempted breakout need not concern us here. Suffice it to say that as early as November 1942 camp officials were conscious of a heightened atmosphere in the camp which housed 800 inmates. One of the underlying anxieties concerned the issue of prisoners working on labour details. From a security aspect, camp authorities realised that it was essential for POWs to occupy their time constructively, whether it was reading, gardening, playing sport or labouring. Idleness bred discontent. It was therefore proposed that the POWs be encouraged to volunteer for work details or be coaxed to pick up those trades previously practised by them prior to the war. Preoccupied, POWs would be less likely to create mischief. However, a number of hardcore militants, most of whom had enlisted in the regular Japanese Army (but also some NCOs from the Imperial Japanese Navy), were extremely aggressive to those prisoners who had been attached to pioneer units in the rear echelon. Intimidation was rife as those Japanese prisoners who wanted to work were bullied and shamed by their more uncompromising countrymen. In the ensuing breakout – which was sparked by the militants who refused to supply a work party for duties inside the camp – forty-eight POWs were killed and approximately sixty-eight others wounded.[49]

[47] NANZ, Army Department 1/336/3/2, conversation on the use by the Americans of Japanese POWs held at Featherston, New Zealand for publicity purposes, held between the US Naval Attaché to New Zealand, Captain J. P. Olding, Pat Frank and Lieutenant-Colonel H. J. Thompson, New Zealand Army; minute sheet, 27 January 1943; AWM 123, item 665, minutes of fourth meeting of the Political Warfare (Advisory) Committee, 16 October 1942.

[48] AWM 54, item 795/3/5, memorandum entitled, 'Japanese Prisoners for Propaganda', Australian Directorate of Air Intelligence, 22 September 1942.

[49] NANZ, Army Department 1, 336/3/11, vol. 1, minute by Lieutenant-Colonel K. H. Donaldson, 29 October 1942; External Affairs Department 1, 89/4/13, part 1, Featherston mutiny, report telephoned by camp commandant, 25 February 1943; External Affairs Department 1, 89/4/13, part 2, proceedings and report on Featherston mutiny by Court of Enquiry, 1943.

Far from slowing down the inducement-to-surrender-campaign, the Featherston mutiny increased the resolve of the Allied Political Warfare Committee to intensify the programme. 'The New Zealand mutiny had been unfortunate', reflected the committee, but 'the best policy from now onwards was to ignore it completely. It was felt that if the Japanese used the mutiny as an anti-surrender deterrent they would undermine their own thesis that Japanese [soldiers] never surrendered.'[50] As a result, Japanese propaganda broadcasts were closely monitored by the Allies fearful of imminent reprisals initiated against Allied POWs in Japanese custody. A few 'offensive' comments from German and Japanese broadcasts were in fact picked up, but the Australians, in particular, were keen to launch their own counter-propaganda campaign. Shortly after the Featherston mutiny, Macmahon Ball informed Colonel W. R. Hodgson, Secretary of the Department of External Affairs, that the number of Japanese prisoners incarcerated by the Allies had to be played up, indicating that Japanese soldiers were surrendering freely. It had to be stressed that these men were well fed, contented and 'happy to be out of the miseries of war'. Moreover, the Featherston incident had to be portrayed as an isolated one which occurred because of the 'misplaced fanaticism' of junior officers who once again had let down their men as they had so often done in past military operations.[51]

In February 1943, Pat Frank, the assistant representative of the OWI who had just completed a tour of POW camps in South Pacific Command, suggested to the Allied Political Warfare Committee that one potentially powerful weapon which could be used in the campaign to overcome the Japanese refusal to surrender was to insert photographs in the propaganda leaflets showing the favourable conditions POWs enjoyed in captivity. By highlighting the humane treatment Japanese prisoners received from the Allies, and demonstrating that there were in fact Japanese POWs in Allied hands, it was anticipated that this might jolt some Japanese out of their suicidal tendencies. As Stokes confided to Michael L. Stiver, OWI's representative on the Allied Political Warfare Committee, the 'no-surrender fanaticism of the Japanese must be broken down, and Japanese POWs [must be] used to that end'.[52]

The use of POW photographs as part of a larger political warfare campaign provides an excellent illustration of how the Allies wrestled with the

---

[50] AA, CRS A989/1, item 43/721/1, minutes of third meeting of the APWC, 20 March 1943.
[51] NANZ, External Affairs Department 1, 89/4/13, part 1, message from London to Batterbee, 9 March 1943; Ball to Hodgson, 7 March 1943. For British concerns over threatened retaliation see PRO, FO 916/791, minutes by G. A. Wallinger, 5 March and 3 May 1943.
[52] AA, CRS A989/1, item 43/721/1, minutes of second meeting of the APWC, 25 February 1943; A1067/1, PI46/2/2/2, Stokes to Stiver, 9 June 1943.

problems of dealing with an Asian culture. When the Allied Political Warfare Committee's draft directive was submitted to General MacArthur, he cautioned the political warfare officers on their use of photographs in the leaflets. In addition, he challenged the whole question of airing selected broadcasts of statements made by Japanese POWs. Apprehensive that these methods ran contrary to the terms and spirit of the Hague and Geneva Conventions, MacArthur informed the Australian Prime Minister John Curtin that the use for propaganda purposes of broadcasts or statements made under compulsion by prisoners was clearly a violation of the laws of war. 'Even though this action be voluntary on the part of the prisoner', he opined, 'few Japanese will believe that it is not the result of intimidation or deception; the conclusion of mistreatment will be drawn and may give rise to reprisal action against our own prisoners in Japanese hands.'[53] This was indeed a serious consideration throughout the Pacific War, and one about which many Australian politicians were gravely concerned.

As to the use of photographs, practically all of the Japanese in Australian custody had objected vociferously to the disclosure of their POW status to their families. The idea that death was preferable to the 'dishonour and degradation of surrender' was deeply ingrained in every Japanese soldier, reiterated MacArthur. Convinced that their families would also face disgrace and retribution if news of their loved one's surrender became known, the general astutely observed that the disclosure of identities was a double-edged sword. He reminded Curtin that regard for family and ancestors was one of the 'most powerful stimuli of oriental life'. This might play into Japanese hands, and could be utilised to stiffen the resolve of the Japanese soldier to die rather than surrender.[54] Events in other theatres of operation were to undermine MacArthur's initial reluctance to use photographs in propaganda literature. In December 1943 MacArthur withdrew his earlier objection to the use of pictures in Allied propaganda. Provided they did not disclose the prisoner's identity, and were subject to prescribed local censorship regulations, approved photographs would be released. This included the release of selected photographs to the daily press for domestic consumption. MacArthur now realised that, if properly handled, shrewd propaganda could modify Japanese reluctance to surrender and ultimately reduce Allied casualties. Such photographs, he insisted, 'should be truthful and factual and not designed to exaggerate'.[55]

By the end of 1943 steady progress had been made in expanding the

[53] AA, CRS A1067/1, PI46/2/2/2, MacArthur to Curtin, 23 July 1943.
[54] Ibid.
[55] Ibid; A663/2, item 0158/1/52, MacArthur to Curtin, 2 December 1943.

Allies' political warfare strategies. As the Australian and American counter-offensive gathered momentum in SWPA, interrogations of new batches of Japanese POWs allowed the Allies to refine and adapt their propaganda policies directed at Japanese forces. The inducement-to-surrender campaign was still a matter of timing and depended largely on local conditions. Well-disciplined troops would not surrender, even in desperate situations, if the flow of ammunition and food was well maintained. If, however, enemy troops could be isolated, their supplies cut off and a severe deterioration in their physical well-being effected, this, in time, would help induce a collapse in their mental resistance. Tired, hungry and weakened by disease, if the enemy could be persuaded that their superiors had left them in the lurch, 'the psychological moment for propaganda to work may be said to have arrived'.[56]

Despite the improvements in processing POW interrogation reports and the synthesis of intelligence for combat operations and psychological warfare, the Australian Department of External affairs struck a cautious note in 1944 about progress made so far.

> The number of Japanese prisoners taken still does not run into many thousands, and, were one to judge on numbers alone, one might question the success of efforts to eliminate Japanese opposition by means other than lethal attack. We have to remember however the extraordinary high rate of suicide amongst Japanese troops. It is true that the enemy normally fights to the death, but it is also true that he frequently fights to an early death. He has been carefully indoctrinated to believe that surrender is dishonourable and that death in battle brings glory and honour to his ancestors and descendants. Small wonder then, that in balancing the advantages of surrender and suicide, he will, so long as he is in the company of comrades, usually elect to destroy himself. On his own, and with none to report his movements, he will sometimes prefer to hold on to life and risk his future in captivity. In such cases he regards himself as technically dead, loyalty gone, and free to start as a new person.[57]

On 5 August 1944, Australians faced the harsh and tragic consequences of an enemy bent on destroying himself. In 'B' compound at No. 12 POW

[56] AA, CRS A1067, item PI46/2/2/2, memorandum by Stokes, 3 June 1943; AWM 123, item 665, 'Directive for Political Warfare Against the Japanese', revised draft, submitted to APWC, 5 June 1944.

[57] AA, CRS A1066/4, PI45/1/1/11, second report on Australian activities concerning political warfare against Japan entitled, 'Nature and Purpose of Political Warfare', n.d. (probably mid 1944). The small number of Japanese POWs held in Australia was revealed in September 1943. Between them, Australian and US forces in SWPA had captured only sixteen officers and 481 men. NANZ, AD 1, 336/3/10, C. A. Berendsen, New Zealand High Commissioner to Australia, to New Zealand Minister of External Affairs, 22 September 1943.

Group, Cowra, New South Wales, a massive breakout was orchestrated by a group of battle-hardened and recalcitrant Japanese POWs angered by the announcement that NCOs would be segregated from the rank and file with the latter being sent to another POW facility at Hay, New South Wales. Japanese casualties were indeed horrific: 234 dead (including forty-eight suicides) and 105 wounded out of a total inmate population of 1085. The 22nd Australian Garrison Battalion suffered four dead and four wounded, expending almost 12,000 rounds of rifle and machine-gun ammunition. About 359 POWs breached the wire while 138 remained inside the compound. Of these, twenty committed suicide just prior to or during the break-out.[58]

The Australians were surprised by the breakout. Measures had been taken since the Featherston mutiny to ensure that a suicidal escape did not reoccur. For example, camp officials were very liberal with daily rations. Not only were prisoners fed on the same scale as their Australian guards (3753 calories per day), but the prisoners were also encouraged to grow their own vegetables to supplement their dietary requirements. Accommodation was built along Australian Army guidelines, huts were heated and no work was required from the prisoners apart from normal camp maintenance and servicing within the compound. ICRC inspections confirmed the good treatment these prisoners received.

Camp authorities were also aware, however, that a large minority of their charge were die-hard fanatics. At the end of March 1943 one intelligence summary noted that a recently arrived group of young POWs, many of them suffering from tinea, scabies and pyrexia, were extremely uncooperative during their treatment, 'giving wrong names and being generally antagonistic'. The camp interpreter, Lieutenant Louwisch, described the junior officer who accompanied the group as an obstructionist. 'He introduced the supposedly religious act of turning to the sun at morning roll call', refrained from telling his fellow prisoners that they had to obey orders from the camp commandant, and began organising English classes, explaining to his men that they needed this skill to understand what their enemy was saying.[59]

Cowra (and Featherston) proved that no matter how closely the Allies followed the 1929 Geneva Convention, there would always be a group of hardcore POWs determined to fulfil their own destiny according to the Samurai tradition. In the United States, this die-hard attitude was

---

[58] Charlotte Carr-Gregg, *Japanese Prisoners of War in Revolt* (St Lucia, Queensland, 1978).

[59] AWM 54, item 780/3/2, part 2, notes from camp intelligence reports, Cowra, 28 March 1943.

demonstrated once again, when in May 1944 at Camp McCoy, Wisconsin, swift action by the camp commandant narrowly averted a potentially ugly situation.[60] In early 1945, at Bikaner in India, tensions were reported to have reached flash point. Indiscipline was rife, according to Admiral Mountbatten, Supreme Allied Commander, South-East Asia Command. He warned that urgent reconsideration of camp policy was vital to thwart the 800 or so Japanese POWs in British custody there from mutinying. In fact, in February 1946 a riot did break out; but this was carried out by Japanese civilians interned at Deoli in which nineteen were killed. Once again, at Hay in early 1945, Australian authorities – learning from the Cowra experience – foiled another suicide breakout by Japanese POWs.[61]

There is no question that by mid 1944, as the intake of surrendering Japanese POWs increased,[62] Allied intelligence and propaganda agencies were amassing an enormous amount of valuable information. In fact, POW interrogation reports disclose that the campaign to break down the suicidal tendencies of the Japanese soldier was beginning to bear fruit. Small parties of soldiers in some operational sectors of SWPA were now capitulating on a regular basis. Waving the surrender leaflets at oncoming Allied soldiers, they revealed during their preliminary interrogations that the leaflets had persuaded them that they had had enough. Even more encouraging was the small but growing number of Japanese POWs eagerly volunteering their services to Australian intelligence and political warfare agencies.

In September 1944 the British government informed Canberra that it was contemplating the establishment of a political reeducation programme using a select number of Japanese POWs. The policy was an extension of one already in operation amongst German and Italian captives held in the United Kingdom and India respectively.[63] To emphasise that the raw material did exist in Australia for just such a project, in early 1945, one External Affairs officer reported to Stokes that he had recently found

[60] Krammer, 'Japanese Prisoners of War'.

[61] PRO, War Office Papers, WO 203/4348, Mountbatten memorandum on his visit to POW camp Bikaner, 24 April 1945; Andrew Easterbrook, 'Japanese Prisoners of War Held by British and Commonwealth Forces in the Pacific War, 1941–1946', unpublished MA thesis, University of the West of England, Bristol, 1996; D. C. S. Sissons, 'The Cowra Break-Out, 5 August 1944', transcript of unpublished paper (1994).

[62] AWM 54, item 780/1/3, Japanese POW statistics August 1942 to September 1944.

[63] M. B. Sullivan, *Thresholds of Peace: Four Hundred Thousand German Prisoners and the People of Britain, 1944–48* (London, 1979); Arthur L. Smith, Jr, *The War for the German Mind: Re-Educating Hitler's Soldiers* (Oxford, 1996); Kent Fedorowich, 'Propaganda and Political Warfare: The Foreign Office, Italian POWs and the Free Italy Movement, 1940–43', in Moore and Fedorowich, eds, *Prisoners of War*, pp. 119–47.

one volunteer, Lieutenant Yoshikazu Furuhata. Not only was the young officer willing to write leaflets to encourage Japanese soldiers to surrender, he was also keen to assist in the broader work of the reeducation programme. Stokes was told that Furuhata, who had been reading economics at Osaka University before receiving his commission, was openly opposed to the military cliques and professed democratic sentiments. He was just the type of candidate the British were looking for to help them establish a special unit in Australia for the political indoctrination of Japanese POWs. 'I am confident', wrote H. A. Graves, 'that there is a sufficient number of *educated* Japanese likely to come over, to make the venture worth while.'[64] It is unclear if this unit in fact got beyond the planning stages. The sudden and unconditional surrender of the Japanese empire in August 1945, and the swift repatriation of all Japanese POWs from Australia by March 1946, suggests that the indoctrination unit remained stillborn. Nevertheless, it reinforces the impression that Japanese POWs were willing to help their captors with this enterprise if the war had continued.

Of course, we must not forget that disease, isolation, starvation and poor leadership were deciding, if not crucial, factors in persuading a growing number of Japanese service personnel to surrender; and it was this combination of factors which led to an increase in the numbers who surrendered to Allied troops in SWPA between 1944–45. But, as Allison Gilmore has so poignantly argued, Japanese POWs were instrumental in drafting propaganda leaflets and assisting American psychological warfare officers in formulating plans for the political indoctrination of their fellow captives.[65] Australian archival material reflects this growing 'rebirth' amongst Japanese POWs too. It also reveals that racial prejudice, apart from individual biases among several Australian officers during the initial stages of the Pacific War, had no place during the interrogation process. Examiners, whatever their personal feelings, had to embark upon a rational and systematic line of questioning. For information coloured by race prejudice was useless and potentially dangerous when applied during combat operations.

Although it remains difficult to assess the application of POW information by field commanders in the SWPA (a subject of ongoing investigation), it must not be forgotten that it was the sterling work of ATIS which provided the various intelligence and political warfare agencies, above all

---

[64] AA, CRS, A1067/1, PI46/2/1/20, S. M. Bruce, Australian High Commissioner to the United Kingdom, to Prime Minister Curtin, 15 September 1944; Evatt to F. M. Forde, Minister for the Army, 9 February 1945; H. A. Graves, Department of External Affairs, to Stokes, 20 February 1945.

[65] Gilmore, 'We Have Been Reborn', pp. 195–215.

those operated by the Americans, with the first insights of their Japanese foe. As the war progressed, it was the painstaking diligence of ATIS officers in Australia and New Guinea who compiled a plethora of increasingly sophisticated and in-depth profiles which a growing number of propaganda and psychological warfare agencies depended upon and deployed with increasing effect. And what of the efforts of the as yet undisclosed number of Japanese POWs who came forward eagerly throughout 1945 to assist the Allies against their former comrades? This overturns earlier conclusions made by Charles Cruickshank, for example, that Japanese POWs provided little in terms of intelligence or propaganda.[66] On the contrary, they were indispensable.

[66] Charles Cruickshank, *SOE in the Far East* (Oxford, 1986), pp. 236–8. The late Louis Allen, scholar and a former intelligence officer who served in Burma with the South-East Asia Translator and Interpreter Centre during the Second World War, acknowledged British efforts to deploy information derived from POW interrogations. He admitted, however, that the information was limited and low grade because the number of POWs captured in Burma amounted to under 3000, the highest ranking captive being a captain. Louis Allen and David Steeds, 'Burma: The Longest War, 1941–45', in Saki Dockrill, ed., *From Pearl Harbour to Hiroshima* (London, 1994), p. 116.

# 5

# POWs and International Law

## Hisakazu Fujita

The treatment of prisoners of war in the Second World War and the question of compensation for their sufferings should be seen in their historical context. While the evolution of laws, customs and usages relating to the status and treatment of prisoners of war dates from the middle ages or earlier in European history, most attention must be paid to more recent times, particularly the period after the Thirty Years War of 1618–48.

During the middle ages, wars were conducted almost as private enterprises between kings, feudal landlords, city states and the church. The chivalrous laws of war, which involved, inter alia, sparing the life of a captured adversary, were applicable only between feudal knights. The rank and file, including archers and crossbowmen, were regarded with contempt by the aristocracy, and were sometimes subjected to wholesale massacre. The civilian population at large was also at the mercy of the aristocracy.[1] On the other hand, warfare was, as a general rule, conducted within some limits. The church from time to time tried to impose restrictions with regard to non-combatants, weapons, church personnel and property.[2] Casualties were also kept down by the relatively small number of actual combatants. The treatment of prisoners of war directly reflected the development of society and warfare. The practice of enslaving enemy prisoners was explicitly forbidden in 1179 by the Third Lateran Council, though only with respect to Christian prisoners.[3]

The most characteristic way of treating prisoners was to hold them in captivity until the payment of a ransom to the captor. This practice, however, seems to have applied only to the aristocracy. Common foot-soldiers, including archers and crossbowmen, although sometimes slaughtered on the battlefield, once their army had suffered defeat were not pursued and

---

[1] Arthur Nussbaum, *A Concise History of the Law of Nations* (revised edition, New York, 1954), pp. 17–44.

[2] Ibid., p. 18.

[3] Miguel A. Marin, 'The Evolution and Present Status of the Laws of War', *Recueil des cours de l'Académie de Droit International* (RCADI), 92 (1957), p. 655; Henri Coursier, 'L'évolution de droit international humanitaire', ibid., 99 (1960), p. 380.

captured at all. They represented no worthwhile economic value. The ad hoc nature of warfare made it difficult to keep large numbers of prisoners for later exchanges with the enemy. The prisoner and the economic value he represented usually belonged to the individual who captured him and not to the state, although the former's captain, lord or king were sometimes entitled to a share of ransom. In the late middle ages especially it was usual to go to court for the settlement of economic disputes between the prisoner (or his family) and the captor, or between persons putting forward conflicting claims to the ransom.[4]

These usages relating to prisoners of war, as well as the laws of war in general in western Europe, were not as such considered applicable in wars with non-Christian societies. The crusades were marked by large-scale atrocities and massacres of the Saracens.[5] Rules relating to the treatment of civilians and prisoners of war also evolved within the Islamic world. In the instructions given by Mohammed's successor, Caliph Abu-Bakr (573–634), to the first Syrian expedition, and in two legal encyclopedias of 1096 and 1280, rules were laid down that civilians and civilian property should be respected. Torture and mutilation of prisoners were prohibited in the code of 1280. Prisoners seem to have been more often exchanged, or even unilaterally released, in Islamic than in Christian warfare. Nevertheless, prisoners captured by Moslems could also be killed, condemned to slavery or released on ransom.[6]

In the sixteenth and seventeenth centuries important changes occurred with the emergence of absolute monarchy and the consolidation of standing professional armies financed by the state treasury and subject to the central administration. War increasingly became a matter between kings and states. Yet wars still retained in practice many characteristics of feudal warfare, particularly over the treatment of prisoners of war. As a general rule the prisoner belonged to the individual who captured him and not to the state. The development of warfare into a relation between states and standing professional armies only gradually led to the prisoner of war being considered as a representative of the regular armed forces of an enemy state.

Among the authors writing in the so-called golden period of international

---

[4] On the practice of ransoming prisoners in the late middle ages, see especially, M. H. Keen *The Law of War in the Late Middle Ages* (London, 1965), pp. 156–85; G. I. A. D. Draper, "The Law of Ransom during the Hundred Years War', *Revue de droit pénal militaire et de droit de la guerre*, 7 (1968), pp. 263–77.

[5] G. I. A. D. Draper, 'The Interaction of Christianity and Chivalry in the Historical Development of the Law of War', *International Review of the Red Cross*, 5 (1965), pp. 8–14.

[6] Ahmed Rechid, 'L'Islam et le droit des gens', *RCADI*, 60 (1937), pp. 449–64, 470–71, 474–77.

legal science, the Swiss jurist Emmerich de Vattel (1714–67) still held that in principle all persons belonging to the enemy nation were enemies. In *The Law of Nations* of 1758, he said: 'Women, children, feeble old men, and the sick are to be counted among the enemy, and a belligerent has a right over them, inasmuch as they belong to the nation with which he is at war'. But he added: 'At the present time war is carried on by regular armies; the people, the peasantry, the towns-folk, take no part in it, and as a rule have nothing to fear from the sword of the enemy'.[7] A few years later J.-J. Rousseau (1712–78), in his famous formulation of the new concept of war, noted that war is a relation between states in which the individuals are not enemies as men, or even as citizens, but as soldiers.[8]

As all prisoners of war came to be regarded as belonging to the state and not to the individuals who captured them, the ransom for their release began to be paid to the state treasury. The state undertook the responsibility for ransoming its own soldiers captured by the enemy. Another trend towards considering the prisoners as belonging to the state can be seen in the practice of releasing all prisoners without ransom and without regard to numbers and rank at the conclusion of peace. A significant example is provided by the Peace of Westphalia of 1648, ending the Thirty Years War. As to the treatment of prisoners of war during captivity, the primary responsibility for their maintenance seems to have lain with the detaining state, while the party which had incurred the greater expenses was compensated by the other party when the prisoners were exchanged or released.[9]

The new ideology that emerged with the French Revolution of 1789 influenced the official French attitude towards prisoners of war during the Revolutionary Wars. The preamble to a decree concerning prisoners of war adopted by the National Assembly on 4 May 1792 noted that the assembly wanted to regulate the treatment of enemy military prisoners 'd'après les principes de la justice et de l'humanité'.[10]

One question on which the French Revolution and to some extent the American War of Independence, had a considerable practical bearing was the scope of the category of persons entitled to the status of lawful combatant

---

[7] E. de. Vattel, *The Law of Nations: or The Principles of Natural Law, Applied to the Conduct and to the Affairs of Nations and of Sovereigns*, trans. G. D. Gregory, Classics of International Law, 3 (New York, 1964), iii, ch. 8, paras 145, 147.

[8] J.-J. Rousseau, *Contrat social: ou principes du droit politique* (Paris, n.d.), i, ch. 4, pp. 244–45.

[9] See article 3 of the treaty of Paris of 1763 between France, Great Britain and Spain, *The Consolidated Treaty Series* (Dobbs Ferry, New York), edited and annotated by Clive Parry, 42, pp. 323–24.

[10] E. Nys, *Etudes de droit international et le droit politique* (Brussels, 1896), pp. 374–75.

and consequently of prisoner of war. The French and American revolutionary forces were to a large extent 'people's armies', consisting of large number of volunteers and later conscripts, as well as bourgeois officers. The existence of these new elements in the French army led the National Assembly to affirm, in a decree of 3 August 1792, that officers and soldiers of the volunteer corps (*la garde nationale*) captured under arms were also to be treated as prisoners of war.[11]

The enlargement and democratisation of the French and American armies did not lead, however, to any drastic changes in the basic distinction between combatants and civilians. Both in the Revolutionary wars and afterwards it seems to have been generally held that persons taking part in hostilities with no authorisation from the state, as well as guerrilla and similar forces operating in occupied territory, were not entitled to be treated as lawful combatants and therefore as prisoners of war.

Military manuals on the law of war began to appear, one of the first being 'Instruction for the Government of Armies of the United States in the Field' in 1863 during the American Civil War. This famous instrument, the so-called Lieber Code, contained a part dealing specifically with prisoners of war.[12]

The codification of the law of war into general multilateral treaties began only in the second half of the nineteenth century. At the same time the pressure for a codification of the customary laws and usages relating to prisoners of war increased. Henry Dunant, the founder of the Red Cross was particularly active in this field. The Geneva Conference, held under the auspices of the Red Cross, adopted the 1864 Geneva Convention for the Amelioration of the Condition of the Wounded in Armies in the Field –

---

[11] M. de Martens, *Recueil des principaux traités d'alliance, de paix, de trêve, de neutralité, de commerce, de limites, d'échange etc, 1791–1795* (Göttingen, 1826), v , p. 363.

[12] *The Law of War: A Documentary History*, ed. Leon Friedman (New York, 1972), i, pp. 158ff. The Lieber Code deals with prisoners of war in section 3. Article 49 defines them as follows: 'A prisoner of war is a public enemy armed or attached to the hostile army for active aid, who has fallen into the hands of the captor, either fighting or wounded, on the field or in the hospital, by individual surrender, or by capitulation'. Article 55 continues: 'A prisoner of war is subject to no punishment for being a public enemy, nor is any revenge wreaked upon him by the intentional infliction of any suffering, or disgrace, by cruel imprisonment, want of food, by mutilation, death, or any other barbarity'. Article 74 lays down: 'A prisoner of war, being a public enemy, is the prisoner of the government, and not of the captor. No ransom can be paid by a prisoner of war to his individual captor or to any officer in command. The government alone releases captives, according to rules prescribed by itself'. Finally article 76 states: 'Prisoners of war shall be fed upon plain and wholesome food, whenever practicable, and treated with humanity. They may be required to work for the benefit of the captor's government, according to their rank and condition'.

the first Red Cross Convention. The Hague Peace Conferences of 1899 and 1907, convoked by the Russian emperor, adopted a series of Hague conventions and declarations on the law of war and neutrality.

Apart from the Red Cross Convention of 1864, the first multilateral convention dealing with prisoners of war was the Hague regulations of 1899 annexed to the convention respecting the law and usages of war on land. This convention was renewed in 1907. The French-German War of 1870–71 had once again highlighted problems relating to the participation in hostilities of persons not belonging to the regular army of the state. This question held an important place on the agenda of the Hague Conference of 1899 and 1907, giving rise to deep controversies between the smaller states and the great powers.

According to the compromise worked out in the Hague regulations of 1899 the following categories were, if captured, entitled to the status of prisoner of war – only the first three being at the same time lawful belligerents:

1. Members of regular armies.

2. Members of militias and volunteer corps not forming part of the army but fulfilling four conditions. [13]

3. Members of so-called mass levies (*leveés en masse*), i.e. civilians offering spontaneous resistance to invading troops, provided these levies respected the laws and customs of war. [14]

4. Individuals accompanying an army without directly belonging to it, such as war correspondents, sutlers and contractors.

As a general rule the civilian population not belonging to any of these categories was exempt from capture. Nor could the medical and religious personnel of the enemy be made prisoners of war according to articles 2 and 3 of the Geneva Red Cross Convention of 1864. Subject to detention and trial, but not entitled to POW status, were such categories as members of irregular forces and mass levies not fulfilling the stipulated conditions, spies and deserters captured by the forces from which they had abandoned. [15]

In addition to the well-established rule, according to which all POWs

---

[13] These conditions, which still exist in article 4 of the Third Convention of 1949, are: (i) that these forces be commanded by a person responsible for his subordinates; (ii) that they have a fixed distinctive emblem recognisable at a distance; (iii) that they carry arms openly; and (iv) that they conduct their operations in accordance with the laws and customs of war.

[14] In the 1907 Hague regulations, the condition was added that the levies carry arms openly.

[15] See articles 29–31 of the 1899 Hague regulations.

were to be repatriated regardless of number and rank at the conclusion of peace, the Red Cross Convention of 1864 (article 6, 3) established a duty to repatriate during the war those wounded and sick prisoners who were recognised as being unfit for further service even when they had recovered.

In 1870 a special information bureau for prisoners captured in the Franco-German War was established at Basel as a complement to the official agency for wounded soldiers, established by the International Committee of the Red Cross (ICRC). It was not until the beginning of the twentieth century, however, that the ICRC, which since 1863 had assumed certain tasks relating to the wounded and sick, also became officially concerned with able-bodied prisoners of war. The Hague regulations of 1899 and 1907 (article 15) recognised the activities of relief societies for prisoners of war but made no specific reference to the ICRC.

The laws and usages outlined above were applicable only in relations between the 'civilised' nations. Prisoners captured in colonial and civil wars were not entitled to the POW status which had evolved in the relations between these states. Nevertheless, it is of interest to remark the application of the laws and usages of war in the Sino-Japanese War of 1894–95. During this war in the Far East, the laws and usages of war, including the treatment of POWs, seemed to have been strictly observed by Japan, with the exception perhaps of the case of Port Arthur. The Japanese government in particular gave orders to its armies to send the Chinese POWs to Japan. The POWs were treated not as criminals but as prisoners and fed in the same way as Japanese soldiers.[16] In the Russo-Japanese War of 1904–5, both the Russian and the Japanese POWs were humanely treated. This was the first case of the application of the POW provisions of the Hague regulations of 1899.[17] The treatment of the POWs and wounded by both countries was recognised as humane by the ICRC.[18]

The escalation of warfare which characterised the First World War involved, *inter alia*, an increase in the number of participating states, the

[16] See Nagao Ariga, *La guerre sino-japonaise au point de vue du droit international* (Paris, 1896), pp. 105 ff; cf. Sakuei Takahashi, *Cases on International Law during the Chino-Japanese War* (Cambridge, 1899).

[17] Nagao Ariga, *La guerre russo-japonaise au point de vue continental et le droit international d'après les documents officiels du grand état-major japonais* (Paris, 1908), pp. 93ff. In this war there were 84,445 Russian POWs and 2083 Japanese POWs. Eight days after the beginning of the hostilities, the Japanese Minister of War published the rules on the treatment of the POWs including thirty-four articles which had for their purpose the application of chapter 2, section 1, of the Hague regulations, ibid., p. 93.

[18] Pierre Boissier, *Histoire du Comité International de la Croix-Rouge: De Solférino à Tsoushima* (Paris, 1963), pp. 432–38.

number of combatants and the duration of the conflict as compared to the wars of the nineteenth century. The total number of POWs captured in the First World War amounted to over five million.[19]

The question of the labour of POWs was of considerable importance in both the First and Second World Wars, where large numbers of POWs helped to alleviate the shortage of manpower of detaining powers.[20] The growing trend towards 'total war' also implied that the value of the prisoners as a labour reserve for the detaining power greatly increased. Yet each power had an interest in reducing to a minimum the exploitation of POWs for the enemy's war effort. The traditional principle, according to which POWs might be utilised for work but only for work of a non-military character, purported to establish an equilibrium between these differing interests. However, the treatment of POWs posed considerable problems of a material and technical nature. There were also frequent allegations of actual ill-treatment of POWs.[21] The sixteen articles of the Hague regulations of 1907 concerning the treatment of POWs during captivity were generally felt to be insufficient in this new situation.

The experience of the First World War led the ICRC, which in 1914 had already established an International POW Agency, to work for the development of the Hague regulations by means of a new multilateral convention specifically devoted to POWs.[22] At the request of the Tenth International Conference of the Red Cross in 1921, the ICRC drew up a draft convention in 1923.[23] The Geneva Conference of 1929, on the basis of the ICRC draft of 1923, drew up the convention relative to the treatment of prisoners of war of 1929. This POW convention in many ways developed and particularised the law as it stood, containing ninety-seven articles as compared to the three articles on lawful belligerents and seventeen articles

[19] During the nineteenth century the highest number of prisoners of war captured in a single war seems to have been approximately 400,000 in the French-German War of 1870–71. A. Mélignhac and E. Lémonon, *Le droit des gens et la guerre de 1914–1918*, i (Paris, 1921), p. 256. This figure is modest compared to the approximately five or six million POWs in the First World War and the perhaps fifteen to twenty million POWs in the Second World War, ICRC, *Report on Activities of the Second World War*, i (Geneva, 1948), pp. 243, 245, 439.

[20] *Report on the Activities of the Second World War*, pp. 327–40.

[21] James Wilford Garner, *International Law and the World War*, ii (London, 1920), pp. 1–57; Mérignhac and Lémonon, *Le droit de guerre et la guerre de 1914–1918* i, pp. 257–306.

[22] Georges Werner, 'Les prisoniers de guerre', *Recueil des cours de l'Académie de Droit International*, 21 (1928), i, pp. 65–73.

[23] See the resolution in *Dixième conférence de la Croix-Rouge tenue à Genève du 30 mars au 7 avril 1921: compte rendu*, pp. 218–21. The International Law Association had already adopted another proposal in the form of a Code for the Treatment of Prisoners of War, *Report of the Thirteenth Conference* (The Hague, 1921), i, pp. 236–46.

on the treatment and repatriation of POWs contained in the Hague regulations.[24] The general principles of the POW convention of 1929 were clearly
derived from nineteenth-century law. In the convention itself it is noted
that it was to be complementary to the Hague regulations in the relations
between the powers bound both by the regulations and the convention
(article 89).

The most important innovations of the convention of 1929 were the
prohibitions on reprisals (article 2, paragraph 3) and collective penalties
(article 46, paragraph 4), the provisions on prisoners' representatives
(articles 43–44), the regulation of judicial and disciplinary proceedings
(articles 54–67) and others. At the same time, the recommendation that
wounded and sick POWs should be repatriated, contained in the Second
Red Cross Convention of 1906, was transformed into an actual obligation
to repatriate seriously ill or seriously wounded prisoners. The forty-seven
participants in the diplomatic conference of 1929 included twenty-five
European states and twenty-two non-European states and British dominions.
The POW Convention of 1929 was formally applicable in the relations
between the major western states, including Germany, during the Second
World War. Japan, not being a party to the convention, had declared itself
ready to apply it *mutatis mutandis.*

The further escalation of warfare in the Second World War, making it ever
more total, brought even greater material and technical problems relating
to POWs than had the First World War. As is well known, the law relating
to POWs (and the law of war in general) was frequently violated, in some
cases on a massive scale. To a certain extent these violations were unavoid-
able, in view of the extensive nature and intensity of the war; but, in the
cases of Germany and Japan, there is ample documentation showing that
the atrocities committed against POWs (not to speak of civilians) were
largely a part of a deliberate and systematic policy of terror.[25]

The treatment of POWs by the western states, notably the United Kingdom
and the United States, was on the whole far better. This does not mean,
however, that the application of the 1929 convention was without problems.

---

[24] At the conference, the ICRC draft of 1923, consisting of 103 articles, was criticised particu-
larly by the United States and Japan for being too detailed. *Actes de la conférence de Genève*
(Geneva, 1930), pp. 433–42.
[25] See, e.g., *International Military Tribunal at Nuremberg: Trial of Major War Criminals*
(Nuremberg, 1947), i, pp. 229–32; 'International Military Tribunal for the Far East', in Leon
Friedmann (ed.), *The Law of War* (New York, 1972), pp. 1055–1123; G. I. A. D. Draper, *The Red
Cross Conventions* (London, 1958), p. 49.

The status of combatants fighting for governments or similar authorities in exile, members of resistance movements operating in occupied territory, and the utilisation of the labour of POW, all caused legal problems. The status of German POWs after Germany's unconditional surrender in May 1945 and that of Japanese POWs after the Japanese surrender in August 1945 was ambiguous.[26]

The experience of the Second World War led the ICRC to include the question of POWs amongst the items requiring new legal instruments. On the basis of the preliminary conference of National Red Cross Societies held in 1946 and the conference of government experts held in 1947, the ICRC submitted, to the Seventeenth International Conference of the Red Cross in 1948, four draft conventions on the wounded and sick in land warfare, on the wounded, sick and shipwrecked in naval warfare, and on prisoners of war and on civilians. These drafts were, with some amendments, submitted to the Geneva diplomatic conference of 1949, which adopted the present four conventions on August 12, 1949.

The Third Geneva Convention (the POW Convention of 1949), with its 143 articles constituted a further development and particularisation of earlier laws and customs relating to POWs. Many of its main principles were based on the POW Convention of 1929, hence also on the Hague Regulations of 1899 and 1907, and on the customary law prevailing at the end of the nineteenth century.

Sixty-four states participated in the diplomatic conference of 1949, as compared with the forty-seven participants in the conference of 1929. Non-European states formed the majority (thirty-four out of sixty-four) in 1949, whereas they had still been in the minority (twenty two out of forty-seven) in 1929.[27] Japan, a participant in 1929, could not attend the 1949 Conference as it was still under Allied occupation.

The convention was a code of legal rules, both fundamental and detailed, for the protection of POWs throughout the period of their captivity. These rules were designed to prevent the appalling experiences of the Second World War. The guiding principle underlying all the articles was that humane and decent treatment was a right and not a favour conferred on men and women of the armed forces captured in the tide of war. There was clear recognition that POWs were the victims of events and not criminals. They owed no

---

[26] *ICRC*, i, pp. 216–403, 228–514.

[27] Dietrich Schindler and Jiri Toman, *The Law of Armed Conflicts: A Collection of Conventions, Resolutions and Other Documents* (Leiden, 1973), pp. 291–92. Even before 1929 the traditional distinction between civilised and uncivilised nations had begun to lose ground as a formal criterion for the application of the law of war.

allegiance to the detaining power and there was recognition of the general principle that both the legal status and the ensuing rights of POWs should be assimilated as closely as possible to those of the members of the armed forces of the detaining power. Provision was made for a comprehensive role to be played by the protecting power, the ICRC, and other relief organisations.[28] POWs must be repatriated at the conclusion of peace regardless of number and rank.[29]

It is on the level of technicalities that a substantial change has occurred, for the Third Geneva Convention contains detailed specifications, adopted mainly on the basis of the experiences of the Second World War. At the same time it is obvious that these rules were designed in the first place for armed conflicts where the participants were developed industrialised states. The additional protocols of 1977 in part met the requirements of developing countries which had gained independence after their struggles for self-determination.

Nowadays it is generally considered that combatants *hors de combat,* whether or not they have 'fallen into the power of the enemy' within the meaning of article 4 of the Third Geneva Convention of 1949, must not be killed but be protected or released if they cannot be held. The provision safeguarding an enemy *hors de combat* in the Hague Regulations does not contain any qualifications relating to military necessity. However, in a case decided by a British military court in 1945, the claim that exceptional circumstances may arise when the killing of a prisoner might be justified was not categorically rejected by the court.[30] But, according to article 130 of the Third Geneva Convention of 1949, acts such as wilful killing, torture or inhuman treatment, including biological experiments, as well as wilfully causing great suffering or serious injury to body or health, are included among the so-called grave breaches of the convention.

During the Second World War, POWs were frequently killed for other than purely operational reasons. Partisans, airmen landing by parachute in enemy territory and commando troops were executed in accordance with the German 'commando order' signed by Hitler in October 1942.

As to torture and other forms of inhuman treatment, the Third Convention contained a number of provisions prohibiting such practice. On the labour of POWs, the traditional principle, according to which POW may be used for work but only for work of a non-military character, forms the

---

[28] Draper, *The Red Cross Conventions,* pp. 50–51.

[29] Allan Rosas, *The Legal Status of Prisoners of War* (Helsinki, 1976), pp. 81–82.

[30] In the Peleus trial (British Military Court, Hamburg, October 1945), *Law Reports of Trials of War Criminals,* The United Nations War Crimes Commission, i (London 1947), pp. 1–21.

basis of article 50 of the Third Geneva Convention of 1949. Its aim, however, was to define more closely the corresponding provision of the POW Convention of 1929 (article 31) by enumerating those types of work which prisoners might be compelled to perform. The question of the labour of POWs was of a considerable importance in the Second World War, where large numbers of POWs helped to alleviate the shortage of manpower of detaining powers.[31] Especially in Germany, POWs were often employed on work of a clearly military character. Sometimes this implied that they were converted into civilians and bereft of the guarantees of the POW Convention of 1929.

The International Military Tribunal for the Far East (the Tokyo War Crimes Tribunal)[32] was established by a special proclamation issued by Douglas MacArthur, as Supreme Commander for the Allied Powers, in January 1946, in order to implement the terms of surrender which required the meting out of stern justice to war criminals. It rendered judgement on the major Japanese war criminals in November 1948.[33] The charter of the Tokyo War Crimes Tribunal had provision for the jurisdiction over persons and offences (article 5) which included three categories of crimes: 'Crimes against Peace'; 'Conventional War Crimes'; and 'Crimes against Humanity.'

While 'Crimes against Peace' and 'Crimes against Humanity' were new categories of international crimes at that time, 'Conventional War Crimes', that is violations of the laws or customs of war, were already well-established ones. The Tokyo Charter did not list war crimes which were included in the Charter of the International Military Tribunal (the so-called Nuremberg Charter). Article 5 of the Nuremberg Charter laid down: 'Violations shall include, but not be limited to, murder, ill-treatment or deportation to slave labour or for any other purpose of civilian population of or in occupied territory, murder or ill-treatment of prisoners of war or persons on the seas, killing of hostages, plunder of public or private property, wanton destruction of cities, town or villages, or devastation not justified by military necessity'. This list was applicable to the category of war crimes in the Tokyo Charter. The Tokyo War Crimes Tribunal confirmed the applicability of the law of war, in particular the POW Convention of 1929, to Japan's activities in the Pacific War, and acknowledged the inhuman treatment of Allied POWs by members of the Japanese Army.

---

[31] *ICRC*, i, 1948, pp. 327–40.

[32] The Tribunal was established in virtue of and to implement the Cairo Declaration of 1 December 1943, the Declaration of Potsdam of 26 July 1945, the Instrument of Surrender of 2 September 1945, and the Moscow Conference of 26 December 1945.

[33] *Treaties and Other Acts Series*, pp. 1586ff.

Japan had not ratified the POW convention before the opening of hostilities on 7 December 1941. But it assured the powers concerned, the USA, Great Britain and others, that, while it was not formally bound by the convention, it would apply the Convention *mutatis mutandis* towards American, British, Canadian, Australian and New Zealand POWs. The judgement stated, 'Under this assurance Japan was bound to comply with the convention save where its provisions could not be literally complied with owing to special conditions known to the parties to exist at the time the assurance was given, in which case Japan was obliged to apply the nearest possible equivalent to literal compliance'.[34] According to the Tribunal, this convention is the 'more complete code of the laws of war' contemplated by the powers signatory to the Hague Convention of 1907. It contained a provision that it should remain in force as between the belligerents who were parties to it, even though one of the belligerents was not a contracting power.

The Red Cross Convention of 1929 was also binding upon Japan, which had signed and ratified it. It contained a provision to the effect that it must be respected by the contracting powers under all circumstances. The parties agreed among other things that officers, soldiers and other persons officially attached to the armies who were wounded or sick should be respected and protected in all circumstances; and that they should be humanely treated and cared for without distinction of nationality by the belligerent in whose power they were.

The Tribunal laid down: 'The general principles of the law exist independently of the said conventions. The conventions merely reaffirm the pre-existing law and prescribe detailed provisions for its application'. A person guilty of inhumanities could not escape punishment on the plea that he or his government was not bound by any particular convention.[35] On conventional war crimes the Tribunal stated (in part B chapter 8), that the evidence relating to atrocities and other Conventional War Crimes presented before the Tribunal established that, from the opening of the war in China until the surrender of Japan in August 1945, torture, murder, rape and other cruelties of the most inhumane and barbarous character were freely practised by the Japanese Army and Navy.

---

[34] Friedman, *The Law of War*, ii, pp. 1047, 1102ff. Japan also assured the belligerents that it would apply this Convention to civilian internees and that, in applying the Convention, it would take into consideration the national and racial manners and customs of POWs and civilian internees under reciprocal conditions when supplying them with clothing and provisions.

[35] Ibid., p. 1106.

In its summary and analysis of the voluminous oral and documentary evidence of atrocities committed by the Japanese Army, the Tribunal cited, among others the examples of the Bataan death march and the Burma-Thailand railway. On the death march, the Tribunal condemned the Japanese Army's non-observation of the laws of war in the movement of POWs from one place to another. Prisoners were forced to march long distances without sufficient food and water and without rest. Sick and wounded were forced to march in the same manner as the able. Those who fell behind on such marches were beaten, tortured and murdered. The Tribunal considered the Bataan march, of April 1942, as a conspicuous example of a breach of the laws.[36] It cited the Burma-Thailand railway as a flagrant example of atrocities over an extended period. Prior to and during the work of the construction of the Burma-Siam railway, POWs were constantly subjected to ill-treatment, torture and privation of all kinds, beginning with a forced march of 200 miles to the construction area under almost indescribable hardships. As a result, in eighteen months 16,000 prisoners out of 46,000 died.[37]

The Tribunal believed the failure of the Japanese government to ratify and enforce the POW Convention of 1929 echoed in the fundamental training of the Japanese soldier.[38] The young men of Japan had been taught that 'The greatest honour is to die for the Emperor', a precept which we find Sadao Araki, the Minister for Education from 1938 to 1940, repeating in his speeches and propaganda motion pictures. In addition they were taught that surrender to the enemy was ignominious. The combined effect of these two precepts was to inculcate in the Japanese soldier a spirit of contempt for Allied soldiers who surrendered, which, in defiance of the rules of war, was demonstrated in their ill-treatment of prisoners. The Japanese government condoned the ill-treatment of POWs of war and civilian internees by either failing or neglecting to punish those guilty of

[36] The American and Filipino POWs on Bataan had been on short rations and the sick and wounded were numerous. They were marched in intense heat along the highway to San Fernando, Pampanga, a distance of 120 kilometres or seventy-five miles. Those who fell by the roadside and were unable to continue were shot or bayoneted. Others were taken from the ranks, beaten, tortured and killed. The march continued for nine days. During the first five days the prisoners received little or no food or water. There were approximately 8000 deaths of American and Filipino prisoners. Ibid., pp. 1077–78.

[37] The railroad running from Bangkok in Thailand was linked with that from Moulmein in Burma, the distance of the gap being about 250 miles or 400 kilometres.

[38] Ratification and enforcement of the Geneva Convention of 1929 would have involved the abandonment of military views. In this connection it is interesting to note that Tojo, giving instructions to chiefs of prisoners of war camps, said: 'In Japan we have our own ideology concerning prisoners of war, which should naturally make their treatment more or less different from that in Europe and America'. Ibid., p. 1107.

ill-treating them or by prescribing trifling and inadequate penalties for the offence.[39]

Can the former POWs win compensation for their ill-treatment by the Japanese army during the Second World War? In 1994 several former POWs from different countries filed lawsuits in the Japanese courts. In denying their claims, the Japanese government has insisted that the issue was resolved by the signing of the San Francisco treaty of 1951. The crucial question is whether a treaty of compensation, which has become international customary law, gives individual persons (in this case, former POWs) the right to claim compensation for the damage suffered by them as a result of acts committed by members of the Japanese armed forces in violation of the law of war.

Article 3 of the Hague Convention of 1907 reads as follows: 'A belligerent party which violates the provisions of the said Regulations [the Hague Regulations annexed to the convention] shall, if the case demands, be liable to pay compensation. It shall be responsible for all acts committed by persons forming part of its armed forces'.[40] Several expert opinions submitted before the Japanese court concentrated on this point.[41] Professor F. Kalshoven stated, 'the purpose of the article has been from the outset, first, to reaffirm the pre-existing customary rule of responsibility of a belligerent state for all acts committed by members of its armed forces in violation of the laws of war; and, second, to put beyond question that any such violations render such a belligerent party liable to pay compensation to the individual victims of the violations'.[42]

---

[39] Ibid., p. 1118. Cf. Solis Horwitz, 'The Tokyo Trial', *International Conciliation*, 465, November 1950.

[40] The authentic text which is French reads as follows: 'La partie belligérante qui violerait les dispositions dudit réglement sera tenue à l'indemnité s'il y a lieu. Elle sera responsable de tous actes commis par les personnes faisant partie de sa force armée'.

[41] In the case of the Dutch ex-POWs and others, four experts from different countries discussed the issue: Fritz Kalshoven, Professor Emeritus, University of Leiden; Eric David, Professor, Université Libre de Bruxelles; Christopher Greenwood, Professor, London School of Economics; and Akira Kotera, Professor, the University of Tokyo.

[42] Kalshoven's opinion supporting this submission is found in the drafting history of article 3. His opinion notes two further points. The first one is that, although its drafters may have been thinking solely of the damage or injury caused to individual persons, the wording of the second sentence of article 3 is broad enough to cover the case of state responsibility as well. The other point is that an international wrongful act which gives rise to a claim of state versus state, under the doctrine of general international law relating to state responsibility, at the same time may constitute an encroachment of the legal interests of an individual person. In such a case, that person can bring his or her own claim for damages against the state responsible for the act of its organ or agent.

Against this, two judgements given recently by Japanese district courts denied the right of individuals to claim compensation. The Tokyo district court on 26 November 1998 gave judgement on a demand for compensation by seven former POWs and civilians from ex-Allied countries (Australia, Britain, New Zealand and the United States).[43] These former POWs as plaintiffs demanded US$22,000 each for what they claimed were violations of their rights under international treaties and conventions on the treatment of POWs. The district court judgement rejected the demand for compensation, arguing that neither article 3 of the Hague Convention of 1907 nor any international customary rule (or even international usage) gave any right to individuals to claim compensation. The presiding judge said that compensation issues must be dealt with on a government-to-government level. Another case was the lawsuit filed by eight Dutch ex-POWs and civilian internees demanding compensation as damages for their suffering during forced marches and other inhumane treatment in the Japanese occupied territory of Dutch East Indies during the Second World War. The Tokyo district court on 30 November 1998 rejected their individual demands for compensation.[44] Nevertheless, the latter judgement admitted, for the first time in the Japanese courts, the fact that the plaintiffs had suffered damages in violation of the law of war, including the POW Convention of 1929, by the Japanese armed forces.

The Japanese courts usually give a very rigid interpretation of the wording of treaty provisions and, as a result, have denied generally the right of individuals to claim compensation before a court.[45] They have recommended in several cases a political solution or new legislation for compensation for the victims of the last world war.

The treatment of POWs has been ameliorated by the development of international humanitarian law, but the belligerents or conflicting parties in recent armed conflicts (particularly the Second World War) did not in general observe humanitarian rules. Innumerable POWs and civilian internees suffered as a consequence. Subsequently the Nuremberg and Tokyo War Crimes Trials provided the precedents for punishing major war criminals for serious violations of the law of war. The International Tribunal for ex-Yugoslavia, and that for Rwanda, which have been established re-

---

[43] Case Heisei 7 Year (wa), no. 1382.

[44] Case Heisei 6 Year (wa), no. 1218.

[45] As a famous precedent, the verdict of the Tokyo District Court in the so-called Shimoda case did not approve the claims of individual victims for damages from the atomic bombs. See Friedman, *The Law of War*, ii, pp. 1688 and 1696.

cently by the United Nations,[46] have been working towards the punishment of individuals considered criminals for serious violation of humanitarian law or for committing crimes against humanity or crimes of genocide. The United Nations hopes, by criminalising serious violations of the international humanitarian law, that the implementation of the law may become more effective. In consequence POWs, for example, might be treated by the belligerents in accordance with the principles and rules laid down.

The problem of compensation for the individual victims who suffered grave damage caused by such violations remains. Neither the Nuremberg and Tokyo Trials, nor other trials in victorious or defeated states of the Second World War, have established individual rights to claim compensation. In consequence, most victims remain uncompensated. To try to remedy this situation, the Rome Statute of the International Criminal Court adopted by the United Nations Diplomatic Conference on 17 July 1998 has a provision on reparations to victims.[47] Unfortunately this will only become applicable after the establishment of the International Criminal Court.

[46] See Statute of the International Criminal Tribunal for the former Yugoslavia, adopted 25 May 1993 by the Resolution 827 of the Security Council of the United Nations (1993); Statute of the International Criminal Tribunal for Rwanda, adopted 8 November 1994 by the Resolution 955 of the Security Council (1994).

[47] United Nations Diplomatic Conference of Plenipotentiaries on the Establishment of an International Criminal Court, *Rome Statute of the International Criminal Court*, United Nations document, A/CONF. 183/9. Article 75 of the Statute provides:

> 1. The Court shall establish principles relating to reparations to, or in respect of, victims, including restitution, compensation and rehabilitation. On this basis, in its decision the Court may, either upon request or on its own motion in exceptional circumstances, determine the scope and extent of any damage, loss and injury to, or in respect of, victims and will state the principles on which it is acting.

> 2. The Court may make an order directly against a convicted person specifying appropriate reparations to, or in respect of, victims, including restitution, compensation and rehabilitation. Where appropriate, the Court may order that the award for reparations be made through the Trust Fund provided for in article 79.

> 5. A State Party shall give effect to a decision under this article (as if the provisions of 109 article were applicable to this article).

# 6

# Culture, Race and Power in Japan's Wartime Empire

## Susan C. Townsend

Though the Second World War in Asia was not essentially a clash of cultures, it was, as John Dower has pointed out, 'a clash of national interests, in which Japan waged war against adversaries of extremely diverse cultural backgrounds'. It was a war over security, wealth and power rather than culture.[1] On the other hand, the conflict was certainly mediated by culture, as the technology of the mid twentieth century offered a host of new possibilities for the dissemination of cultural propaganda.

Japanese ideas of an historical and cultural mission in East Asia and later South-East Asia have often been dismissed as empty rhetoric. Indeed, popular wartime slogans such as *hakko ichiu* (eight corners of the world under one roof), and *kyoei* (co-prosperity) undoubtedly sound hollow in the ears of the citizens of Japan's erstwhile colonies who suffered the excesses of Japanese so-called cultural policy. Japanese cultural and racial ideology arose partly in response to Japan's increasing isolation in the international sphere as condemnation of Japanese expansionist policies in China increased, leading ultimately to Japan's withdrawal from the League of Nations. This, together with the rise of Fascism in Europe, resulted in profound disillusionment with western ideas such as liberalism, democracy and individualism among Japanese scholars and government leaders. Japanese intellectuals therefore began to re-examine Japan's own history, culture and traditions in the search for answers to the problem of identity.

An examination of some of the theories predominant among Japanese intellectuals at the time about Japan's cultural mission on the Asian continent and, after 1942, in South-East Asia throws light on the factors which influenced Japanese policy. How did intellectuals and politicians justify Japanese expansion in East and South-East Asia? How did they set about achieving cultural dominance in Asia? Finally how compatible was Japan's cultural ideology with her economic and strategic goals?

---

[1] John Dower, *Japan in War and Peace: Essays on History, Culture and Race* (London, 1995), p. 33.

After the First World War the problem that all imperial powers faced was rising nationalism in their colonies, protectorates and spheres of interest. This had in part been encouraged by the increasing influence of American anti-imperial rhetoric – particularly the rhetoric of Wilsonian idealism which proclaimed the goal of national self-determination for all. Japan's first problem was how to legitimise continuing expansion, indeed overexpansion, in a world where colonialism was considered illegitimate and unjustified.[2]

Japan's second problem was that, although the Fourteen Points speech showed US commitment to the ideal of free trade and open door policy, free trade policies began to break down. The Japanese government's attempts to integrate the Japanese economy into the free trade world order was frustrated by world depression in the early 1930s and by the increasing economic nationalism and protectionism in the west which placed barriers on trade with the British, Dutch and American colonial markets. The alternative, therefore, was a self-sufficient economic bloc consisting of Japan (at this time the concept of Japan included her formal empire in Taiwan and Korea), China and Manchukuo. Thus from the early 1930s a rhetoric of community or *Gemeinschaft* and co-prosperity was formulated and encompassed within concepts such as East Asian Federation (*toa renmei*) and East Asian *Gemeinschaft* (*toa kyodotai*). In 1938 the Japanese Prime Minister, Fuminaro Konoe declared a New Order in East Asia (*toa shin chitsujo*). Later, as the USA began to impose embargoes on the export to Japan of key strategic materials in 1939–1940, an extended economic bloc which would include parts of the European empires in South-East Asia was defined by the rhetoric of the Greater East Asia Co-Prosperity Sphere (*daitoakyoei-ken*).

In the 1920s many American and British observers were sympathetic to Japan's economic aims.[3] After the Manchurian Incident of 1931, however, the tide of opinion began to flow against Japan, especially in the United States, and it became evident that it was not enough to cite Japan's economic needs as a justification for expansion. Therefore Japanese intellectuals and politicians began to formulate a more coherent expansionist ideology which sought to circumvent charges of aggressive imperialism and to appeal instead

---

[2] Peter Duus 'Introduction', in Peter Duus, Ramon H. Myers and Mark R. Peattie, editors, *The Japanese Wartime Empire, 1931–1945* (Princeton, 1996), p. xix.

[3] For example, in 1921 shortly before the Washington Conference, Victor Wellesley in the British Foreign Office expressed sympathy for the Japanese 'confined within a restricted area exceedingly poor in natural resources'. Japan also suffered 'the policies of exclusion adopted by the British Dominions and the United States ... forcing her to take the least line of resistance'. *General Survey of Political Situation in Pacific and Far East with Reference to the Forthcoming Washington Conference*, DBFP, first series, 14, Far Eastern Affairs (April 1920 to February 1922), no. 404.

to the supposed 'oriental' ideals of community and benevolent rule. They professed the cultural commonality of the Asian races and deployed the rhetoric of Pan-Asianism, reinventing traditional concepts such as 'the harmony of the five races' (*kyowa*) 'the kingly way' (*odo*) and 'the eight corners of the world under one roof' (*hakko ichiu*). In 1936 Masayoshi Miyazaki, an economist working for the South Manchurian Railway, and a leading proponent of an East Asian Federation, stated that 'in brief it will be the achievement of the great mission of *hakko ichiu*'. The first task was to liquidate the 'vestiges of the idea of imperialistic aggression and return [to] the rule of righteousness'. He attacked western influenced ideologies stating that 'we orientals know that such western ideas as freedom, equality, democracy, etc. are based on the concept of racial and class differences'. Japan's role, on the other hand, was to achieve a genuine 'Asia for Asiatics'; then it would 'lead a revived China towards the great goal of the New Order in East Asia', replacing 'western concepts of freedom ... with the eastern concept of morality'.[4]

In 1933 one group of intellectuals, the *Showa Kenkyukai* or Showa Research Association, came together to form a think-tank which, it was hoped, would come up with a scientific justification for Japanese expansion on the Asian continent. Dubbed 'Prince Konoe's Brains Trust' membership was diverse, consisting of scholars, journalists, politicians, bankers and representatives of the semi-official Federation of Youth Groups of Greater Japan (*Dai Nippon Rengo Seinendan*). Because of its associations with the Imperial Rule Assistance Association, however, and because some members such as Shumei Okawa were associated with ultra-nationalist groups in Japan, the organisation has been labelled 'fascist'. At the same time it was labelled 'communist' because another member, Hotsumi Ozaki, was executed for his role in the pro-Soviet Sorge spy ring.[5]

In 1938 the association established a task force to determine the 'meaning' of the China Incident of 7 July 1937 which had led to undeclared war with China. It was decided that a new China policy should be formulated which abandoned ideas of national gain and self-interest and would instead promote special ties with China, Japan and Manchukuo predicated on the principles of freedom, equality and cooperative relations. It was necessary to promote a new sense of national mission. A culture study group was

---

[4] Masayoshi Miyazaki, 'Tôa Renmei-ron' (A Theory of East Asian Federation), in Joyce Lebra, *Japan's Greater East Asia Co-Prosperity Sphere in World War II: Selected Readings and Documents* (Kuala Lumpur, 1975), pp. 4–7.

[5] James B. Crowley 'Intellectuals as Visionaries of the New Asian Order', in *Dilemmas of Growth in Prewar Japan*, ed. James Morley (Princeton, 1971), p. 321.

assigned the task of elaborating the cultural and philosophical basis for a regional bloc of Asian nations. The group was headed by the eminent philosopher Kiyoshi Miki, a former student of the leader of the Kyoto school of philosophers Kitaro Nishida. In August 1938 Miki presented his ideas in a lecture entitled 'The World Significance of the China Incident' (*Shina jihen no sekaishiteki igi*) and in 1939 the Culture Study Group published 'The Philosophical Principles of the New Japan' (*Shin Nihon no Shiso Genri*).[6] The document began with a recommendation on the internal reform which was necessary to prepare Japan for leadership in Asia.[7] The key to Asian unity, however, was the modernisation of China to be brought about through Japanese intervention:

> Oriental culture belongs to a treasure house which has not as yet been sufficiently exploited. Opening this treasure house is a duty to the world incumbent upon Orientals. However, East Asian unity cannot be achieved if we allow the continued existence of feudal elements or a return to feudalism ... It is necessary for China to advance within a new culture which allows it to modernise whilst at the same time eliminating the evils of modern capitalism. East Asian unity will make it possible for China to free herself from the yoke of European and American imperialism. Japan, through the China Incident, must work for the liberty of China ... Japan has not carried out an imperialist invasion substituting itself for America and Europe. Rather, Japan is demanding the progress to a new system which goes beyond the profiteering of capitalist economics and views the China Incident as a means to this end.[8]

Miki advocated an East Asian *Gemeinschaft* linked to the cultural traditions of East Asia. He called for a 'revival' or a renaissance of oriental culture: not in the sense of a mere revival of classical culture, such as the Renaissance in the west, but as the creation of an entirely new modern culture. Miki was not therefore dismissing western culture but seeking to 'learn from its scientific spirit' and to reappraise it in relation to Oriental culture.[9]

On 3 November 1938 Konoe, in a radio broadcast, adopted much of this type of rhetoric in his proclamation of the New Order in East Asia which stated Japan's main pledges: to cooperate with China, without subjugating it; to carry out the mission of a united Asia leading to a regenerated China;

---

[6] Crowley, 'Intellectuals as Visionaries', p. 367.

[7] Kiyoshi Miki, 'Shin Nihon no Shiso Genri' (The Ideological Principles of the New Japan) (1939) in *Miki Kiyoshi Zenshu* (The Collected Works of Kiyoshi Miki), ed. Hyoe Ouchi et al. (Tokyo, 1968), xvii, p. 507.

[8] Ibid., p. 510.

[9] Ibid., p. 515.

and to ensure that the Chinese people would share in the great peaceful undertaking of the new East Asian Order.[10]

Two years later the New Order in East Asia was to be expanded into the Greater East Asia Co-Prosperity Sphere as the advocates of *nanshin* or the 'southward advance' began planning to turn a romantic and nebulous dream into reality.[11] At first, however, *nanshin* literature expressed a wish to operate within the orbit of western powers – if only they would agree to open up markets and allow Japanese immigration. The extension of an East Asian Order into the Greater East Asia Co-Prosperity Sphere was not the result of a long-term plan or a widely-held interest in the fate of the peoples of the south. Even in July 1940, when the New Order in East Asia became the Greater East Asian Order, nothing about South-East Asia was implied in the documents. It was only an unforeseen turn in international events and Japanese opportunism that caused a radical change in Japanese policy.[12] On 1 August 1940 Foreign Minister Yosuke Matsuoka proclaimed the Greater East Asia Co-Prosperity Sphere and this was followed by a radio address by Konoe a few days later. Japan's empire was to extend to Borneo, Dutch East Indies, Philippines, French Indochina, Timor, Thailand and Malaya in the southward advance giving Japan formal and informal dominion over about 350,000,000 people.[13]

Existing cultural policy in Korea and Taiwan was characterised by an uncompromising policy of assimilation (*dokashugi*), premised on Japanese racial and cultural superiority and an almost total disregard of the cultural heritage of the colonised. In effect the policy consisted of Japanisation. The Japanese were aware of the French concept of *assimilation* but, whereas the French colonial empire made a pragmatic adjustment toward the principle of association rather than assimilation at the end of the nineteenth century, Japanese policy appeared to move in exactly the opposite direction.[14] The Japanese idea of assimilation had a strongly moral flavour supplied by the Chinese Confucian tradition which was expressed in the phrase *isshi dojin* meaning 'impartiality and equal favour'.[15] Despite the rhetoric of *isshi dojin*, however, Japanese rule degenerated into a ruthless regimentation which entered its final phase in the late 1930s when assimilation gave way to *kominka*

[10] Lebra, *Japan's Greater East Asia Co-Prosperity Sphere in World War II*, p. 10.

[11] Mark R. Peattie '*Nanshin*: The "Southward Advance", 1931–1941, as a Prelude to the Japanese Occupation of Southeast Asia', in *The Japanese Wartime Empire, 1931–1945*, pp. 193–94.

[12] Peattie, '*Nanshin*', p. 212.

[13] Lebra, *Japan's Greater East Asia Co-Prosperity Sphere in World War II*, p. 10.

[14] Mark R. Peattie, 'Japanese Attitudes towards Colonialism, 1895–1945', in *The Japanese Colonial Empire, 1895–1945*, ed. Ramon H. Myers and Mark R. Peattie (Princeton, 1984), p. 97.

[15] Peattie, 'Japanese Attitudes', p. 97.

(the transformation of colonial peoples into imperial subjects), with its enforced worship at Shinto shrines and the taking of Japanese names by Koreans and Taiwanese.[16] The aim of *kominka* was to instil 'the spirit of the military nation' (*gunkoku seishin*) into the indigenous population, as it was realised that colonial subjects were absolutely vital to Japan's war effort.[17] Though the ideology of cultural commonality lent itself less well to the peoples of Micronesia and South-East Asia, Japanisation and *kominka* were the hallmarks of Japanese cultural policy in every corner of the Greater East Asia Co-Prosperity Sphere.

The underlying myths behind Japanese cultural and racial ideology of the Fifteen Years' War first came to light during the literary movement of the eighteenth and nineteenth centuries which became known as the Shinto revival. 'Pure Shin-tau', according to Ernest Satow, was the religious belief of the Japanese prior to the introduction of Buddhism and Confucianism into Japan and the attempts by scholars known as the *wagakusha* or *koku-gakusha* (scholars of things Japanese) to eliminate these alien influences.[18] They sought to reclaim Japanese history and culture from predominant Chinese influences by reviving ancient Japanese texts which by the eighteenth century had fallen into such a state of neglect that much of the literature was scarcely intelligible. The recovery of the texts was a painstaking operation and was the result of almost obsessive dedication resulting, on the one hand, in commendably rigorous scholarship but, on the other hand, in some underlying racial and cultural beliefs which to the modern eye seem not only irrational but grotesque.[19] Two principal myths evoked by the Shinto revival were the 'Golden Age' and the 'Chosen People'. The myth of a 'Golden Age' or 'Paradise' at the beginning of time is found in every continent. The *kokugakusha* believed that Japan's fall from innocence came with the introduction of Chinese learning, particularly Confucianism.[20] In ancient times Japanese people were simple and guileless, requiring no complicated system of morals. On the other hand, the Chinese were so wicked (despite their moral teachings) that society was thrown into disorder and the country was in a state of perpetual civil war. Chinese philosophy was therefore founded upon a false system and had led to the degradation of

[16] Ibid., p. 121.

[17] Wan-yao Chou 'The Kominka Movement in Taiwan and Korea: Comparisons and Interpretations', in *The Japanese Wartime Empire, 1931–1945*, p. 42.

[18] Ernest Satow 'The Revival of Pure Shiñ-tau', *Transactions of the Asiatic Society of Japan*, 3, appendix (from 14 October 1874 to 23 December 1874), revised in 1882 (London, 1905), p. 1.

[19] Carmen Blacker, 'Two Shinto Myths: The Golden Age and the Chosen People', in *Themes and Theories in Modern Japanese History: Essays in Memory of Richard Storry*, ed. Sue Henny and John-Pierre Lehman (London and Atlantic Highlands, New Jersey, 1988).

Japanese society and even the Emperor, who had been reduced 'to the intellectual level of a woman'.[21]

Motoori Norinaga (1730–1801), widely acknowledged as one of the greatest of *kokugakusha* scholars, drew on the ancient chronicles of Japan, the *Kojiki*, originally compiled in the eighth century to prove Japan's cultural and racial superiority to all other peoples. He believed that as Japan was the country which had given birth to the goddess of the sun, Amaterasu-oho-mi-Kami, that 'proves its superiority over all other countries which also enjoy her favours'. Japan's superiority was also enhanced by the fact that it had been ruled over by an unbroken line of sovereigns since the goddess had endowed her grandson Ninigi no Mikoto with the three sacred treasures,[22] proclaiming him sovereign of Japan for ever and ever.[23]

From the beginning of the Meiji period, however, the limitations of *kokugakusha* scholarship, which was confined to ancient Japan and forgotten China, became all too apparent and it lost credibility as scholars turned to the west in order to develop a new world history based on scientific methods in which Japan too could take her place.[24] Japanese historical schools swung somewhat erratically between the Orient and the Occident during the Meiji and Taisho (1868–1926) periods and the mythology of the Shinto revival was largely overlooked; however, it was revived, as one of the pillars of State Shintoism when it was enshrined in 1937 in the *Kokutai no Hongi* (the Cardinal Principles of the National Polity).[25] To the ideologues of expansion it explained why Japan was uniquely fitted to free Asia from western imperialism in a 'holy war'.

Within Japan itself propaganda about Japan's mission in Asia was widely circulated during the 1930s. After the war an investigation of the Japanese pre-war education system was carried out by the Civil Information and Education Section of SCAP Headquarters.[26] Lieutenant-Colonel Donald

[20] Blacker, 'Two Shinto Myths', pp. 66–67.

[21] Satow, 'The Revival of Pure Shin-Tau', p. 13.

[22] The sword, the mirror and the jewel.

[23] Satow, 'The Revival of Pure Shin-Tau', pp. 21–22.

[24] Stefan Tanaka *Japan's Orient: Rendering Pasts into History* (Berkeley, California, 1993), pp. 37–38.

[25] Blacker, 'Two Shinto Myths', p. 77.

[26] The study consisted of 'an examination of elementary middle and higher school textbooks; of an examination of teachers' manuals, teachers' guides, and other instructional material; of an examination of laws pertaining to education, of directives, and orders of the ministry of education, and such other ministries as were concerned with education; of interviews with hundreds of Japanese educators, students, and graduates, covering the period from 1925 until the conclusion of the war'. *The Tokyo War Crimes Trial: The Complete Transcripts of the Proceedings of the International Tribunal for the Far East in Twenty-Two Volumes*, ed. R. John Pritchard and Sonia Magbanua Zaide (New York and London, 1981), i, transcript no. 829.

Ross Nugent, who served in Japan as an educator for four years just prior to the bombing of Pearl Harbor, was a witness for the prosecution at the Tokyo War Crimes Trial. When asked what in his opinion was the effect of pre-war education and military training upon Japanese students, he replied:

> The result, in my opinion, was that such teachings did, in fact, impress upon the students of Japan a belief in the so-called divine mission of the Japanese Empire, a belief in the superiority of Japanese culture over the cultures of other countries [and] what was called 'all the world under one roof'.[27]

As lawyers acting for the defence rightly protested, it is very difficult to judge with any great confidence the precise effect that such propaganda had on a population. The testimony of Professor Tokiomi Kaigo, assistant professor of education at Tokyo Imperial University, threw doubt on its effectiveness. He stated that, whereas in primary and secondary schools pupils tended to believe whatever their teachers taught, he had noted a 'critical attitude' to such teaching by students in high school and in the higher grades of secondary school.[28]

Outside the education system, propaganda regarding Japan's divine mission in Asia was disseminated through all the usual media channels: newspapers, books, posters, photographs and cartoons, as well as through the relatively new and highly effective media of radio and film. One film producer, Kimbei Nakai, who had worked for the Nippon Newsreel Corporation during the war, stated at the trials that:

> Numerous propaganda films were produced following the Manchurian Incident, which pictures were so made as to justify Japan's position in Manchuria, and also to prepare the Japanese people for further military aggression, glorifying the military life, divine worship of the Emperor, depicting Japanese culture and habits as superior to all other nations, and attempting to inculcate into the minds of young and old alike the belief that if was Japan's mission to rule the Great Far East and ultimately the world.[29]

Such testimonies can be misleading, however, and Japanese war films when examined in the United States both by Hollywood directors and the government during the war were found to be highly skilful and sophisticated pieces of work and, though expressly made for propaganda purposes, betrayed the filmmakers' roots in the humanism and liberalism of more peaceful times. More often than not the heroes of films, such as Kenzaburo

[27] Ibid., i, no. 835–36.
[28] Ibid., i, no. 898.
[29] Ibid., i, no. 159–60.

Yoshimura's highly acclaimed 1940 film *Tank Commander Nishizumi* (*Nishizumi Sensha-cho Den*), are humble conscripts or young officers who distinguish themselves in the service of their country. What is emphasised is their humanity and their purity and, according to Ruth Benedict who reviewed the films at the time, they are remarkable for their realism.[30] Other films were more avowedly militarist, such as *The War at Sea from Hawaii to Malaya* (*Hawai-Marei Oki Kaisen*), but in general there was a minimum of rhetoric as to why Japan was at war and few references to the Emperor. Unlike cartoon images of the enemy, the celluloid enemy tended to be amorphous rather than specific, although occasionally the Japanese did produce 'hate the enemy' films such as *The Opium War* (*Ahen Senso*), released in 1943, which targeted the British.[31] The ideology of a racial harmony is presented in films depicting interracial love, such as *China Night* (*Shina no Yoru*), made in 1940. This film is unique because it had different endings depending on which part of the wartime empire it was shown in.[32]

At the beginning of 1942 the Japanese were singularly unprepared for establishing a cultural policy in South-East Asia and, therefore, had to rely on their experiences in Korea, Taiwan and China or on the model of Nazi German propaganda.[33] In South-East Asia, moreover, they were faced with largely illiterate rural populations and thus promoted media which had auditory or visual appeal; movies, performing arts, paper picture shows (*kamishibai*) and music were especially important.[34]

A major Japanese innovation in this region was the drafting of hundreds of *bunkajin* (men of culture), writers, artists, university professors, scholars and musicians, sent to ensure the smooth running of the Japanese propaganda operation under the orders of military officers committed to the Japanese principles of *kodo* (way of the emperor) and *hakko ichiu* (eight corners of the world under one roof). Many Japanese assumed that the newly conquered populations either had no culture of their own or that they were culturally inferior or backward.[35] Other *bunkajin*, such as Kiyoshi Miki who was drafted to the Philippines in 1942 as a punitive measure for

---

[30] Dower, *Japan in War and Peace*, pp. 35–37.
[31] Ibid., p. 35
[32] Aiko Kurasawa, 'Films as Propaganda Media on Java under the Japanese, 1942–45', in *Japanese Cultural Policies in South-East Asia during World War 2*, ed. by Grant K. Goodman (Basingstoke, 1991), p. 76.
[33] Ibid., pp. 2–3.
[34] Kurasawa, 'Films as Propaganda Media on Java', p. 36.
[35] Goodman, *Japanese Cultural Policies in South-East Asia during World War 2*, pp. 3–4.

his 'liberal' ideas,[36] suggested that the peoples of South-East Asia had merely been corrupted by years of European or American colonial rule.[37]

A programme which appeared actually to benefit South-East Asians, however, was the *Nanpo Tokubetsu Ryugakusei* (Special Overseas Students from the Southern Region) which had been based on a study begun just before the outbreak of the Pacific War. The objective of the scheme was:

> to have promising young people from various regions of the world, with major emphasis on the Orient, come to our country ... not only to learn of our excellent academic and artistic achievements but also to come into direct contact with the essence of our national character so they will perceive that the realisation of Japan's ideals of a New Order is the best way for their own motherlands as well and so that they will come forward to cooperate with us.[38]

These attempts to turn the students into Japanophiles seem not only to have failed but to have stoked up the fires of nationalist sentiment in their own countries. Many students, however, remembered with fondness the kindness of their hosts and the people they met in Japan.[39] Indeed even the rigorous and sometimes brutal military-style training in special camps intended to instil the students with the *Yamato damashii* or Japanese spirit were deemed useful since the participants considered that it strengthened both body and soul, giving them self-confidence and eliminating myths of white supremacy. Though many participants remained both critical and sceptical of cultural propaganda elements, many of the students who later

[36] Apparently some former 'liberal leftists' such as Kiyoshi Miki were drafted as *bunkajin* as a punitive measure including Kenzo Nakajima and Soichi Oya, together with known Marxists such as Ikutaro Shimizu and even deserters from military service such as Kinzo Satomura. See Yoji Akashi, 'Japanese Cultural Policy in Malaya and Singapore, 1942–45' , ibid., p. 155n.

[37] See, for example, Kiyoshi Miki, 'Hitojin no Toyoteki Seikaku' (The Oriental Characteristics of the Filipinos) in Miki Kiyoshi Zenchu, xv, pp. 478–519. This originally appeared from July to October 1942 in eight parts in the *Minami Jujisei* (Southern Cross) a newspaper for Japanese soldiers. The version printed in the Zenshu appeared in February 1943.

[38] 'Ryunichi Gakusei Shido Yoryoan' (Outline of Guidance for Foreign Students in Japan) drafted by the Ministry of Education 28 November, 1942 and cited in Kenichi Goto, '"Bright Legacy" or "Abortive Flower": Indonesian Students during World War 2', *Japanese Cultural Policies in Southeast Asia during World War 2*, p. 9.

[39] Yoji Akashi noted that when he attended a round table discussion between Japanese and sixty-seven former *nantokusei* (special students) in 1983, the consensus among them was that they and the Japanese during the Second World War were mutually poor in material life but were rich in their human relations, because they were bound together by *kokoro-to-kokoro no tsunagari* (linked by heart to heart relationship). 'Japanese Cultural Policy in Malaya and Singapore, 1942–45', in Goodman, *Japanese Cultural Policies in Southeast Asia*, p. 149.

achieved prominence in independent South-East Asia felt that this training had benefited them in their careers.[40]

Japan's cultural programmes implemented in her wartime empire came to an abrupt end in 1945. Cultural propaganda was for the most part ill-planned, insensitive and crude, and the former colonial subjects were quick to reject everything associated with Japan. The ideal of a Greater East Asia Co-Prosperity Sphere became associated with the memory of a mortal fear of the *Kempeitai* (police force) and forced labour or prostitution. Many South-East Asians remembered the Japanese for one very singular act which for them symbolised the hollowness of Japanese cultural and racial ideology. This was the practise of *binta* or the slap in the face which was of particular abhorrence, since in most of South-East Asia and the Philippines the head is sacred.[41] The ideology of *hakko ichiu* (eight corners of the world under one roof) frequently translated as 'all the world under one roof', which at one time symbolised 'universal brotherhood', was taken to mean world domination.[42] The ill-treatment of prisoners of war was associated with the codes of *bushido* (the way of the warrior) which were formulated during the early Tokugawa period (1615–1868). While it was often suggested, mistakenly, by western observers that *bushido* was an invention of the twentieth century,[43] the *Hagakure*, a book of narratives told by Tsunetomo Yamamoto and compiled in the early eighteenth century, was widely circulated among Japanese serving officers as well as militarists and ultra-nationalists during the Fifteen Years War.[44] It is perhaps unfortunate that the *Hagakure*

[40] Ibid., pp. 148–49.

[41] See Theodore Friend, *The Blue-Eyed Enemy: Japan against the West in Java and Luzon, 1942–1945* (Princeton, 1988), pp. 188–89, and Ba Maw, *Breakthrough in Burma: Memoirs of a Revolution, 1939–1946* (New Haven and London, 1968), p. 177.

[42] At the Tokyo War Crimes Trial Mr Sugawara, counsel for the defendant Sadao Araki, objected to the translation of the *hakko ichiu* as 'all the world under one roof', stating that in Japan the phrase had a cultural meaning which had no aggressive implications whatsoever. IMFTE, i, no. 850.

[43] See for example Peter de Mendelssohn, *Japan's Political Warfare* (London, 1944), p. 146. The famous Japanese internationalist Inazo Nitobe was the great proponent of *bushido* and popularised the concept in the West in *Bushido: The Soul of Japan,* which first appeared in 1900. Basil Hall Chamberlain, the British pioneer of what can only be described as 'Japanology', maintained all along that *bushido* was essentially a twentieth-century fabrication. In 1912 he wrote that, 'The very word appears in no dictionary, native or foreign, before the year 1900'. He certainly convinced many scholars. Cyril H. Powles, '*Bushido*: Its Admirers and Critics', in *Nitobe Inazo: Japan's Bridge Across the Pacific,* ed. John F. Howes (Boulder, Colorado, 1995), pp. 107–18.

[44] Eiko Ikegame *The Taming of the Samurai: Honorific Individualism and the Making of Modern Japan* (Cambridge, Massachusetts, 1995), p. 279.

represents one of the most extreme and aggressive expressions of *bushido* with its fixation on death. Its opening line is famous: 'The way of the warrior is to be found in death'.[45] Thus far from encouraging a worldwide appreciation of Japanese culture, the cultural propaganda of the wartime empire did exactly the opposite, subjecting Japanese cultural concepts to hatred and ridicule.

Yet in South-East Asia in particular Japan had offered a real promise of hope. The Burmese leader Ba Maw stated that:

> India was the first to recognise the Japanese destiny in Asia, that is, the decisive part Japan would play in destroying the Western domination of the continent ... Rabindranath Tagore ... and a stream of others visited the country and found the heart of Asia beating there too. All returned with a wider Asian feeling, with their faith increased in the reality of the Asian bond, and especially the historical necessity for it.[46]

Japanese leaders simply could not square Japan's economic and strategic aims, primarily the maintenance of peace and order and the acquisition raw materials, with her greater ideals. This dichotomy was not lost on Sun Yat-Sen when, shortly before his death, he made a speech in Kobe entitled 'Great Asia Spirit' in October 1924, citing the Japanese example in Asia as turning point – a starting point in Asia's resurgence. But then he stated:

> You, the Japanese nation, possess the essence of the kingly way of Asia but have already set a foot on the dominating way of America and the West. Before the tribunal of world culture, you, the Japanese nation, will have to make a serious choice whether from now on to become an agent of the western dominating way or a bulwark of the eastern kingly way.[47]

Intellectuals as well as militarists and politicians suffered charges of fascism and ultra-nationalism to the extent that the history of inter-war Japan became distorted in the struggle to apportion blame or avoid blame. However, a substantial body of research is now surfacing which, based on detailed research of the works of a number of intellectuals, now offers a revisionist view of the position of intellectuals in relation to the Fifteen Years War. A recent reappraisal of Miki's teacher Kitaro Nishida, for example, has challenged criticism that he was rabidly nationalistic and pro-militarist. When asked in May 1943 by the army to write his ideas about Japan's role in East Asia, Nishida complied because, although he disliked

---

[45] *Hagakure*, ed. Takeshi Naramoto (Tokyo, 1984), p. 58.

[46] Ba Maw, *Breakthrough in Burma*, p. 48.

[47] Cited in Shizuteru Ueda, 'Nishida, Nationalism, and the War in Question', in *Rude Awakenings: Zen, the Kyoto School and the Question of Nationalism*, ed. James W. Heisig and John C. Maraldo (Honolulu, 1995), pp. 80–81.

the military, he believed that he had a duty to comment on such matters since the principles behind them were of the gravest importance to the state.[48] Many intellectuals found themselves in this position and were aware of the gap between cultural concepts and the military's abuse of them. Nishida is reported to have thundered at one army officer:

> You call it a 'Co-Prosperity Sphere', but how can it be co-prosperity if it doesn't meet the needs of all the peoples involved? If it means giving to our side the right to make all the decisions and tell the other side to 'Do this and don't do that', it is a simple coercion sphere, not a co-prosperity sphere.[49]

Intellectuals were in reality divorced from the decision-making processes and, for those who could see the writing on the wall, the voice of caution turned to the voice of despair. In 1937, shortly after the Rape of Nanking, the Christian and pacifist Tadao Yanaihara was forced to resign for entreating Japanese to 'bury our country for a while so that her ideals may live'.[50]

---

[48] Ibid, pp. 88–89.
[49] Ibid, p. 90.
[50] Tadao Yanaihara, 'Kami no Kuni' (God's Country), in *Yanaihara Tadao Zenshu* (The Collected Works of Yanaihara Tadao), ed. Shigeru Nambara et al. (Tokyo, 1963–65), xviii, p. 652.

# 7

# Japan's Racial Identity in the Second World War: The Cultural Context of the Japanese Treatment of POWs

## Harumi Furuya

Why was Japan's treatment of its prisoners of war in the Second World War so atrocious? Japan's treatment of 'white' POWs — among them, Americans, Australians, the British, the Dutch, Canadians and New Zealanders — was inhumane enough. But its treatment of Asian POWs — Chinese, Malay, for instance — was considerably worse.[1] Why was this so? The aim of this essay is to look at the cultural context for the POW issue, specifically through an examination of Japan's racial identity in the Second World War from a global perspective. Given that race was a salient issue both in Japanese diplomacy and in international politics of the 1930s, an inquiry into Japan's racial identity can shed light on its policies and actions in the Second World War.

By the 'racial identity' of a nation, I mean an identity based on the nation's self-conceived racial worthiness weighed against other races. Japan's racial identity as discussed in this essay is not to be confused with Japan's rhetoric as to what its racial identity was, or with the racial identity of individual Japanese citizens. To examine Japan's racial identity at any time, one must study Japan's relationship with the rest of the world in racial terms, for no country carves out its racial identity on its own. In the first section, the international forces which shaped Japan's racial identity from the end of the nineteenth century into the 1920s are examined in brief, followed by an analysis of its new, double-edged racial identity as 'honorary white' which manifested itself on the Asian continent in the 1930s and 1940s. The second, longer section shifts to the European stage, focusing on Nazi racism toward the Japanese, the myth of the 'honorary Aryan' status and the Japanese reaction to it. The final section presents a brief analysis of

---

[1] See also the comments in Clifford Kinvig, 'Allied POWs and the Burma-Thailand Railway', Kazuaki Saito, 'Towards Reconciliation', and Philip Towle, 'The Japanese Army and Prisoners of War'.

Japan's policy on the Jews, which adds yet another dimension to the highly convoluted and contradictory nature of the Japanese racial consciousness. Japan's role in international politics as a villain throughout the 1930s and during the war was closely tied to its racial identity. This may be best summed up as a racial inferiority complex resulting in a general policy of antagonism toward all.

The 'rest of the world' for Meiji Japan was the west, which, in racial terms, represented the 'white'. Following the opening of its doors in 1868, Japan tried to win a status equal to that of the 'white' nations, mainly by means of industrialisation and imperialism. It is well known that Japan's victories in the Sino-Japanese War in 1895 and in the Russo-Japanese War in 1905 marked Japan's emergence as the first non-white international power. It was precisely at this time, however, that any racism toward the 'yellow' race that had existed ever since the age of expansion in the sixteenth century suddenly took on a political significance. The Triple Intervention in 1895, in which Germany, Russia and France forced a victorious Japan to surrender the Liaotung peninsula, signified both a national and racial humiliation of Japan. Shortly thereafter, Wilhelm II introduced a racial element in his Weltpolitik: *die gelbe Gefahr*, or the 'Yellow Peril'. Wary of Japanese progress, Wilhelm II commissioned the artist Knackfuss in 1895 to work on a picture entitled 'The Yellow Peril' from his own design of an European in a toga, with the Archangel Michael behind him, resisting a Buddha — a symbol of barbarism and heathenism — sitting on flaming clouds across the sea. Impressed with the result, he ordered all ships of the Hamburg-America and Norddeutscher Lloyd lines to display a copy on board.[2]

How many Japanese actually saw Knackfuss's picture is unknown. Nevertheless, Japan was not blind to the existence of the mounting racist resistance on the part of the west. In 1919, at the Treaty of Versailles, Japan asked that a declaration of racial equality be incorporated into the covenant of the League of Nations — a proposal which was vetoed by the 'white' Europeans and Americans.[3] Another racial humiliation for Japan was the US immigration law of 1924 which, in excluding Asians, was clearly racist. Racial discrimination against Japanese-Americans prior to and throughout the 1920s seemed to confirm the Japanese conviction that the racial boundary was perhaps the most difficult of all the hurdles that Japan had to surmount in

---

[2] Frank Iklé, 'Japan's Policies towards Germany', *Japan's Foreign Policy, 1868–1941: A Research Guide*, ed. James W. Morley (New York, 1974), p. 281.

[3] Ernst Presseisen, 'Le racisme et les Japonais', *Revue d'histoire de la Deuxième Guerre Mondiale*, 51 (1963), p. 1.

its ordeal to join the league of modernised, white nations. Japan's interaction with the rest of the world from the end of the nineteenth century to the 1930s therefore resulted in a national identity marked by plummeting racial self-esteem.

The apparent rise of racism toward the Japanese coincided with the world wide trend to recognise and legitimise racism in various forms. From the turn of the century to the 1930s, not only internationalism but also racism — both by-products of imperialism in a sense — gained recognition and respectability in Europe and North America. According to Akira Iriye,

> while international organisations mushroomed, anti-Semitism revived in Europe, eugenics as a scientific investigation of hereditary traits so as to 'perfect the race' was established as an academic discipline, anti-Chinese and anti-Japanese immigration movements gained strength in the United States, and brutal colonial wars were fought in Africa, the Pacific and the Caribbean against non-white races.[4]

The vogue for race and racism in society and even in the universities, as well as the institutionalisation of racism signified, therefore, a pandemic phenomenon which found its ultimate expression in the emergence of Nazi Germany in 1933. This international trend favouring racism and racial hierarchy, reaching its peak in the 1930s, not only exacerbated Japanese problems of racial identity but further proclaimed — it seemed to the Japanese — their racial inferiority.

How did Japan react and respond to white racism toward the 'yellow' race? How did it react to the seemingly insurmountable boundary called race in its effort to be 'one of the west'? Japan defied the international order by withdrawing from the League of Nations in March 1933, setting an example followed by Nazi Germany, and pursued unlimited military expansion. Japan did not, however, challenge the international *racial* status quo. On the contrary, Japan accepted, embraced and applied the west's racial hierarchy which preached the superiority of the white over other races. Japan had long internalised the idea of white supremacy, convinced that the white nations — highly industrialised societies with enormous power overseas — were justified in laying claims to superiority. Based on the premise that Japan had become a modernised, industrialised country on a par with the white nations by the turn of the century, Japan saw itself as one of the 'white' nations, or more accurately, as an 'honorary white' nation: the Japanese had the right to act as though they were white. The

---

[4] Akira Iriye, *Cultural Internationalism and World Order* (Baltimore and London, 1997), p. 40.

corollary of this new, self-authorised racial status was that the Japanese increasingly distanced themselves from other Asians who, in the Japanese eyes, were 'backward' and therefore 'inferior' peoples over whom the Japanese could justifiably exercise control.

Previous historians have interpreted Japanese imperialism as part of Japan's self-promotion to the rank of the white race and efforts to distance itself from other Asians. John Dower in *War Without Mercy* discussed the self-Caucasianisation of the Japanese, which he traced back to the first Sino-Japanese War at the end of the nineteenth century. Japanese cartoons during the Second World War depicted Asians as dark-skinned and the Japanese themselves as light. Japanese soldiers dispatched to South-East Asia were reluctant to acknowledge that their skin colour was the same as that of the natives.[5] While such evidence may be interpreted as merely indicative of the Japanese traditional preference for the fair skin, Japanese military actions in Asia throughout the war emphasise their self-demarcation in their racial identity from other Asians in the late 1930s and onwards. However sincerely some Japanese statesmen and citizens may have embraced the idea of 'Asian race solidarity' in their rhetoric about the Greater East Asia Co-Prosperity Sphere,[6] it failed to materialise in practice, as massacres of Asian civilian populations, biological tests on Asian captives and indiscriminate use of chemical weapons on Asian subjects demonstrate clearly.

Japan's inhumane treatment of Asian POWs is all the more revealing of its racism toward non-Japanese Asians. While white POWs were treated inhumanely enough, the treatment of Asian captives was incomparably more severe.[7] Pursuant to a law for the 'provisional punishment of bandits' passed in September 1932 in Manchukuo, the Japanese puppet-state in Manchuria, the Japanese army, the Manchukuo army and the police were allowed to kill captives without trial if they were regarded as guerrillas or anti-Japanese. These procedures, *genju-shobun* (severe punishment by law) and *genchi-shobun* (on-the-spot punishment), were applied by Japanese troops throughout China during the course of the second Sino-Japanese War, which began in 1937. With the excuse that no war had been officially declared against China, neither a POW administration nor POW camps

[5] John Dower, *War Without Mercy: Race and Power in the Pacific War* (New York, 1986), p. 210.

[6] See Susan Townsend, 'Culture, Race and Power in Japan's Wartime Empire'.

[7] See Clifford Kinvig, 'Allied POWs and the Burma-Thailand Railway', Kazuaki Saito, 'Towards Reconciliation'. See also Hirofumi Hayashi, 'Japanese Treatment of Chinese Prisoners, 1931–1945', *Nature-People-Society: Science and the Humanities*, 26 (January 1999), pp. 39–52.

were set up for Chinese captives. *A Study of Ways to Fight the Chinese Army*, published by the Infantry Academy in 1933, stated that Chinese captives should either be killed or deported.[8]

Japanese internalisation of white supremacy and their racism towards other Asians did not automatically translate into a sense of equal brotherhood with the white races. After all, Japan's inhumane treatment of its white POWs was in a sense a reflection of anti-white racism, or of racial retaliation against the whites. Japan's racial identity, therefore, was a contradictory combination of self-identification with the 'superior' white race and latent antagonism toward the white race.

Japanese anti-white hatred, however, should not be overemphasised – as it is qualified in two ways. First, Japanese racial animosity toward the whites cannot be summed up as pure hatred because it was heavily tinged with envy. The Japanese could not, whatever they wished, discard their respect for white nations who had served as their mentors for the previous decades. Their national aspiration, after all, had been to join the ranks of the whites. Respect survived even after Japan had left the international game with its 'western rules', and reappeared in the form of envy in their hatred toward the white race. Secondly, Japan's inhumane treatment of white POWs was not merely or primarily racial revenge. It was more a means by which Japan tried to show its racial superiority over the whites to the audience of Asians.[9] In July 1942 the Minister of Army stated in his address to the chief officers of POW camps that 'excessive' humanity in the treatment of POWs would be dangerous and that they should use POWs to display the superiority of the Japanese race to the native people of the occupied territories.[10] An underlying assumption betrayed here is that the Japanese had become superior only because they have succeeded in subjugating the previously superior white race. The same can be said of the Japanese military officials' reason for using Taiwanese and Koreans guards for white POWs: to foster a sense of respect for Japan and to bring about 'a sense of good fortune in being the subjects of the Empire'.[11] How was acting as guards for white POWs supposed to make Taiwanese and Koreans respect Japan? They would see with their own eyes that Japan was successfully subjugating

---

[8] See also the quotation from Amleto Vespa in Towle, 'The Japanese Army and Prisoners of War'.

[9] Howard S. Levie, ed., *Documents on Prisoners of War* (Newport, Rhode Island, 1979), pp. 460–61.

[10] Yoshio Chaen, *Dainihon Teikoku Naichi Furyo Shuyojo* (Tokyo, 1986), p. 78.

[11] *Kyokuto Gunji Saiban Sokkiroku*, no. 146. Cited in Aiko Utsumi, 'Prisoners of War in the Pacific War: Japan's Policy', in Gavan McCormick and Hank Nelsen, ed., *The Burma-Thailand Railway: Memory and History* (St Leonards, Australia, 1993), pp. 68–83.

the white race, the all-time 'superior' race. The superiority of the white race was not a contested issue. By treating white POWs inhumanely in the presence of Asian onlookers, the Japanese hoped to flaunt their superiority over the whites and legitimise themselves as the 'substitute whites' in Asia. With their new, self-established identity as 'honorary whites', Japan imposed on Asian peoples the racial hierarchy authored and enforced by the true whites, of which Japan itself had been a victim. In short, Japan's racial identity as reflected in its treatment of POWs in the Second World War reflected its inferiority complex vis-à-vis the real whites, which manifested itself in the forms of retaliation against the 'superior' whites and subjugation of the 'inferior' Asians.

Ironically, just as Japan applied the idea of white supremacy in Asia, Japan was simultaneously its victim. The enemy, American soldiers, re-garded the Japanese as 'yellow sons of bitches', 'vermin' and 'a curious race – a cross between the human being and the ape'.[12] A study conducted by the US Army confirmed the racist motivation of American soldiers in their battle against the Japanese. For instance, among American soldiers fighting in the Pacific surveyed in the spring of 1944, 35 per cent of officers and 42 per cent of enlisted men felt like 'wiping out the whole Japanese nation' after the war, while only 13 per cent of officers and 22 per cent of enlisted men felt like 'wiping out the whole German nation' after the war. Likewise, among American soldiers fighting in Europe, 44 per cent of officers and 61 per cent of enlisted men felt like wiping out the Japanese, while only 15 per cent of the former and 25 per cent of the latter felt like wiping out the Germans.[13] Even Japan's ally, Nazi Germany, claimed that all 'non-Aryans', including the Japanese, were inferior to the 'Aryans', the ultimate superior race. Hitler's Third Reich passed racial laws in its territories that officially prevented those with 'non-Aryan' blood from holding public office and marrying, while punishing 'Aryans' who had any social contact with them.

The next section examines Japan's racial identity as reflected in its interaction with Nazi Germany. Nazi racism towards the Japanese is analysed in some detail, followed by an examination of the Japanese reaction to Nazi racism and to the myth of the 'honorary Aryan' status. This sheds light on Japan's double-edged racial identity.

[12] Dower, *War Without Mercy*, pp. 69–71.
[13] Samuel Stouffer et al., ed., *The American Soldier: Combat and its Aftermath*, ii (Princeton, 1949), p. 158.

Hitler set about codifying National Socialist racial doctrine as early as April 1933, less than one month after the Nazi electoral victory.[14] In the following months, a series of racial laws were passed which excluded those who could not prove their 'Aryan' descent and their spouses from various private and public offices. This affected lawyers, jurors, governmental officials, professors, dentists in state social-insurance institutions and many others. The Justice Ministry's draft for the Criminal Law Reform of September 1933 proposed the prohibition of sexual relations and of marriage between 'Aryans' and 'non-Aryans'. The racial laws were targeted primarily at Jewish people but also applied to other 'non-Aryans'. Nazi officials' public speeches which railed against 'coloured' races led to protests from the Japanese government as early as October 1933. There were also instances of racial discrimination against Japanese and German-Japanese in Germany, such as the case of a Japanese businessman's young daughter being struck by German children because of her skin colour, and the dismissal of a Japanese-German scientist from the Reich Institute of Biology for Landscape and Forestry.[15] Japanese Ambassador Nagai demanded clarification from the German Foreign Ministry on the race question, asking whether the term 'coloured' would apply to the Japanese and whether the draft for the Criminal Law Reform would affect the Japanese.[16] Major Japanese newspapers such as *Nihon, Hochi Shinbun* and *Yomiuri Shinbun* published Alfred Rosenberg's speech on the white race's struggle under the headings, 'The Arrogant Nazis! The Chief of the Foreign Office Pronounces Hatred against the Coloured Races!'[17] and 'Anti-Jews! Anti-Yellow Race! Say the Nazis'.[18]

While the Third Reich had not yet formed a military alliance with Japan, the Nazis were determined on reversing the Wilhelmstrasse's decades-old pro-China foreign policy to one favouring Japan. For this reason, some party officials voiced the diplomatic inconvenience of pursuing racial politics with regards to the Japanese. The most fervent proponent of the realpolitik — a 'race-free' foreign policy — was curiously none other than Johann von Leers, a Nazi expert on the Jewish question. In the memorandum of 25 October 1934 sent from the Deutsch-Japanische Gesellschaft (German-Japanese Society) in Berlin to various ministries, von Leers, the true author,

[14] The following section on Nazi racism is based on Harumi Furuya, 'Ideology vs. Realpolitik: Nazi Racism Toward the Japanese. German-Japanese Relations in the 1930s', *Nachrichten der Gesellschaft für Natur- und Völkerkunde Ostasiens* (1995), pp. 17–76.

[15] 'Besprechung mit Botschaftsrat Fujii am 21. November 1933 betreffend Rassenfrage', German National Archives, Koblenz (BA, Koblenz), R 64 IV/31, pp. 44–45.

[16] Letter from von Bülow of the Foreign Ministry to the Minister of Justice, no. V14036, 24 October 1933. German National Archives, Potsdam (BA, Potsdam), R 43 II/720a, 6.

[17] Alfred Rosenberg was the Chief of the Nazi Party's Central Department for Foreign Policy.

demanded that the Japanese be excluded from the racial doctrines, based on the far-fetched premise that they traced their roots back to the 'Aryan' race. The diplomatic exigencies were also noted: 'the only obstacle between Germany and Japan', von Leers contended, was 'this unfortunate race question, which — if not solved or if solved unsatisfactorily — threatens to destroy the good relationship'. The replacement of the controversial term 'coloured' by 'Jews and those belonging to primitive races' would accomplish this goal.[19]

The German Foreign Ministry agreed with von Leers and attempted to restrict the racial laws to Jews in November 1934, November 1936 and February 1937. Each time, the Foreign Ministry was met with resistance from the other ministries, most notably the Racial Policy Office headed by Alfred Gross and the Auslands-Organisation, a Nazi Party apparatus for overseas. Vehemently opposing the Foreign Ministry's claim that the exemption of non-Jewish 'non-Aryans' would not seriously harm 'the domestic interest', given the small number of non-Jewish mixed marriages, the Interior Ministry argued along Gross's lines that any exemption would be impossible because 'the ultimate goal of the National Socialist movement is to eliminate all people of foreign blood from the German population'.[20] Consequently, all Nazi racial laws, with the exception of the Nuremberg Laws of 15 September 1935 which singled out Jews, generally referred to 'non-Aryans' and were thus applicable to the people of Japanese descent and their spouses. While there was no law which explicitly restricted non-Jewish 'non-Aryan' mixed marriages, a draft for such a law was ready as of 11 August 1939; only the outbreak of the war persuaded Hitler that the draft's passage into law should be postponed to the end of the war given the inconveniences such a law would incur for Germany's foreign relations.[21] This postponement was

[18] Letter from the German Embassy in Tokyo to the German Foreign Ministry in Berlin. 7 September 1933. German Foreign Ministry Archives (AA), R 85941 Pol. IV 725/4, vol. 3, January 1932 to December 1934.

[19] 'Denkschrift der DJG zur Frage der Anwendung der Rassensetzgebung auf die Abkömm-linge aus deutsch-japanischen Mischehen', 25 October 1935, BA, Koblenz, R 64 IV/31, 26–37.

[20] Letter from Pfundtner of the Interior Ministry to the Foreign Ministry, 22 April 1937, AA, R 99182, E 257242.

[21] Letter from Lammers of the Reich Chancellery to Gürtner of the Justice Ministry, 31 January 1940, BA Koblenz, R 22 9/465/ 104. Letter from the Interior Ministry to the Reich Chancellery, 19 March 1943, BA Koblenz, R 22 9/465/ 129.

compensated for by a series of decrees depriving Germans marrying 'non-Aryans' of vital civic and socioeconomic privileges, and by propaganda which branded those who dared enter into 'undesirable' marriages as traitors forsaking their *völkische Pflicht* (folkish or ethnic duty) to protect their blood.[22] It follows, therefore, that all 'non-Aryans', including those of Japanese descent and their spouses, were subject to racial discrimination in the Third Reich.

An average of five hundred Japanese citizens resided in Germany throughout the 1930s, the majority of whom were government officials, army and navy personnel, businessmen and students.[23] Apparently, very few of them reported racial discrimination. The application of racial laws to people of Japanese descent in Germany was overwhelmingly targeted at German-Japanese people – half-Japanese German citizens ('Japanese mixed-offspring of the first degree'), and quarter-Japanese German citizens-('Japanese mixed-offspring of the second degree') – and their spouses. According to the German-Japanese Society's files, there were approximately fifty German-Japanese people in Germany. At least one-third of this population reported various forms of racial discrimination, as is evident in the files of the German-Japanese Society and the files of the German Foreign Ministry Archives.

Without going into the details of the cases, it is worth noting that racial discrimination took three forms: humiliation in public, which was exacerbated by the fact that any friendly interaction with 'non-Aryans' was considered a *Rassenschande* (racial disgrace) and punishable; institutional discrimination, which most often translated into unemployment and dismissal from educational institutions and civic associations; and marriage prohibition. The reasons why German citizens of Japanese descent were more often victimised than Japanese citizens thus become apparent: institutional racial discrimination was generally not applicable to Japanese citizens employed by the Japanese government or companies; and the Nazis had no particular desire to offend the Japanese 'guests' who were temporarily stationed in Germany as representatives of the Japanese government, military and major corporations. Nevertheless, Japanese citizens were equally susceptible to racial discrimination in public and subject to the unofficial

---

[22] 'Die Politik ist kein Feigenblatt', *Das Schwarze Korps*, 12 February 1942, BA, Koblenz: R 22 9/465, 127. *Das Schwarze Korps* was an SS newspaper.

[23] 'Populations of Japanese citizens domiciled abroad, categorised by occupations. 1 October 1935' ('Kaigai kakuchi zairyu honpo naichijin shokugyobetsu jinko hyo. Showa 10nen 10gatsu 1 tachi'), Inquiry Commission of the Foreign Ministry, Archives of the Foreign Ministry of Japan.

prohibition of mixed marriages, as the few discrimination cases against Japanese citizens attested.

The general rule for the application of racial laws on people of Japanese descent (German citizens and Japanese citizens) and their spouses was summed up in the decree of 18 April 1935: those 'non-Aryan' individuals, against whom racial discrimination would jeopardise Germany's diplomatic interests, would be exempt from the racial laws.[24] In other words, Japanese and Japanese-German individuals were to be dealt with case by case, with the exemption from the racial laws to be granted to some and not to others. In practice, the decisions, if ever issued at all, were slow to come. The majority of the discrimination cases in the late 1930s and early 1940s had to wait years, sometimes forever, for the Nazi authorities' decisions. This meant that they continued to face discrimination, be it in the form of unemployment or marriage prohibition, throughout the duration of their waiting. The slow decision-making process resulted from the uncertainty as to who was officially in charge of the *Rassenfrage* as regards the Japanese, and the inter-ministerial disagreements as to what extent they were willing to compromise their racial ideology. More importantly, however, the 'inefficiency' in dealing with discrimination cases was precisely the strategy by which the Nazis tried to avoid, as far as possible, having to issue decisions exempting Japanese-Germans from the racial laws. In a rare testimony to Hitler's personal stance on Japanese-German mixed marriages, the Chief of the Reich Chancellery, Hans Lammer, recorded that he had persuaded Hitler to grant a Japanese-German woman her request to marry an 'Aryan' German because of diplomatic considerations. Hitler insisted, however, that such marriages should not take place in the future for any reason, since maintaining the purity of the 'Aryan' blood was the priority, to which Lammers responded that they would postpone similar cases in the future so as to prevent such mixed marriages without having to issue official disapproval.[25]

In addition to this strategy of procrastination in issuing decisions, which amounted to authorising racial discrimination against Japanese-German individuals and their spouses in the meantime, what greatly helped the Nazis in their effort to continue discriminating against them while denying the existence of such practice to the Japanese government was their own, ingenious creation: the semi-true myth of the 'honorary Aryan' status for the Japanese. The myth was, in fact, semi-true because no Japanese, apparently, were sent to concentration camps, and *if* and *when* the Nazi authorities

[24] Notes of the Foreign Ministry, 17 November 1936, AA, R99182; E 257182.
[25] Duplicate signed Lammers, 21 September 1940, BA, Potsdam, R 43 II/1456a, 9.

did issue decisions on the racial discrimination cases of German-Japanese and Japanese individuals, they often ruled in favour of the victims. Nevertheless, their 'honorary Aryan' status was a myth in that the Japanese were subject to the racial laws of the Third Reich. The testimony of some of those involved reflected the Nazi authorities' successful endeavour to spread the rumour abroad, especially in Japan, of the 'honorary Aryan' status of the Japanese. In trying to persuade the Nazi authorities to grant him a marriage certificate, a German-Japanese individual, H. v. K,[26] noted that his uncle in Japan, a major-general in the Japanese army, had been told that the German racial laws did not apply to the Japanese. 'How can it be that what is said by the German Embassy in Japan is the opposite of what is said in Berlin?'[27] The half-German daughter of the former Japanese Foreign Minister, Aoki, also brought up the racial discrimination against the Japanese, noting 'I have heard from various sources that following a certain incident ... the government has issued a formal decree in which all Japanese and their offspring would be considered *honorary Aryans* ...'[28]

The 'certain incident' referred to was probably the initial uproar in October 1933, which prompted German Foreign Minister von Neurath to issue a statement that was published both in *The Times*,[29] and *New York Times*: 'the Japanese were not included among coloured peoples' and the German government would 'rectify the supposed inclusion of Japanese in measures prohibiting Germans from marrying Jews or 'coloured persons'.[30] It is evident from the tone in which the articles were written that both newspapers published von Neurath's statement to jeer at the Nazis, who, it seemed, were induced against their will to curb their racial ideology to accommodate realpolitik. However unintended, their publication proved highly beneficial to the Nazi authorities in terms of German-Japanese relations, as it had the effect of internationalising the myth of the 'honorary Aryan' status of the Japanese as early as 1933. The world, including Japan, was made to believe, contrary to reality, that the Nazis had decided to exempt the Japanese from the racial laws. The myth therefore served as a useful tool by which the Nazis tried to evade the race controversy with Japan.

---

[26] Except for persons who are sufficiently renowned to be regarded as historical figures, the names of the individuals discriminated against have been abbreviated so as not to invade their privacy.

[27] Letter from H. v. K. to the German-Japanese Society, 10 July 1939, BA, Koblenz, R 64 IV/31/: 279.

[28] Letter from H. v. H-A. to Dr Hack of the German-Japanese Society, 20 April 1934, BA, Koblenz, R 64 IV/31/ 101.

[29] John P. Fox, *Germany and the Far Eastern Crisis, 1931–1938* (Oxford, 1982), p. 86.

[30] 'Reich Reassures Japan', *New York Times*, 23 October 1933, p. 9.

Curiously, not only Nazi Germany but Japan also reaped *diplomatic* profits from the 'honorary Aryan' status. This special status served to save Japan's face: its white ally, notorious for its staunch racism against all 'non-Aryans', had promoted the Japanese to a rank equating them, if only in honorary terms, to the all-time superior 'Aryans'. The 'honorary Aryan' status was, one might even say, a coveted gift to the Japanese in that it seemed to project to the world their new, self-carved racial niche in the whites' league. Whether the world swallowed this projection is altogether another question. Furthermore, the status, tailor-made for the Japanese, went hand in hand with the Japanese racial identity which asserted superiority over other Asians. By singling out the Japanese, the Nazis had helped the Japanese in their efforts to dissociate themselves from the 'inferior' and 'backward' Asians. We may recall that that the Japanese government's rage against Nazi racism in the autumn of 1933 on behalf of the *Japanese* people, not the yellow race. Had the rhetoric for the Greater East Asia Co-Prosperity Sphere of the 'all-Asian racial solidarity' any substance, Japan would have found it in its interest — if not in 1933, in the late 1930s — to act as the spokesman for the Asian race and oppose Nazi racism on behalf of all the Asians, of whom it claimed to be the leader. In view of the improvement in German-Japanese relations throughout the 1930s, and accordingly worsening German-Chinese relations, the Chinese government's protest against Nazi racism fell on deaf ears. Chinese living in the Third Reich met with severe racial discrimination, with many sent to the concentration camps.[31] Japan's failure to speak on behalf of all Asians attested once again to their racial identification with the whites and their racial dissociation from other Asians — which, as we have already seen, was reflected in Japan's policy and actions on the Asian continent.

The overall significance of Japan's complacency about its 'honorary Aryan' status should not be overestimated, as it was indeed strictly limited by its narrowly defined diplomatic benefit. Any blatant violation in practice of the 'honorary Aryan' by the Nazis, after all, would only bring international racial humiliation to Japan. Therefore, from both the racial and diplomatic standpoints, it was in Japan's interest to ensure that there was some truth in the 'honorary Aryan' status. By making official protests against Nazi racism in autumn 1933, the Japanese authorities had successfully made it clear to the Nazis that the race question was a highly sensitive issue for Japan. Probably in response to the protests of the autumn of 1933, Goebbels

---

[31] Dagmar Yü-Dembski, 'Verdrängte Jahre: einige Fragen der deutsch-chinesischen Beziehungen während des Nationalsozialismus', unpublished manuscript, 1989.

forbade the German press to mention the *Rassenproblem* in association with the Japanese in early 1934.[32]

Behind the Japanese authorities' tacit, diplomatic complacency with the 'honorary Aryan' status were their continued efforts throughout the 1930s to remind the Nazis, in implicit ways, of the potentially explosive issue of race. Japan's relative success in warning the Nazis of the deleterious consequences of a potential race controversy was evident in the apparent over-sensitising of the Nazis to Japan's easily piqued racial pride. Upon investigating the background of a Japanese-German living in Hamburg, the Nazi local authorities judged it unlikely that this particular individual 'whose physical appearance resembles that of a Malaysian more than a Japanese' maintained close contacts with the Japanese relatives, and therefore 'the refusal to grant a marriage certificate would probably neither provoke an outcry by the Japanese public, nor have negative consequences on German-Japanese relations'.[33] The Nazis ruled against the victim in the above case. Even so, the time and energy they spent on assessing the diplomatic cost of the continued discrimination against German-Japanese, as evidenced by copious paperwork for the above case and others, seem to show their serious efforts to avoid another uproar from Japan. Indeed, the Nazis' paranoia about offending the Japanese government and public persuaded them eventually to exempt more Japanese-Germans and Japanese citizens from the racial laws than they would have liked.

Not only did Japan press Nazi Germany with limited success to adhere to the policy of the 'honorary Aryan' status for the Japanese, it also resisted Nazi racial ideology as a principle by erecting barriers to the spread of Nazi political propaganda in Japan. Erich Kordt, a minister at the German Embassy in Tokyo, noted after the war:

> A flood of propaganda directives was poured over the Embassy in Tokyo ... But Ribbentrop's bright ideas did not sell well with the Japanese press. The paper shortage and inborn distrust by the Japanese of every kind of foreign propaganda limited these attempts to influence the people. The government consciously made difficulties for the spread of this propaganda by refusing mail deliveries, forbidding the printing of non-Japanese war news, censorship, etc.

The limit to the Nazis' efforts to infiltrate Japan with their propaganda were also noted by a German specialist on Japan, Hankow, who had travelled there in May 1937:

---

[32] F. W. Iklé, *German-Japanese Relations, 1936–1940* (Berkeley, 1953), p. 15. Goebbels himself noted on this prohibition in his diary in January 1942, Joseph Goebbels, *Goebbels' Diaries*, trans. and ed. Louis P. Lochner (Garden City, New York, 1948), p. 51.

[33] Notes signed von Hahn, Referat D III LS, 26 February 1943, AA, R 99176.

one could read in leading Japanese newspapers — even after the conclusion of the Anti-Comintern Pact — sentences such as 'it is a scandal that the old Japanese Empire concluded a pact with a parvenu-state [Nazi Germany] which has existed only for three years and had driven away its own Emperor' (from *Chugai*, the leading newspaper on economy), or 'Germany and Italy have fallen back to barbarism ... Japan could never have sunk this far' (from *Asahi Shinbun*, the biggest Japanese newspaper).[34]

As of May 1937, only the War Ministry had promised to try to minimise the number of 'unfriendly' articles, he noted. In examining German in-fluence in Japan, Hankow cited 'medicine and law' for German science, only 'music' for German culture, and 'nothing' for both German political ideology and political organisation. He deplored the fact that 'German music was making more friends in Japan than all other German achievements combined'.[35] While Japan's resistance to Nazi political propaganda might be seen as merely another testimony to the lack of cooperation between the two countries, Japan's objection specifically to political propaganda, which was almost synonymous with propaganda for the racial ideology, attests to its implicit rejection of the idea of 'Aryan' racial supremacy.

In short, Japan's racial identity manifested itself as a contradictory com-bination of the self-identification with the white 'Aryans', through its acceptance of the 'honorary Aryan' status, on the one hand, and the rejection of the racial ideology preaching 'Aryan' supremacy, on the other hand. Just as Japan's self-promotion to the status of 'honorary white' on the Asian continent did not translate into its embracing the real whites, Japan's tacit acceptance of the 'honorary Aryan' status by no means signified its advocacy of the Nazi racial ideology. The double-edged nature of Japan's racial identity explains at least partly why Japan's wartime policies were antagonistic toward both fellow Asians and its 'fellow' whites.

An examination of Japan's conflict-ridden racial identity is not complete without at least a cursory reference to Japan's puzzling attitudes toward the Jews. Initially imported to Japan from Russia during Japan's Siberian Intervention in 1920,[36] antisemitism in Japan was given a new stimulus by

---

[34] Erich Kordt, 'German Political History in the Far East during the Hitler Regime', translated by E. A. Baines. Unpublished manuscript, Nuremberg, May 1946, p. 66. Hankow's report on 'Fremdenhaß und deutsch-japanische Beziehungen', sent by Hankow to Berlin, 31 January 1938, AA, R 104880, 130898–130903.

[35] AA, R 104880; 130902.

[36] Françoise Kreissler, 'Antisemitische Propaganda in Japan und die japanische Politik ge-genüber den Juden in China', *Symposium: Die deutsch-japanischen Beziehungen in den 30er und 40er Jahren 22–24.6.1992* (Berlin, 1993), pp. 107–11.

Nazi Germany in the course of the 1930s. Major Japanese newspapers such as *Asahi*, *Hochi*, *Yomiuri* and especially *Mainichi* published antisemitic articles in the late 1930s, with *Osaka Mainichi* sponsoring an Anti-Freemason Exhibition in Tokyo in January 1943 among other antisemitic events.[37] While Japan had its own share of antisemites,[38] it is doubtful whether they had a significant impact on the Japanese citizenry as a whole. Moreover, Japan's antisemitism cannot be judged apart from a passion more important for most Japanese: nationalism. Japan's imported, cliché-ridden antisemitism had to be subordinated to nationalistic goals. The resulting policy was one that benefited the Jews, for Japanese military officials came to believe that making an enemy out of the internationally influential Jewry would run counter to Japan's national goals.[39] The curious irony of antisemites arguing in favour of the Jews is evident in the following incident: on 24 November 1940 the Jewish newspaper in Shanghai, the *Jewish Chronicle*, published the speech by a navy captain, Koreshige Inuzuka – a noted antisemite – on Japan's position on the Jewish question which had been broadcast earlier, praising his claim that 'under the fundamental principle of the Japanese – equality and justice for all races – Jewish refugees would be taken care of'.[40] Japan allowed Jewish emigrants from Europe, mostly those escaping Nazi persecution, into Manchuria, North China and Shanghai. From 1938 to 1939 alone 13,527 Jewish immigrants registered in Shanghai, with other unregistered persons estimated at 4000.[41] Jewish refugees continued to make their way to Shanghai by boat and to Kobe as late as May 1941.[42]

Not surprisingly, Japan's policy on Jews became a source of conflict between Germany and Japan. Not only did the German Foreign Ministry under the Nazi influence protest at Japan's policy of admitting Jewish

---

[37] Ibid., p. 109. David Goodman and Masanori Miyazawa, *Jews in the Japanese Mind* (New York, 1995), p. 109. This gives an extensive account on the antisemitic discourse in Japan in the 1930s and 1940s.

[38] Japanese antisemites in the 1930s and 1940s included Arihisa Kumamoto, Hokuzan Atago, Nobutaka Shioden, Norihiro Yasue and Takeo Koyama among others, ibid., pp. 106–34.

[39] Norihiro Yasue believed that given the Jews exercised decisive influence on the press, economy and politics as they did, Japan should not drive them to become its enemy. Kreissler, *Antisemitische Propaganda in Japan*, p. 110. Norihiro Yasue, Koreshige Inuzuka and Shirô Ishiguro aspired to harness Jewish power to influence the United States, the so-called 'Fugu Plan', which was not adopted by the Japanese government. Goodman and Miyazawa, *Jews in the Japanese Mind*, pp. 132–33.

[40] Letter from the German Consulate in Shanghai to the German Foreign Ministry, 27 November 1940, AA, R99423.

[41] 'Statistik der Shanghaier Immigration. Frauenmangel — Überalterung. Höhere Sterblichkeit der Österreicher', *Gelbe Post*, 15 June 1940, AA, R 99423.

[42] Goodman and Miyazawa, *Jews in the Japanese Mind*, pp. 111–12.

refugees to territories under its rule,[43] it also actively tried to persuade the Japanese government to monitor Jews in Japan. The German Embassy in Tokyo preoccupied itself with dissuading the Japanese from hiring prominent Jewish professionals in Japan. Twenty per cent of all foreign teachers at the secondary school level were Jewish, and so were half of all foreign doctors, lamented the German Embassy in March 1939.[44] The case of the German Jewish conductor Klaus Pringsheim, the director of the national music conservatory, the Ueno Academy, is but one example illustrating the German Embassy's exasperated attempt to impose antisemitic policies on Japan. On Richard Strauss's seventieth birthday, on 30 October 1934, Germany and Japan planned a radio exchange in which performances of Strauss's pieces by the Berlin Philharmonic and by the orchestra of the Ueno Academy would be broadcast as one concert in both countries. The German Embassy's efforts to replace Pringsheim with a Japanese or non-Jewish conductor for this concert availed them nothing after ten months of bargaining with the Japanese authorities. They insisted throughout that Pringsheim was the best suited to conduct a very difficult piece, Strauss's sixteen-voice a capella hymn, and dismissed the Nazis' preoccupation with the fact that Pringsheim was Jewish.[45]

The conflict was, nonetheless, serious enough for the Nazis: a major ulterior motive behind their proposal for the German-Japanese Cultural Pact, concluded on 25 November 1938, was to enable them to exercise more control over Japanese domestic policies, specifically to encourage antisemitic policies in Japan.[46] The Nazis, however, never succeeded in the 1930s and 1940s in persuading the Japanese authorities that Jewish professionals could not possibly convey German culture. Furthermore, the Nazi efforts to play down the race question in German-Japanese relations in order not to puncture Japanese racial pride, as discussed earlier, prevented them from actively and openly advocating antisemitism in Japan. In this sense, Japan had leverage over Nazi Germany in pursuing a non-antisemitic policy.

Individual Japanese citizens helped Jews in Japan and abroad, although the only example of a high-ranking Japanese official who actively participated in the rescue of the Jews was Chiune Sugihara. Sugihara and other Japanese citizens were moved by their consciences and by certain values embedded

[43] Ibid., pp. 112–113.

[44] 'Die Juden in Japan', signed de la Trobe, German Embassy in Tokyo, AA, R 99423.

[45] Correspondence between the German Embassy in Tokyo and the German Foreign Ministry in Berlin, March to October 1934, AA, R 85963, vol. 2.

[46] Letter from the Ministry of People's Enlightenment and Propaganda to the Foreign Ministry, 10 May 1939, AA, R 61439, vol. 2. Also 'Die Juden in Japan', AA, R 99423.

in Japanese culture, notably personal ties and obligation to return the *on*: gratitude for something they had received in the past. Many Japanese who had studied medicine and music in Germany before the 1930s had Jewish teachers. When their former teachers were persecuted by the Nazi regime it was natural for them, as former students, to come to their help. Given the lack of enthusiasm on the part of the Japanese government in helping Nazi Germany implement antisemitic policies in Japan, these Japanese in-dividuals had all the more reasons not to shirk their duty of returning their *on* to their former mentors. While such individual acts were neither com-monplace nor well-organised, informal rescue networks, such as the one led by Professor Akihiko Sata in Osaka,[47] attested to the failure of the Nazis to induce cooperation from Japan and the Japanese on the Jewish question.

Japan's deaf ear to Nazi protests against Japan's 'indulgent' policy on the Jews and Japan's refusal to implement an antisemitic policy in Japan testified not only to its avowal of national sovereignty in formulating its own domestic policies but to Japan's resistance against the Nazi racial ideology which preached the supremacy of the 'Aryan' race. At the Privy Council preceding the conclusion of the German-Japanese Cultural Pact in Novem-ber 1938, both Councillor Ishizuka and Foreign Minister Arita expressed doubts as to the appropriateness of the cultural alliance, suggesting that 'the racial and national life of Germany' conflicted with 'our [Japanese] spirit' which ' maintains the equality of all races without prejudice'.[48] To be sure, Japan's 'pro-Jewish' policy was motivated by a combination of realpolitik and nationalism rather than of moral integrity. It is ironic that Japan lived up to its rhetoric of equality for all races not in its policy toward fellow Asians, for which it was initially intended in the Greater East Asia Co-Prosperity Sphere, but in its policy toward the Jews.

Japan's racial identity was like a coin with two contrasting sides: it was marked, on one side, by its aspiration to be the 'white', the superior race, and on the other side, by its latent animosity toward the white race which had subjugated and continued to denigrate the Japanese as a 'yellow' race. Japan's promotion to the white status — if only in form — by means of the self-inaugurated 'honorary white' status in Asia, reinforced by the Nazi-consigned 'honorary Aryan' status, was diplomatically convenient as it could

[47] Correspondence between Akihiko Sata and former German Ambassador to Japan, Wilhelm Solf, March to August 1933, BA, Koblenz, Nachlaß Solf, pp. 6–7, 35, 58.
[48] The quote is from Ishizuka's 'Minutes of the Conference on the Conclusion of Agreement for Cultural Cooperation between Japan and Germany', 22 November 1938. Archives of the Japanese Foreign Ministry, IMT, 135 IPS, 956-B.

be used to justify Japan's supremacy over other Asians, and accordingly, to legitimise Japanese imperialism. Not surprisingly, the promotion of the Japanese to the 'honorary white' rank translated into a policy of physical and racial subordination of other Asians, as evident in Japan's numerous atrocities committed against Asians, among them the absolutely base and inhumane treatment of its Asian POWs. The other side of the coin, namely Japan's latent antagonism toward the white race, led to its retaliatory policies and actions against the whites, as manifested in Japan's efforts to prevent inroads of Nazi political propaganda into Japan, and its obstinate refusal to cooperate with the Nazis on the 'Jewish Question' beyond authorising the circulation of antisemitic literature in Japan. Last but not least, was Japan's inhumane treatment of white POWs. The convoluted nature of Japan's racial identity was but one facet of the highly irrational, unstable and ineffectual politics that Japan carried out at home and abroad in the Second World War. In a broader historical perspective, Japan's double-edged racial identity may be interpreted as just one attestation to the racist international politics of the first half of the twentieth century — traces of which thrive to this day.

# 8

# *Japanese Treatment of British Prisoners of War: The Historical Context*

## Yoichi Kibata

A large photograph which covers almost two-thirds of a two-page spread shows a scene in which many soldiers with beaming faces are dashing forward. The accompanying caption reads:

> Cheering their hearts out, more than 3000 British POWs rush from a German camp towards their American liberators in April 1945. Most were fit and well; they received Red Cross parcels and often had more luxuries – chocolate, jam, cigarettes – than their German guards, with whom in general they got on.

In a much smaller photograph beside it sixteen people with very thin bodies and expressionless faces are watching the camera. The caption compares them with those in the other photograph:

> A horrifying contrast was revealed when British and Indian troops in Burma liberated a Japanese prison camp in Rangoon. The British POWs were emaciated and listless, some too shocked to smile. They had no medical supplies and no food but rice; the guards treated them as animals. Worse would be found before the Japanese war was won.[1]

These photographs and captions, in a recent book which looks back upon the British history in the twentieth century and is intended for wide readership, are good examples of the persistence in Britain of the terrible memories about the maltreatment of British POWs in Japanese hands. It is noteworthy that in relation to the treatment of POWs such a contrast between the Germans and the Japanese is often brought out in Britain. For example, immediately after the fiftieth anniversary of VJ Day in 1995, the *Independent* pointed out in a leading article that, whereas 5 per cent of prisoners captured by the Germans died, more than a quarter of those held by the Japanese succumbed to disease or were murdered.[2] It then

---

[1] Brian Moynahan, *The British Century: A Photographic History of the Last Hundred Years* (London, 1997), pp. 202–3.

went on to argue that the reason why the wound caused by this historical experience had not healed was the strong feeling that the Japanese, unlike the Germans, regretted not their aggression but their defeat: that they had not apologised because they were not sorry.[3]

While it is arguable whether the difference between the Germans and the Japanese in their treatment of POWs and their postwar attitudes can be drawn so clearly,[4] the point made about Japan is not so far off the mark. For the problem of the Allied POWs is more or less forgotten or ignored in today's Japan. While it is true that for the past ten years or so various aspects of misconduct and atrocities carried out by Japanese forces during the Asia-Pacific War,[5] especially the tragic fate of so-called 'comfort women', has come to be hotly discussed in Japan, little attention has been paid to the experience of British POWs.

The Japanese neglect of this poignant problem became evident at the time of the Emperor's visit to Britain in May 1998. Foreseeing that this problem would cause much trouble during the royal visit, both the British and Japanese governments tried hard to soothe the atmosphere in Britain beforehand. Prime Minister Ryutaro Hashimoto's letter to the *Sun* in January 1998 apologising for the maltreatment of POWs was the most remarkable gesture brought about by the occasion.[6] Needless to say, makeshift attempts like this could not dampen the anger of former POWs, and they took protest action during the Emperor's visit. What is noteworthy was that, while this action was widely and often sensationally reported in Britain, Japanese mass media carried far more muted reports about it. The glaring gap in the reaction of the mass media displayed on this occasion was a clear indication of the difference in public reaction to this problem in the two countries.

It can be said that even those Japanese who are aware of the existence of this problem tend to regard it as merely a troublesome thorn in the

[2] According to the judgement of the Tokyo War Crimes Trial, 27 per cent of the British and American POWs captured by the Japanese died, while about 4 per cent died in German and Italian hands.

[3] *Independent*, 21 August 1995.

[4] It is true that the number of British POWs who died in German hands was not great, but about 58 per cent of Soviet POWs who were captured by Germany did not survive the captivity. In the postwar period, the Germans have certainly been much more self-critical than the Japanese, but it cannot be said that they have completely overcome their past.

[5] The use of this expression for what has long been called the Pacific War is now fairly widespread in Japanese historical works, since it can denote both Japan's war against China and its war against the United States and Britain.

[6] Hashimoto used the following expression: 'our feelings of deep remorse and heartfelt apology for the tremendous damage and suffering of that time', *Sun*, 14 January 1998.

otherwise smooth Anglo-Japanese relations of today. It is, nevertheless, a significant issue which has profound implications not only for painting the true picture of Anglo-Japanese relations but also for assessing the nature of the modern Japanese state in the nineteenth and twentieth centuries.

The aim of this essay is to discuss the historical context which led to the cruel treatment of British POWs, focusing on the way in which Japan emerged as an imperialist power during the late nineteenth century and on the nature of the Asia-Pacific war. In doing so stress will be placed on two aspects: Japan's attitude to international law; and racial factors in Japan's international behaviour. It is needless to say that various other elements lay behind Japan's bad treatment of Allied POWs. Charles Orlando enumerates the following factors: bad faith; revenge for racial slurs by western nations and individuals; lack of respect for POWs because of the Japanese belief that being taken prisoner is totally disgraceful; maladministration by the relevant Japanese government departments and military services; logistical failure due to overstretched lines of communication and to increasingly effective Allied attacks on these lines; individual cruelty; and others.[7] But, when we search for the long-term background of the POW issue, these two factors, which were in fact closely interrelated, seem to be most crucial.

It is often said that until the First World War Japan observed the rules for the treatment of POWs and was regarded as a model country in this respect. At the time of the Sino-Japanese War of 1894–5 about 1500 Chinese POWs were kept in camps in Japan, but they were not forced to work. The number of Russians taken as POWs during the Russo-Japanese War of 1904–5 was much larger and nearly 80,000 Russians were housed in POW camps at Matsuyama (Ehime prefecture) and elsewhere.[8] Japan's good treatment of them was highly praised in various quarters, including the International Red Cross.[9] During the First World War of 1914–18, in which Japan played a subordinate but important role, about 4600 German POWs were captured at Tsingtao in China and brought to Japan. The Japanese treatment of these POWs was also in line with international conventions, and the Bando camp

[7] Charles G. Roland, 'Allied POWs, Japanese Captors and the Geneva Convention', *War and Society*, 9 (1991), p. 101 n. 83.

[8] For the Matsuyama camp, see Tokio Saikami, *Matsuyama Shuyojo* (The Matsuyama POW Camp) (Tokyo, 1969).

[9] Ikuhiko Hata, 'From Consideration to Contempt: The Changing Nature of Japanese Military and Popular Perceptions of Prisoners of War Through the Ages', in Bob Moore and Kent Fedorowich (eds), *Prisoners of War and their Captors in World War II* (Oxford, 1996), p. 257.

(Tokushima prefecture) became famous for cultural activities performed by German POWs.[10]

The contrast between the fair treatment of POWs up to the First World War and the brutalities inflicted on Allied POWs during the Second World War in fact provides a good lead for considering the historical context of this problem. What needs to be examined first is the motive which prompted Japan to take a law-abiding stance in the first three wars.

The answer can be found in Japan's aspiration to enter into the European international system as an active participant. In his famous memoirs written after the Sino-Japanese War, Foreign Minister Munemitsu Mutsu empha-sised that Japanese people had made strenuous efforts to introduce numerous reforms after the Meiji Restoration and, as a result of those endeavours, Japan had come to embody European civilisation, whereas China still clung to the traditional habits of Asia.[11] Japan thus justified its war against China over Korea as an attempt to introduce the principles of European international society, which was composed of modern nation states, into an arena where China continued to treat Korea as a vassal state in the old Chinese-centred world view.

To be recognised as a member of the international society which was dominated by European powers, Japan had to behave like them, and the observance of international law was a crucial element in this undertak-ing.[12] As long as Japanese leaders felt that Japan was yet to catch up with European powers, they regarded it as imperative that Japan's activities conformed to the standard set by the European international system, espe-cially when Japan dealt with the advanced countries of Europe. Fair treatment of POWs was a significant aspect of this basic attitude.

This does not mean that Japan abided by international law in all circum-stances. As Tadashi Tanaka argues in a perceptive article about Japan's adoption of international law, Japan's stance of observing it was nothing but a smoke-screen to conceal its forceful conquest of and rule over weaker countries. Put differently, Japan used international law only as a tool for realising its ambition, not as a norm to be always observed.[13] This had two

---

[10] For the Bando camp, see Hiroshi Tomita, *Bando Furyo Shuyojo* (The Bando POW Camp) (Tokyo, 1991).

[11] Munemitsu Mutsu, *Kenkenroku* (A Diplomatic Record of the Sino-Japanese War) (Tokyo, 1941), pp. 44–45.

[12] See Gerrit W. Gong, *The Standard of 'Civilization' in International Society* (Oxford, 1984), ch. 6.

[13] Tadashi Tanaka, 'Waga Kuni ni Okeru Senso-ho no Juyo to Jissen' (The Introduction and Practice of International Law of Wars in Japan), in Yasuaki Onuma (ed.), *Kokusai-ho, Kokusai Rengo to Nihon* (International Law, the United Nations and Japan) (Tokyo, 1987), p. 415.

implications. One is that, even during these early wars, the Japanese took a different attitude towards the Asian peoples whom they looked down on as inferior beings and did not always observe international law in dealing with them. A typical example was the unlawful occupation of the Korean royal palace by the Japanese army two days before the start of actual fighting in 1894.[14] The other implication is that, once Japan achieved its initial aim of entering into the European international system as a latecomer, the political and psychological restraint which prompted Japan to observe international law could easily disappear. This process of entry into the European international system was more or less completed by the end of the First World War. Japan not only gained victories against China and Russia, it also acquired Taiwan, Korea and south Sakhalin as its colonies, and thus successfully joined the club of imperialist powers.

In building up the Japanese empire, Japanese leaders tended to assert that the relations between Japan and its dependent territories were unique and should be distinguished from European colonial rule. What was regarded as constituting the core of this uniqueness was geographical proximity and racial similarity between Japan and its colonies. Though these characteristics came to be increasingly stressed during the course of Japanese expansion, they were at the heart of Japanese imperialism from the very beginning. When the colonial rule of Taiwan began, Shuji Izawa, a famous educationist who took charge of education in Taiwan, maintained that Taiwanese and the Japanese were almost of the same stock.[15] This kind of parlance was quite common in Japanese imperial discourse, but, despite the basic assumption that the peoples in colonies were of the same stock as the Japanese, Japanese rulers and the Japanese public at large always embraced a sense of racial superiority towards the colonised peoples.[16]

This twisted racial feeling of the Japanese people towards the peoples in their colonies went hand in hand with the lingering sense that, despite their elevated position in international society, the Japanese were not treated as complete equals by the Europeans. It is against this background that the Japanese delegation at the Paris Peace Conference in 1919 proposed to insert a provision about racial equality into the Covenant of the League of Nations.[17]

---

[14] See Akira Nakatsuka, *Rekishi no Gizo wo Tadasu: Senshi kara Kesareta Nihon-gun no 'Chosen Okyu Senryo'* (Rectifying a Falsification of History: Japanese Occupation of the Royal Palace in Korea Unmentioned in the Official War History) (Tokyo, 1997).

[15] Shi Gang, *Shokuminchi Shihai to Nihongo* (Colonial Rule and the Japanese Language) (Tokyo, 1993), p. 41.

[16] See Yoichi Kibata, 'Igirisu no Teikoku Ishiki: Nihon to no Hikaku no Shiten kara (Imperial Mentality in Britain: A Comparison with Japan), in Kibata (ed.), *Daiei-Teikoku to Teikoku Ishiki* (The British Empire and Imperial Mentality) (Tokyo, 1998).

As can be easily discerned, this proposal was essentially of a hypocritical nature, for most Japanese were not ready to treat the peoples under Japan's colonial domination as truly equal human beings. That said, the major powers' refusal to accept this principle certainly showed that they were not willing to embrace something which might jeopardise the very foundation of the international system dominated by European powers. A British diplomat expressed the basic motive of the European powers in rejecting Japan's demand in a document on racial discrimination in 1921: after conceding the fact that Japan was the only non-white first class power, he pointed out that, however powerful Japan might eventually become, the white races would never be able to admit its equality.[18] This view is all the more instructive, as the diplomat who wrote this had worked in the British Consular Service in Japan and was well versed in the Japanese language and culture.[19] In challenging a world which was sustained by such a view, Japan opted for a path of aggression and aggrandisement in Asia and the Pacific, which led to the Sino-Japanese conflict after the Manchurian Incident of 1931, the Sino-Japanese War from 1937 and finally to the Asian-Pacific War.

By then many Japanese leaders had come to think that Japan was no longer inhibited by the rules set by the west. It was thought that, as a big imperial power in Asia and the Pacific with wide dependent territories stretching from south Sakhalin through Korea and Taiwan to mandated islands in South Pacific, Japan could pursue its own way in international affairs. The military, whose power and influence in Japanese society increased considerably in the course of Japan's expansion, started to enunciate more clearly its opposition to European standards. What was crucial was that the negative stand taken by the military was decisive in Japan's decision not to ratify the 1929 Geneva Convention about the treatment of POWs. Immediately before the meeting in Geneva, the Ministers of Army, Navy and Foreign Affairs jointly wrote to the Japanese delegates: 'in view of the difference between our way of living and that of European peoples, it is impossible to implement the detailed measures contained in the codes for the treatment of POWs'.[20] Later the Japanese navy explicitly stated its reasons

---

[17] See Yasuaki Onuma, 'Haruka naru jinshu byodo no riso' (The Distant Ideal of Equality among All the Peoples), in Onuma (ed.), *Kokusai-ho, Kokusai Rengo to Nihon.*

[18] Memo by F. Ashton-Gwatkin, 10 October 1921, quoted by Frank Furedi, *The Silent War: Imperialism and the Changing Perception of Race* (London, 1998), p. 30.

[19] See Ian Nish, 'In One Day Have I Lived Many Lives: Frank Ashton-Gwatkin, Novelist and Diplomat, 1889–1976', in Nish (ed.), *Britain and Japan: Biographical Portraits* (Folkestone, Kent, 1994).

[20] Fuhito Kanda, 'Kindai Nihon no Senso: Horyo Seisaku wo Chushin to shite' (Wars of Modern Japan: With Special Emphasis on the POW Policies), *Senso Sekinin Kenkyu*, 9 (1995), p. 15.

for its opposition to the ratification of the Geneva Convention. The central argument was that Japanese soldiers never expected to become prisoners, whereas foreign fighting men thought it inevitable to become POWs once captured by the enemy, and that as a result of this difference in the military ethos the Convention would function as a one-sided regulation which impose obligations only on the Japanese side.[21]

In contrast to the posture taken during the period up to the First World War, when Japan tried to show that it was capable of behaving just like the European powers which set the standard of behaviour in international society, Japan's stance turned into a wilful neglect of international law under the pretence of the historical and cultural divergence between the European and Japanese tradition and world view. This change was reflected in military education: at the time of the Russo-Japanese War, Japanese soldiers were taught international law concerning the conduct of war and the International Red Cross treaty, but in the changed atmosphere instruction about these subjects came to be neglected.[22]

The result was abundantly clear in the brutal behaviour of Japanese soldiers in their fight against the Chinese in the 1930s, the Nanking Massacre in December 1937 being the most blatant expression of this brutality. We must not forget that latent racism, with which Japanese people looked down on the Chinese, lay behind Japanese actions.[23] A remark made around that time by Lieutenant-Colonel Ryukichi Tanaka, an eminence grise in the Japanese Army, to Shigeharu Matsumoto, a liberal journalist, epitomised this racism: 'Frankly speaking, you [Matsumoto] and I have diametrically different views of the Chinese. You may be dealing with them as human beings, but I regard them as swine. We can do anything to such creatures'.[24]

It should be also noted that the period after the outbreak of the Sino-Japanese War saw strong expressions of blatant anti-British opinion, with mass demonstrations against Britain in many parts of Japan. In these demonstrations Britain was attacked as a country obstructing Japan's

---

[21] Yutaka Yoshida, *Tenno no Guntai to Nankin Jiken* (The Imperial Army and the Nanking Incident) (Tokyo, 1985), p. 47.

[22] Fumio Shiromaru, 'Tenno-sei kyogaku ron' (On the Education under the Emperor System), in Eiichi Matsushima and Fumio Shiromaru (eds), *'Jiyushugi Shikan' no Byori* (Maladies of the 'Liberal View of History Group') (Tokyo, 1997), p. 215.

[23] During the Asian-Pacific War Japanese soldiers occupying Indonesia spread a rumour about the different prices of comfort women: Indonesian 1 yen; Chinese 10 yen; Korean 100 yen; Japanese 1000 yen. Of course this was an exaggerated difference, but this story is informative about the accepted hierarchy of races under Japanese rule. Aiko Utsumi, *Chosen-jin BC-kyu Senpan no Kiroku* (Stories of Korean Minor War Criminals) (Tokyo, 1982), pp. 143–44.

[24] Shigeharu Matsumoto, *Shanhai Jidai* (My Days in Shanghai), ii (Tokyo, 1974), p. 209.

development in Asia.[25] Though there were people who lamented this situation, and tried to promote Anglo-Japanese rapprochement, they were powerless. Japan shook off its pose of behaving as a friend of the European powers in Asia and tried to replace them by recourse to war.

It is not entirely correct to depict the period between 1931, when the Manchurian Incident occurred, and 1945, the year of Japanese defeat, as an unbroken continuum of Japanese expansion, for there were times in the mid 1930s which offered Japan alternative courses. The most significant phase was the period of the 'Sato Diplomacy' in the spring of 1937, when Foreign Minister Naotake Sato attempted to combine a new and conciliatory attitude towards China with the improvement of Anglo-Japanese relations. The logic of Japanese expansion, however, which culminated in the outbreak of the Asian-Pacific War, was certainly consistent: Japan attempted to build up its empire in Asia and the Pacific. The so-called Amau Statement of April 1934, in which an influential diplomat stressed that Japan had a special mission in East Asia, and that in order to realise peace and order in this region Japan would act independently and oppose foreign interference in China, was a clear expression of Japan's 'Asian Monroeism'. Indeed the slogan of 'The Great East Asian Co-Prosperity Sphere', which began to be circulated from 1940, was nothing but an ingenious label to conceal Japan's imperial ambition.

Japan's thrust into China and southward advance were justified by the argument that Japan was liberating Asian peoples from the yoke imposed by European powers. In fact, the Japanese government and the Japanese military were not thinking about the liberation of Asian peoples from their subordinate position. A policy directive about the administration of occupied territories, issued in November 1941 shortly before the outbreak of the Asian-Pacific War, overtly exhibited Japan's basic posture: 'It is necessary to inculcate the feeling of respect for the imperial army in the minds of native peoples, and discourage their movements for independence'.[26] The Great East Asian Co-Prosperity Sphere, constructed under such Japanese tutelage, was to be a new empire with the Japanese in the commanding position.

It was inevitable that the war fought between Japan, which was intent on ousting European powers from Asia and building an Asian empire, and the Allied countries led by America and Britain would assume the character of

[25] See Kazu Nagai, '1939 Nen no Han-ei Undo' (Anti-British Movements in 1939), *Kindai Nihon Kenkyu*, 5 (Tokyo, 1983).
[26] *Nihon Gaiko Nenpyo Narabi ni Shuyo Bunsho* (Chronology of Japanese Diplomacy and Major Documents), ii (Tokyo, 1966), p. 562.

a race war. As John Dower vividly described in his pathbreaking book on the Asian-Pacific War, both belligerents employed a variety of means to defame the enemy as racially abhorrent and detestable.[27] Dower stressed that the Japanese strenuously depicted the enemy as demons or beasts, or simply despicable people, while representing themselves as perfect.[28] In this picture of a race war, European people, who had occupied the superior position in the racial hierarchy in Asia, were degraded, but it did not mean that the status of other Asian peoples whom the Japanese had regarded as inferior was elevated.

Both the use of Asian peoples as *romusha* (labourers) for forced labour in constructing the Burma-Thailand railway and the bad treatment of Allied POWs, many of whom were also forced to work to build that railway, can be placed in the context of this race war. The existence of white POWs provided the Japanese leaders with a convenient means to demonstrate that Japan was destroying the past order dominated by Europeans. Such a motive was clearly stated in a report sent in March 1942 from Seishiro Itagaki, Commander in Chief of the Korean Army, to Hideki Tojo, acting both as Prime Minister and Minister of War, about the plans for the internment of POWs in Korea:

> It is our purpose by interning American and British prisoners of war in Korea, to make the Koreans realise positively the true might of our Empire as well as to contribute to psychological propaganda work for stamping out any ideas of worship of Europe and America which the greater part of Korea still retains at bottom.[29]

It is not surprising that the Allied powers detected this factor in Japanese treatment of POWs. A British army memorandum written in 1944 stated: 'Some evidence indicates an official policy of humiliating white prisoners of war in order to diminish their prestige in native eyes'.[30]

---

[27] John W. Dower, *War Without Mercy: Race and Power in the Pacific War* (New York, 1986). This perspective about the character of the race war was put forward earlier by Christopher Thorne, *The Issue of War: States, Societies and the Far Eastern Conflict of 1941–1945* (London, 1985). For a recent argument, see Furedi, *The Silent War*, ch. 6 ('The Second World War as Race War').

[28] Dower, *War Without Mercy*, pt 3.

[29] John R. Pritchard and Sonia M. Zaide (eds), *The Tokyo War Crimes Trial*, pt 6 (New York and London, 1981), pp. 14, 514–15. Aiko Utsumi draws attention to the importance of this report, Utsumi, 'Prisoners of War in the Pacific War: Japan's Policy', in Gavan McCormick and Hank Nelson (eds), *The Burma-Thailand Railway: Memory and History* (St Leonards, New South Wales, 1993), p. 73; Utsumi, 'Senjika no Gaikokujin no Jinken' (Human Rights of Foreigners during the War), *Senso Sekinin Kenkyu*, 3 (1994), p. 7.

[30] 'Allied Prisoners of War in Japanese Hands', 24 August 1944, PRO, WO 208/3485.

The biggest irony in this undertaking was that many Taiwanese and Koreans, who continued to be ruled by Japan as second-class citizens, were placed in the position of dealing with POWs directly as guards in POW camps. On the surface they apparently volunteered to work for the Japanese army, but in fact many of them were either compelled to 'volunteer' or chose to serve in this capacity in order to avoid forced emigration to Japan.[31] Before being posted in POW camps, those Koreans and Taiwanese were not taught the proper way of treating POWs. Instead, exposed daily to harsh training accompanied by physical maltreatment by men of superior rank, they were inculcated with the idea that they should not be soft with their charges and inferiors.[32]

The lack of training and knowledge about the rules for the treatment of POWs was combined with the suppressed anger which the Taiwanese and the Koreans nursed under the Japanese domination and which could be easily vented on somebody in a weaker position, often making these guards behave brutally towards POWs. For example, in Sandakan camp in Borneo the treatment of British POWs worsened after the replacement of Japanese guards by Taiwanese in April 1943.[33]

As a result of Japan's deployment of Korean and Taiwanese guards, and their role in brutalising POWs, many of them were tried in the minor war crimes trials after the war: of the 129 people found guilty, fourteen were sentenced to death.[34] What should be emphasised here is that they were tried as Japanese subjects, their special position as colonial subjects not being taken into consideration by the Allied powers. It can be said that the Allied powers, which were after all imperialist powers intent on regaining their influence in Asia-Pacific after the war, overlooked this aspect of Japan's conduct.[35]

The case of Korean and Taiwanese guards exemplifies the working of racial factors behind the treatment of Allied POWs. The ordinary Japanese people whom POWs encountered, while more or less free from the complex racial feelings of the Koreans or the Taiwanese, also often displayed arrogance towards the white people whom they had used to admire. This attitude

[31] See Aiko Utsumi, *Chosen-jin BC-kyu Senpan no Kiroku*, pp. 121–40.

[32] Ibid., pp. 128–32, 230–31.

[33] 'Allied Prisoners of War Captured in the Far East and Hong Kong: Narrative Written by Miss M. M. Baird', PRO, CAB101/199.

[34] Utsumi, 'Senjika no Gaikokujin no Jinken', p. 16.

[35] In a recent book, Hirofumi Hayashi argues that Britain regarded the minor war crimes trials as an important means of recovering its imperial prestige in South-East Asia. Hirofumi Hayashi, *Sabakareta Senso Hanzai: Igirisu no Tai-nichi Senpan Saiban* (War Crimes that were Tried: British Trials of Japanese War Criminals) (Tokyo, 1998).

was buttressed by the emphasis on the idea that to become a POW was totally disgraceful. As mentioned earlier, Japanese soldiers were not taught the international regulations about the treatment of POWs. What was stressed in their education was the unique spirit of the Japanese military epitomised in the Field Service Code (*Senjinkun*) of 1941, which included a passage: 'You shall not undergo the shame of being taken alive. You shall not bequeath a sullied name'.[36] While it is true that this kind of attitude had certainly existed in traditional Japanese military activities,[37] it surfaced plainly in the process of Japan's pursuit of the leading position in Asia and the Pacific under the pretext of liberating Asia from European domination. International rules about the treatment of POWs were set aside as an embodiment of a European value system to be replaced by a Japanese one. Hideki Tojo said in his address to the chiefs of POW camps in June 1942:

> In Japan, we have our own ideology concerning POWs, which should naturally make their treatment more or less different from that in Europe and America ... you must place the prisoners under strict discipline and not allow them to lie idle doing nothing but eating freely for even a single day.[38]

Though the Japanese Foreign Ministry replied to the inquiry by the British government that Japan would apply the Geneva Convention of 1929 *mutatis mutandis*,[39] the actual treatment of POWs never conformed to international law. It is useful to remember that the Imperial Rescript about the declaration of war in December 1941 did not contain a reference to Japan's willingness to observe international law, unlike those for the preceding three wars (the Sino-Japanese War of 1894–95, the Russo-Japanese War and the First World War). Instead of following international regulations, Japanese leaders stuck to what was regarded as Japan's own and unique value system, ignoring the convention on the treatment of POWs.

This does not mean that in dealing with Allied POWs all Japanese behaved badly. The fact that there were people who treated POWs in a humane way can be glimpsed in various records.[40] But, as Charles Roland points out,

---

[36] Hata, 'From Consideration to Contempt', p. 255.

[37] The most comprehensive account of the history of POWs in Japan is still Shin Hasegawa, *Nihon Horyo Shi* (History of POWs in Japan) in *Collected Works of Hasegawa Shin*, ix (Tokyo, 1971). Hasegawa wrote this during the last phase of the Asia-Pacific War, but it was not published until 1949, when it appeared in the form of a series of journal articles.

[38] John R. Pritchard and Sonia M. Zaide (eds), *The Tokyo War Crimes Trial*, vi, pp. 14, 427.

[39] See Hisakuzu. Fujita, 'POWs and International Law', below p. 98

[40] For example, the author of a report about his experience as a POW concludes his account with the following observation: 'The individual Nippon guards controlling my camps were with a very few exceptions sympathetic and patient with our difficulties, but owing to the

'these instances shine out in an otherwise grey panorama of injustice, indifference and inhumanity. Transgressions of the Geneva Convention were commonplace and, in many locations much of the time, the rule'.[41]

It is worth contrasting British handling of Japanese surrendered personnel (JSP), taken into custody after the Japanese surrender in August 1945, with Japanese treatment of their Allied equivalents.[42] Just as the Asian-Pacific War was for Japan a war for realising its expansionist ambition, for Britain it was a war for recovering its power and influence in Asia and the Pacific. When the war came to an end, Britain not only hastily reestablished its control over its own colonial territories, but also helped France and the Netherlands to regain their dominant position in their respective territories in Indochina and Indonesia. It is not well known that in doing so Britain extensively used JSP. The degree of their use can be detected in the following remark of Lord Mountbatten, who directed the South-East Asia Command, at the time of his visit to Sumatra in April 1946:

> I of course knew that we had been forced to keep Japanese troops under arms to protect our lines of communication and vital areas ... but it was nevertheless a great shock to me to find over a thousand Japanese troops guarding the nine miles of road from the airport to the town.[43]

The retention of JSP by the British forces was carried out in spite of the repeated questioning of its validity by the American side.[44] Britain was determined to make JSP work as hard as possible, as a directive at the end of 1945 stated: 'The maximum use is to be made of Japanese surrendered personnel for work for the Services'.[45] Until they were finally repatriated to Japan in 1947, JSP were used for various purposes, such as maintaining roads, preparing ground for farming and mending roads and railway systems for plantations. Sometimes they were ordered to dig up the corpses of Allied

*continued*
nature of the task were often unable to assist us to any degree. The officers and staff at Nippon Head Quarters always treated me with the greatest courtesy and sympathy'. 'Report by AIF Section of H Force', PRO, WO 32/14550.

[41] Roland, 'Allied POWs, Japanese Captors and the Geneva Convention', p. 94.

[42] In the areas which were put under the control of South-East Asia Command after the end of the war there were 738,000 JSP, of whom about 100,000 were retained in South-East Asia until 1947. Peter Dennis, *Troubled Days of Peace: Mountbatten and South-East Asia Command, 1945–46* (Manchester, 1978), pp. 225–26.

[43] Ibid., p. 226.

[44] See the correspondence in PRO, CO 537/1257.

[45] 'HQ SACSEA Administrative Directive No. 36', 31 December 1945, PRO, WO 203/2727.

soldiers for proper burial, work which former JSP remember with the utmost disgust.

The reason why the JSP problem needs to be emphasised here is that in dealing with JSP the British displayed racial prejudice. A famous episode in Yuji Aida's reminiscence of his days as a JSP, in which a naked British woman soldier completely ignored his presence, when he went into her room to clean it, and continued to comb her hair, is an example of the deep racial prejudice felt by the British and the depersonalisation of their captives.[46] On the other hand, Indian soldiers working in JSP camps tended to deal with JSP in a much more friendly way. In his memoirs, a former JSP went as far as to say that it was thanks to the Indian soldiers that he survived and came safely back to Japan.[47] During the Asian-Pacific War many Indian nationalists fought with the Japanese to achieve their wish for independence. Though Japan did not think seriously about India's independence and only utilised their cooperation for its own imperialistic purposes, this relationship between the Indians and the Japanese in JSP camps certainly pointed to the importance of racial factors dealt with in this essay.

To refer to the experience of JSP is not to trivialise Japanese brutality towards Allied POWs. It is necessary to take into account all the ramifications of changing power relations and shifting perspectives on race. JSP are discussed so as to put the historical nature of the POW issue into clear relief. A study of the POW problem in the larger context of the interactions between imperialist powers in Asia and the Pacific and between those powers and Asian peoples is yet to be undertaken.

[46] Yuji Aida, *Aaron Shuyojo* (The Alon Concentration Camp) (Tokyo, 1962), p. 39.
[47] Hiroyoshi Honma and Toshiaki Niwa (eds), *Ryoshu no Uta* (Poems of the Captured) (private publication, 1997), pp. 178–79.

# 9

# Religion, the Red Cross
# and the Japanese Treatment of POWs

## Margaret Kosuge

Press reports in autumn 1997 suggested that the International Committee of the Red Cross (ICRC) was giving up its traditional emblem and 'adopting another design such as a red diamond'. The ICRC corrected the reports and stressed that 'the red cross emblem has no religious connotation whatsoever, being a reversal of the colours of the Swiss flag'. It has been its symbol since the birth of the Red Cross Movement at the 1863 International Conference.[1] The incident was reminiscent of another problem with the emblem almost a century earlier in Japan.

In 1886 the Japanese government agreed to adhere to the Geneva Convention of 1863. The Japanese Red Cross Society (JRCS) was established in 1887.[2] The JRCS was concerned to emphasise that the symbol had no religious connotation. The emblem ran the risk of provoking anti-Christian opposition because there was anti-western feeling in Japan in the late 1880s as a reaction to westernisation. This mood was exacerbated early in 1891 when a Christian, Kanzo Uchimura, refused to pay homage to the pre-war Japanese totem, the Imperial Rescript on Education and to the Imperial Portrait. The JRCS semi-official bulletin of December 1891, *Hakuai*, stated in the preface to the first volume that:

> Because the cross is the sign of *yaso* [Jesus], one might suspect the Red Cross Society could be associated with that religion. Apparently, there is a European

---

[1] The information is derived from the ICRC, 'The Red Cross Emblem', 22 September 1997, press release 97/26. On the emblem issue, see François Bugnion, 'The Red Cross and Red Cross Emblem', *International Review of the Red Cross*, 272, pp. 208–19; ICRC, *The Emblem of the Red Cross: A Brief History* (Geneva, 1977).

[2] On the Japanese Red Cross, see Olive Checkland, *Humanitarianism and the Emperor's Japan, 1877–1977* (London, 1994); John F. Hutchinson, *Champions of Charity: War and the Rise of the Red Cross* (Boulder, Colorado, and Oxford, 1996), chapter 5; Michiko Kameyama, *Kindainihon Kango-shi, i Nihonsekijujisha to Kangofu* (History of Nursing in Modern Japan, and The Japanese Red Cross Society and Nurses) (Tokyo, 1983). The concise account of the Japanese Red Cross in Hans Haug, *Humanity for All: The International Red Cross and Red Crescent Movement* (Geneva, 1993), pp. 299–308, is also useful.

country where their society is solely organised by Christians and pagan participation is forbidden. However ... in our country, it has no smell of religion and
it is purely founded for the good purpose of relief, honorably recognised by His
Imperial Majesty the Emperor and Her Imperial Majesty the Empress.

The JRCS was anxious not to antagonise Buddhists, especially the West and
the East Honganji priests and their adherents, who had fought so hard against
the movement for 'abolishing Buddhism and destroying Buddha '*haibutsu
kishaku*''.[3] Buddhism had revived since the 1870s, and Buddhist intervention
might become a barrier to the JRCS's efforts to organise local branches.[4]

In spite of this trouble, the JRCS established itself with astonishing
rapidity. Historians are agreed that this can be explained by the Japanese
character: the Japanese had a top-down society where imperial patronage
promoted progress and was employed to boost the national policies of
'entering into the west' and 'making the fighting forces stronger'. Checkland
points out that the JRCS was just one of the state and imperial agencies,
'never independent and ... always subject to the will of government'.[5]
According to Hutchinson, 'a master-servant relationship' was constructed
between the military and the Red Cross Society, instead of the latter becoming an independent service in wartime.[6]

Kameyama examines modern Japan's nursing history chiefly in terms of
the development of the JRCS and the education of nurses.[7] She argues that
the JRCS initially encountered difficulties because it was started as a civilian
voluntary movement. These problems were compounded by the allegedly
religious nature of the Red Cross. For its humanitarian work to proceed
smoothly, the JRCS was often required to emphasise its non-religious status
and its close relations with the military and the government. The subsequent
dramatic development of the Japanese Red Cross was paradoxically enhanced
by the apparently western and Christian connotation of its emblem, whether
or not it actually had any connection. Checkland is among those who raise
the question of whether the cross, the Christian symbol, was 'embraced so
eagerly in Japan because of an urgent need to join a world club rather than
as an expression of genuine concern'.[8]

---

[3] Yoshio Yasumaru, 'Kindaitenkanki ni okeru Shukyo to Kokka' (Shinto and the State at
the Turning Point) in Yasumaru and Masato Miyachi ed., *Shukyo to Kokka, Nihonkindai-
shiso-taikei*, 5 (Religion and the State, 5, The Compendium of Modern Japanese Thought)
(Tokyo, 1988), pp. 490–564.

[4] Ibid., pp. 513–14 and 541; see also Kameyama, *Kindainihon Kango-shi*, p. 39.

[5] Checkland, *Humanitarianism and the Emperor's Japan*, pp. 11, 173–74.

[6] Hutchinson, *Champions of Charity*, p. 211.

[7] Kameyama, *Kindainihon Kango-shi*, especially pp. 18–19, 38–39.

[8] Checkland, *Humanitarianism and the Emperor's Japan*, p. xvii.

Japanese ambivalence over the cross was related to the problem of recognising Christianity, a problem which the new government inherited from the Tokugawa who had worried that this peculiar denomination would disrupt their established social order. Western religion was also feared as a trigger for denationalisation.[9] Yet, as long as Japan's leaders desired to enter into the circle of power dominated by the west, it was required, as a civilised nation, to display tolerance towards western Christianity. Japan decided to adopt the red cross rather than any new design such as the red crescent, which the Turks had adopted during their war with Russia, both from an element of theatre and the need to impress western observers. Tokyo wanted above all to be admitted to the table of the civilised nations and to revise the unequal treaties which the western powers had forced it to accept.

Some Europeans were reluctant to expand the Red Cross to non-Christian Far Eastern countries such as Japan. Gustave Moynier, the Swiss organiser and administrator of the movement, was amongst them. Fukiura points out that Moynier's hesitation about Japanese involvement was due to the religious differences, which he supposed were a 'serious barrier' to the Japanese Red Cross pioneers who had somehow succeeded in obtaining their own government's agreement.[10]

Differences over the symbol had to be resolved. In order to do so, a myth was introduced:

> On the occasion in 1887 when the title of the Society was changed from 'Hakuaisha' to 'The Japanese Red Cross Society', the then President, Count Sano, asked the Empress Shoken to suggest a new crest for the society. She graciously responded with the gift of her ornamental hairpin decorated by a sculpture of a phoenix with paulownia and bamboos. The crest of the society was taken from that design.

This legendary story implies that imperial patronage overcame the opposition which would have been likely if the symbol of the cross had been adopted. Contributions by the general public were also encouraged by the fact that the society had imperial benefactors. Empress Shoken herself was regarded as a strong sympathiser with the humanitarian movement, contributing enormous funds to various organisations apart from the ICRC. After her first courtesy call at the palace in Tokyo in May 1889, one British diplomat's wife felt that, because she had no children of her own, this had

---

[9] See Yasumaru, *Shukyo to Kokka*; Masato Miyachi, 'Kokka-shinto Keisei-katei no Mondaiten' (The Points at the Formation of State Shinto), ibid., pp. 565–93.

[10] Tadamasa Fukiura, *Sekijuji to Henry Dunant* (The Red Cross and Henry Dunant) (Tokyo, 1991), pp. 172–74.

encouraged the Empress to devote herself ever more energetically to charitable activities.[11] Her role as patroness of the Red Cross also echoed the role of German Kaiserins such as Auguste Viktoria.[12] The Emperor and the Empress jointly patronised humanitarian organisations, setting an example by demonstrating imperial humanity and mercy (*jinji*).

The imperial connection with humanitarian movements dates back to the 1877 rebellion. When he learnt of the first conference of the Red Cross in Paris of 1867, Count Sano was moved to organise a humanitarian society intended to aid casualties on both sides in the rebellion. The government rejected Sano's proposal partly because he wished to treat the rebels as well as the government wounded, and partly because of their suspicion of the Christian affiliations of the Red Cross. Sano then made a direct appeal to Prince Arisugawa, the Commander-in-Chief of the imperial forces during the 1877 Satsuma rebellion, mentioning the benefits of imperial patronage: 'If you could give us permission [to operate] that would make it possible to demonstrate the tolerance of the Imperial Court (*chotei*) both to foreigners and to the Japanese people.'[13] The Prince promptly allowed the organisation of Hakuaisha, the forerunner of the JRCS. The role played by the imperial family was decisive.

Until Hakuaisha was founded, relief activities had been organised on an ad hoc basis throughout the civil war (*Boshin Senso*). Though help was given to both sides in Aizu and Hakodate, the organisers met with opposition because of their aid to 'the rebels against the Emperor' (*zokugun*). A notable example was the relief activities by William Willis, a British medical officer. Willis had been involved with the imperial forces' medical service for five months during the early civil war and had treated a total of 600 wounded soldiers and 1000 patients on both sides, teaching his students, Japanese medical officers, European methods of treatment.[14] The Hakuaisha emblem was 'a sun and a horizontal stripe' because Sanetomi Sanjo, Minister of

---

[11] Mary Crawford Fraser and Hugh Cortazzi eds, *A Diplomat's Wife in Japan: Sketches at the Turn of the Century* (original edition published in New York and Tokyo, 1982; Japanese edition translated by Toshio Yokoyama, *Eikokukoshi-fujin no mita Meiji Nihon*, Tokyo, 1988), see pp. 41–42.

[12] On the petition for expanding the Red Cross activities from Prince Arisugawa, President of the JRCS to Count Ito, Minister of Imperial Household, 1 January 1887, see Seiichi Kawamata, *Nihonsekijujisha Hattatsu-shi* (History of the Japanese Red Cross Society in Development) (Tokyo, 1916), p. 51–52.

[13] Ibid, p. 42–3.

[14] Kaori Nishioka, 'Nihonrikugun ni okeru Guni-seido no Seiritsu' (The Establishment of Army Medical System of Modern Japan), *Gunjishigaku*, 26, pp. 24–39.

State, showed strong antipathy toward the sign of *yaso*.[15] Also the term *yaso* (Jesus) itself often meant 'others' in Japanese and a few years earlier, before the civil war of the early 1870s, the imperial court as well as the new government were equivalent to *yaso* in some rural parts of Japan.[16] The birth of the Empress myth after the 1877 rebellion reflected the rapid spread of the idea of the Emperor's divinity. In non-Christian Japan the tradition of the Emperor's divinity took root at the same time as Christianity was reinterpreted as the religion of the west, instead of being thought of as some incomprehensible and unnatural denomination. The Japanese constitution of 1889 recognised freedom of religion, provided it did not interfere with stability and order, and the obligations of the subject. At the same time, article 28 implied recognition of the absolute superiority of State Shintoism.[17]

Japanese recognition of the Red Cross involved the divine ruler and his imperial entourage as patrons of the western Christian institution. In contrast, ordinary Japanese subjects were sometimes hostile to Christianity, which was a reversal of the situation in the pre-modern age, when it had been the government which was intolerant. At the same time the JRCS was reconciled with the Buddhists by Prince Komatsu, and his round of visits greatly helped the rapid development of the regional organisations.[18] The Catechism for Privates (*Heisotsu-kyojusho*) of 1889 stated that, if anyone violated the Red Cross Convention, it meant they rebelled 'against the great heart of Emperor'. It also stressed that the Red Cross ideology was reflected in Japan's ancient traditions. A handbook on Japan edited in English in 1896 traced the work of the Red Cross in Japan back to the legendary reign of the Empress Jingu: 'a code of martial law was drawn up on this occasion … including the following: suffer not a traitor to live. Kill not one who has asked for quarter (*shizen*). Henceforth no Japanese could kill any one, even an enemy, who refused to fight'.[19]

Despite the rapid development of the JRCS under imperial patronage,

---

[15] Fukiura, *Sekijuji to Henry Dunant*, p. 11. Already in 1871, Ryojun Matsumoto, the head of the army's medical services, suggested the design, 'a red cross on white', for the sanitary section's emblem, but his suggestion was opposed by the Minister of State; see Kameyama, *Kindainihon Kango-shi*, p. 44 n. 5.

[16] On the discussion, see Yoshio Yasumaru, *Kindai Tennozo no Keisei* (Formation of the image of Modern Emperor) (Tokyo, 1992), especially pp. 210–23.

[17] Article 28 requires that 'Japanese subjects shall, with limits not prejudicial to peace and order, and not to antagonistic to their duties as subjects, enjoy freedom of religious belief'.

[18] Kameyama, *Kindainihon Kango-shi*, p. 39.

[19] F. Warrington Eastlake and Yoshiaki Yamada, *Heroic Japan: A History of the War between China and Japan* (Yokohama, Shanghai, Hong Kong and Singapore, 1896), p. 465.

there was little attempt to stress the notion of equality in modern Japan. In western humanitarian traditions from the eighteenth century onwards, preceding the birth of the Red Cross, the emphasis was placed on equal respect for slaves, the poor, prisoners, patients, the disabled and children. We might include animals on the list after 1820. Particular respect was to be paid to prisoners of war as well as the wounded and sick. In pre-war Japan, by contrast, the top-down society was unfamiliar with the idea of 'equality' except as inspired by the new divine ruler's 'humanity and mercy'.

The Japanese Red Cross movement was launched before there was any real experience of a full-scale external war. Once the movement was established, the structure on which it was based, with a branch in every administrative district, was the model for the organisation of the local military aid groups, the Patriotic Women's Association (*Aikoku Fujin Kai*) in 1901.

The merciful treatment of Russian POWs in 1904–5 was the high point of the Japanese Red Cross. As Philip Towle indicates in his earlier analysis of the British officers' observations of the 1904–5 war, Japanese behaviour was designed to avoid the 'Yellow Peril' scare and to earn the applause of western observers, especially the British.[20] The image of Britain as an important observer of Japanese behaviour had been portrayed earlier in a Meiji romantic novel published in 1896, shortly after Japan's first international war with the Chinese empire.[21] In the novel a young Japanese Red Cross man, who had been taken prisoner by the Chinese, is freed to return to his own unit, and then arrested by a party of Japanese military employees. These patriots fiercely criticised the former prisoner for treating Chinese wounded and presumably leaking military intelligence to his captors. The Red Cross man pleaded that he never has, and never would, do anything other than his duty. The furious employees rape and kill a Chinese girl as a warning to the Red Cross man. A British journalist, who has witnessed the events from his hiding place, then writes a report for his newspaper on what he has seen.

It was during the war with Tsarist Russia, which was Japan's first struggle with a white enemy, that the Japanese were most worried that the west would unite against the 'Yellow Peril'. After the Japanese triumphed in that

---

[20] Philip Towle, 'Japanese Treatment of Prisoners in 1904–1905: Foreign Officers' Reports', *Military Affairs*, October 1975.

[21] Kyoka Izumi, *Kaijo Hatsuden* (A Telegram from Haicheng) (Taiyo, January 1986). This point is argued by Margaret Kosuge, 'A Historical Background of the Japanese Mistreatment of Allied POWs in the Pacific War: Development and Decline of the Red Cross in Japan', *Sophia Historical Review*, 37 (1992), pp. 79–100.

war and western nations showed a good deal of sympathy with their achievements, this anxiety faded. It was Russia which was disparaged. Nikolai, a Russian missionary to Japan, lamented in his diary in 1904:

> They say Russia is really brutal, really mean, so that it would not be sufficient even if the country were swept away and erased from the surface of the earth. Their hatred is horrible. It is as if all the races in the world hated her. Even the Italians were delighted that the Japanese destroyed the Russian fleet. Have we ever done anything wrong towards them? And they say the British were beside themselves with rejoicing.[22]

The British emphasised Japan's humanitarianism when they wanted to introduce their non-Christian ally to the western powers at the time of the Anglo-Japanese alliance. Their response to Japan's atrocities against British subjects in the Second World War was more confused. They hesitated to emphasise Japanese maltreatment of white POWs chiefly because the 'Japanese would immediately exploit this [racial hate] as a reason for Asiatic solidarity against white races'.[23] They believed, consequently, that Japan's brutal treatment of western POWs 'must always be linked with atrocities against Asians, never reported alone' in broadcasts to the Japanese occupied Asian territories, India and, especially, China.[24] British sensitivity to the racial aspects of the Asian conflict can be seen in an analysis by the British embassy to Chunking in mid February 1944, shortly after the Allies publicised the Japanese atrocities. Pointing out Chinese 'relative lack of interest' in the Western disclosures of the Japanese brutalities against Allied POWs, the analyst concluded that:

> This is undoubtedly accounted for in part by the fact that atrocity stories leave relatively unmoved a country which has already endured six and a half years of war at Japanese hands, including such experiences as the Nanking outrages

---

[22] Kennosuke Nikamura, *Senkyoshi Nikolai to Meijinihon* (Nikolai, the Missionary and Meiji Japan) (Tokyo, 1996), p. 206. According to Nakamura, Nikolai or, to use his real name, Ioan Dimitrovich Kasatkin, the missionary of the Russian Orthodox Church to Japan contributed greatly to the relief activities for the Russian POWs, despite religious persecution during the war with Russia.

[23] 'Committee of Enquiry into the Treatment of British Subjects in Japanese Controlled Territories', 5 December 1942, PRO, FO 371/31840.

[24] 'Publicity about Treatment of British and Allied Prisoners and Internees by the Japanese', 24 January 1944, PRO, FO 371/41787. On the discussion of the British publicity aspect of the Japanese atrocities of the POWs, Margaret Kosuge, 'Publicity Aspect of the IJA's Atrocities during the Second World War', unpublished, 1997; Margaret Kosuge, 'Endless War of the British POWs', *Sekai*, November 1997; Margaret Kosuge, 'Publicity and the Racial War', *Ippankyoikkuburonju*, 21 (1999), pp. 143–60. See also John W. Dower, *War Without Mercy: Race and Power in the Pacific War* (New York, 1986).

of 1937 ... It is also possible that the Chinese appreciate–and secretly sympathise with–the fact that one Japanese aim in perpetrating these atrocities was the humiliation of the white man, as part of the plan for his expulsion from East Asia.[25]

Philip Towle suggests that the dramatic change in the Japanese treatment of western POWs was the result of what happened in Japan in the 1930s. He points out that 'the Japanese knew perfectly well how the Europeans behaved towards prisoners' in 1904. However, because of the rise of anti-western feeling in the period, the Japanese had been persuaded that, in contrast to the western code, death rather than capture was in fact traditional Japanese behaviour on the battlefield. Even without any knowledge of international conventions on POWs, the average Japanese knew that western ideas on POWs were derived from Christianity or European ideology. To the Japanese such ideas were in opposition to, and even threatened, their 'traditional' attitude towards prisoners. To demonstrate their cultural superiority, some told their western victims, 'we are knights of the *Bushido*, of the Order of the Rising Sun, we do not execute at sundown, we execute at sunrise'.[26]

When the Japanese had treated their POWs well in the First World War, the Japanese felt that their conditions were unduly lenient, when compared with the treatment of their own soldiers. In 1916, the chief of the POW Information Bureau commented at a bureau conference that:

> It is agreeable with *Bushido* to treat the enemy braves leniently, and it is necessary for us, as a great nation, to demonstrate our behaviour on behalf of our national pride. At the same time, as nations in this empire, we should fight harder, should be honoured with death, and never be shamed by being taken prisoner.[27]

The duality of these views did not lead to revision but reinforcement of the state of affairs. Infamous Japanese militarist practices such as 'respectfully bowing' (*keirei*), 'roll calling' (*tenko*) and 'thanks for beating' (*binta*) were introduced as part of the process of establishing a national army.

[25] 'Chinese Reactions to British and American Publicity about Japanese Atrocities', 15 February 1944, PRO, FO 371/41789.
[26] GHQ/SCAP ed., 'History of the Non-Military Activities of the Occupation of Japan, 1945–1951', v, 'Trials of Class 'B' and Class 'C' War Criminals' (typescript), p. 24. (trans. and annotated by Margaret Kosuge and Hitoshi Nagai, *GHQ Senryo-shi*, v, *BC kyu-senso-hanzai-saiban* (Tokyo, 1996.)
[27] Furyo-johokyoku, 'Taisho 5 nen 9 gatsu, Furyoshuyojocho-kaigi ni okeru Kunji narabi ni, Taisho 5 nen Rikugunsho Zatsuroku, Furyoshuyojo ni kansuru Tsuzuri; quoting in Akira Fujiwara, 'Are ha Inujini datta!' (Their Death was Meaningless), Shukan Kinyobi, 3 December 1993.

Obedience under duress and mysticism about Japan's cultural singularity were considered essential for the continued existence of the national army.

The 1941 field code was introduced initially to avoid the moral corruption which had appeared in the Chinese theatre of war in the late 1930s. Fujiwara indicates that a few Japanese Communist leaders had tried to organise Japanese POWs in Chinese hands for an anti-war campaign in 1939.[28] The Chinese armies, especially the Eighth Road, encouraged these activities. They were only on a small scale, although they worried the IJA authorities. As a result of the Communist campaign, they knew that the Chinese would not kill enemy POWs but reeducate them. This information spread amongst the Japanese soldiers in the China North theatre, where approximately 2000 surrendered into Chinese hands.

Some of the Japanese fighters in China suffered from post-traumatic stress. According to Yoshida, one of the causes was their involvement in brutality towards the Chinese population.[29] The other troubles faced by the military authorities included serious dietary deficiencies experienced by the Japanese Army in China. Japanese soldiers were already suffering from malnutrition in the late 1930s, although the military authorities would not admit there was a shortage of rations.[30]

Japanese characteristics had changed especially amongst the younger generation. They were far removed from the reality of the Meiji civil war and even from that of the present war, which was skilfully obscured by the control of information. To the Japanese, the First World War was very remote. It had not awakened Winter's 'apocalyptic imaginations'.[31] The younger generation were only concerned with the war in their imaginations, which had been romanticised by so many 'moving war stories' (gunkoku-bidan).

State Shintoism lacked any view of the afterlife, unlike Christianity, but the deification of the war dead went some way to fill the lacuna. Funerals emphasised the militarist ideal. The crowd, all in formal clothes, solemnly received the remains of the war dead at the local station, and the subsequent funeral ceremony was conducted at the local school. An official record of such a funeral for war dead in 1932 shows the Army Minister sent his name-card. The card was probably handed over by his agent. Even so, the

---

[28] Akira Fujiwara, *Shiryo Nihongendai-shi 1* (Documents of Japanese Modern History) (Tokyo, 1980), pp. 420–21.

[29] Yutaka Yoshida, *Gendai-rekishigaku to Senso-sekinin* (Modern Historiography and War Responsibility) pp. 85–89.

[30] Goichi Nagao, *Senso to Eiyo* (The War and Nutrition) (Tokyo, 1994).

[31] Jay Winter, *Sites of Memory, Sites of Mourning: The Great War in European Cultural History* (Cambridge, 1995).

average participant saw the ritual as a triumphalist ceremony rather than a defeatist funeral.

These frequent civilian rituals and countless popularised war stories show the extent of the losses Japan suffered during the war. The figures rose steeply after 1937, and even before the outbreak of war with the Allied forces, approximately 200,000 were killed in the Chinese theatre. This was too many to be deified according to strict ritual. Local ceremonies were gradually simplified. Villages were even encouraged to cultivate cemeteries, where the graves were used for growing 'wartime-plants'.

According to Japan's wartime conventions, the bereaved were compelled to admit that the war dead now rested in the Yasukuni shrine, delivered from the bondage of ancestral worship by their families. National ceremonies for the war dead were held at the national shrine and the bereaved were invited. Some of these were broadcast throughout Japan and its wartime colonies. Murakami explains that radio reporters sometimes had to cut the laments of the bereaved and the cries of 'murderers' and 'bring back my son'.[32] Japanese gallantry in various theatres of war as imagined by the Japanese at home was increasingly questioned before the outbreak of the war with the western Allies. During the China Incident, instructions were sent to the garrison there by Yoshijiro Umezu, Vice Minister of the Army Ministry, stating that 'it was not appropriate to conduct the war rigorously observing to the last letter' of the international laws of war.[33] On the other hand, a few days after the beginning of the war with the western Allies, Akira Muto, chief of the IJA military affairs section, told both the China Expeditionary Army and the Southern Army: 'We hope the POWs captured in the present war will be reasonably treated applying international laws accordingly'.[34]

Mikio Uemura, the first chief of the POW information bureau, was worried about applying international standards to POWs, and concerned about possible diplomatic friction with Japan's white ally, Nazi Germany, if white POWs were forced to work.[35] On the other hand, the JRCS was

---

[32] Shigeyoshi Murakami, *Yasukunijinja, 1869–1945–1985* (The Yasukuni Shirine, 1869–1945–1985) (Tokyo, 1986), pp. 28–29.

[33] Rikushimitsu dai 198, Senshisosho, Shinajihen Rikugun-sakusen 2, appendix 7 (Tokyo, 1975).

[34] Furyo-johokyoku, Furyo-toriatsukai no Kiroku (The POW Information Bureau, The Record of the Treatment of POWs) (1955), p. 3.

[35] On the Japanese views of the international laws of war in the Second World War, see Hitoshi Nagai, 'Ajia-Taiheiyosensoki no Horyo-seisaku, Rikugunchuo to Kokusai-joki' (Japan's Policy towards POWs in the Asian Pacific War, the IJA and International Standards), *Senso Sekinin Kenkyu*, no. 9.

opposed to Japan accepting the Allies' proposal to apply the 1929 Geneva Convention on the treatment of POWs, which Tokyo had signed but not ratified. To the JRCS, it seemed that, in the light of the experiences in the Chinese theatre, it was much better to reject the proposal than to violate the convention with their proclamation that they would apply it *mutatis mutandis*.[36]

Despite these dilemmas and tensions, the 1937–45 war was the peak of JRCS membership.[37] Statistics shows that, during the war with China in 1937, total membership was 2,930,000, and this increased to 4,010,000 in 1940 and 5,840,000 in 1942. At the time of the defeat in 1945, it stood at 15,210,000. Compared with the total annual contribution to the Red Cross in 1935, that in 1945 was fourteen times as great, but because of increasing wartime inflation its actual value had only increased by a factor of four. The total amount disbursed, inclusive of special accounts from 1935 to 1945, was two and a half times that distributed in the past ten decades. From 1937 to 1945, 960 relief shipments organised by 33,156 servicemen were sent to the hospitals in Japan, the hospital-ships, China and the South Pacific areas, though many were lost on the way.

Before the defeat some topics regularly included in school textbooks concerned the Red Cross, including a poem about the friendly meeting at Suishiei between General Nogi and the captured Russian commander, General Stoessel. Stories of Red Cross philanthropy and imperial patronage also circulated.[38] Before their departure from their homeland, Red Cross nurses were thanked by pupils for their impartial service on the battlefields to enemy soldiers as well as Japan's.[39]

Despite the reality, the people were told that western POWs were treated according to international law. Thus, when the Japanese publicised the Allies' brutalities and their neglect of the Red Cross emblem, such behaviour was furiously denounced by the Japanese people. At the same time, the military often warned the people against being moved by 'a mistaken idea of humanitarianism or swayed by personal feelings towards the prisoners'.[40]

[36] Masao Ichimata, 'Senpansaiban-kenkyu-yoron, 1, 1929 Horyo-joyaku Junyo-mondai' (Essay on the War Criminal Trials, 1, the 1929 POW Convention Issue), *Kokusaiho Gaiko Zasshi*, 66, no. 1.

[37] The figures are shown in *Nihonsekijujisha Shashiko*, 5 (Tokyo, 1969), pp. 40, 219, 455–62.

[38] Ibid., p. 114–6. See also Toshio Nakauchi, *Gunkokubidan to Kyokasho* (War Stories and School-Textbooks) (Tokyo, 1988). Unless they read it in army college, soldiers had already lost the opportunity to learn international law since the 1932 revision of the army educational system.

[39] Yamanashi-nichinichi, 15 September 1937.

The IHQ spokesman warned in his radio speech in 1942 against showing mercy to the enemy who had tried to subvert Japanese culture long before the fighting.[41]

In a picture painted in 1944, now in the war museum in the Yasukuni shrine, we are shown a party of Red Cross nurses.[42] The picture, measuring six foot by nearly ten foot, was the joint production of forty-four members of the Women Artists Service Corps. It is a genre painting in wartime clothes, where the nurses occupy a focal point, with their Red Cross armbands, buttons and medals. Looking at them closely, we find the Red Cross members bowing to a shrine with the Imperial Chrysanthemum. According to Japan's wartime conventions, the nurses are dedicating themselves to the Emperor; unless the war ends in victory, their ultimate 'good fortune' will be to 'die for the Emperor' in the theatre of war. It may be worth mentioning that the first women enshrined at the Yasukuni in 1907 were Red Cross nurses.

In the final stages of the Burma campaign, in the spring of 1945, after the Japanese defeat at Imphal, a crashed Allied airman was delivered to an IJA field hospital. A Japanese Red Cross nurse recalled:

> Just once, an enemy airplane crashed and then an enemy airman suffering all over his body was carried into us, the surgery section. This pilot must have strafed us just before, so we cannot hate him enough, though we now have an obligation to give him medical treatment once he comes to our hospital. 'Save the medicine, rather let him die, kill him', many patients said after surrounding him. He was big enough for us to hide behind his back to play hide-and-seek. We did treat him kindly, filming a tincture over his body. That is the Red Cross Spirit.[43]

Here we see in practice the pre-war ideal of the Japanese Red Cross. The Red Cross Spirit was the young nurses' support throughout the long war years even when it was thought better by the Japanese to be killed rather than to be taken prisoner.[44]

The acceptance of the Red Cross by Japan was important for the non-Christian latecomer's standing with the western Christian civilised nations, especially Britain, and also for Japan's integration with the western powers. Imperial patronage and the repeated claim that the Red Cross was not

---

[40] 'Tojo's personal instruction to the commander of Zentsuji Camp', 30 May 1942.
[41] *Asahi*, 5 December, 1942.
[42] 'Kokokufujo kaido no zu, shuto no bu' (1944).
[43] Ichizo Miyabe ed., *Hakui no Tenshi* (Angels in White) (Tokyo, 1972), p. 213–14.
[44] Louis Allen, *Burma: The Longest War, 1941–1945* (London, 1986).

religious popularised the movement across Japan. The Regular Assembly of the JRCS in 1908 was one of the earliest occasions for a crowd of up to 41,000 to listen to the national anthem, '*kimi-ga-yo*', in the Empress's presence.[45] The Red Cross was rapidly embraced into pre-war Japan's patriotism. What the emblem represented as time went on was equated both with the imperial virtues and the subjects' duties. The significance of this was seen on various ceremonial occasions, in cities, towns and villages, in schools, when official funerals were performed for those killed in the war, and in the Yasukuni shrine when rituals were held for 'inviting in souls of the war dead'.

The ceremonies for the war dead were intended to allow the bereaved to uphold the family's honour. To 'mourn' their loss was strictly forbidden. The core of 'war dead' worship was woven around their imagined battlefield glory and the romanticised image of the ultimate reunion of the war dead at the Yasukuni shrine.[46] After this reunion, the war dead, now reincarnated into cherry blossom flowers, would fall again as if on the field, symbolising absolute loyalty to the Emperor's state (*shichisho hokoku*).

It was the apocalyptic defeat under the mushroom clouds that released ordinary people from their obsession with 'honourable death in war' (*meiyo no senshi*). Ironically, at this moment of Japanese liberation from the anti-western militarist myth, western POWs now embraced a nuclear triumphalist myth that average Japanese found difficult to accept.[47]

[45] Kawamata, *Nihonsekijuji-sha Hattatsu-shi*, p. 429.
[46] Winter, *Sites of Memory, Sites of Mourning*, especially p. 15–28.
[47] This discussion was presented at the Summer Seminar of Modern History in Nagano in 1999: 'We shall remember them – Igirisu ni okeru Senso no Kioku, Kioku no Ba, Ninaite-tachi' (We shall remember them – Britain, Remembrance and the Carriers of War Memories).

# 10

# The Post-War Treatment
## of Japanese Overseas Nationals

### Hideo Kobayashi

In August 1945 Japan accepted the terms of the Potsdam Declaration and surrendered unconditionally to the Allied Forces. The Allied armies forced the Japanese to give up their colonies. At this time, the population of Japanese residing in its former overseas territories had reached six million, half of whom were military the other half civilian. The Japanese had to surrender to the Chinese army in China, to the American, British, Dutch, Australian and French armies in South-East Asia, and to the Soviet army in North-East Asia. It was estimated that three years would be needed to repatriate these people. By 1947, however, that is within two years, approximately 90 per cent of them had been returned to Japan. These Japanese returned home with only the clothes on their backs, carrying a few pieces of hand luggage.

The courteous treatment the Chinese showed towards the Japanese left the latter with fond memories of their Asian neighbour. Those returning from the Soviet Union and Soviet-controlled territories, in contrast, were less fortunate due to the sufferings they endured, including rape, plunder and other violent acts committed by the Soviet army. This antipathy was intensified by the general ill treatment the Japanese prisoners received from their Soviet captors, treatment that included forced hard labour in territory controlled by the Soviet Union.

This essay will first present a general view of the conditions that Japanese prisoners of the Allied forces endured following their country's surrender in 1945. It concentrates on the differences in treatment experienced by those captured by the Chinese and those captured by the Soviets at this time.[1]

As the Second World War ended, the Japanese surrendered to the Allied forces led by the United States. Having lost their influence and interests in

---

[1] The Japanese people's impression of the Soviet Union is poor in comparison with their impressions of China and the USA. This stems from the post-war treatment of overseas Japanese. On the bibliography of this subject see Yasuo Wakatsuki, *Sengo Hikiage no Kiroku* (Documents on the Post-War Treatment of Japanese Overseas) (Tokyo, 1991), pp. 375–84.

Asia, the Japanese returned home. Although Japanese enterprises today have also lost some of their influence and interests in Asia, because of the currency crisis of July 1997, they have certainly not withdrawn and returned home. Japan's defeat in 1945 was undoubtedly a far greater change in Japan's relations with Asia.

The twentieth century in East Asia started with the break-up of the Chinese Empire and the rise of the modern Japanese Empire. Japan encroached on the old Chinese Empire by making war on China and Russia (the Sino-Japanese and Russo-Japanese Wars), and, in the process, expanded its power to incorporate Taiwan and Korea, as well as north-eastern China. At the end of the nineteenth century, China was still powerful but based its diplomacy on an out of date tribute system and on the belief of its superiority to others. Japan criticised China and adopted European ideas of free trade and international public law. It also caught up with the great powers.

Japan took possession of Taiwan, part of Sakhalin and Kanto state through the Sino-Japanese and the Russo-Japanese Wars. From 1910, it made Korea a formal part of its empire. During the First World War, the Manchurian Incident, the Sino-Japanese War and the Pacific War, Japan extended its territory. In the end, the Japanese Empire, or Greater East Asia Co-Prosperity Sphere, extended from the Aleutian Islands in the north to the Thymol Islands in the south, from Burma in the west to the Bismarck Islands in the east.

In August 1945 the Allies defeated Japan and ended the Greater East Asia Co-Prosperity Sphere. However, Japan's sphere left east Asia with a legacy of centralised government, bureaucratic systems, a powerful judicature, a strong police structure, a primary education system and industrial organisations such as national corporations, joint stock companies, banks, and trading companies, as well as a pyramid of owners, managers and labourers. Japanese civilians also left a vacuum after they were repatriated.

Table 2 gives the total number of Japanese nationals residing in the Greater East Asian Co-Prosperity Sphere in 1945. The Japanese civilian population in the colonies at this time was almost 3,130,000, of whom 1,148,000 were in Manchuria (36.7 per cent), 712,000 in Korea (27.8 per cent) and more than 355,000 in Taiwan (11.7 per cent). The largest percentage of the Japanese overseas population was concentrated in Manchuria and, if the population in the Kanto state is included, would reach 44.3 per cent, about half of this overseas population. Almost 489,000 (15.6 per cent) of the overseas Japanese lived in mainland China, 67.7 per cent of these living in north China, 28.7 per cent in Central China, and only 3.6 per cent in south China. 3 per cent of all overseas Japanese lived in South-East Asia. The largest number of these were concentrated in Indonesia, followed by the Philippines, which together accounted for 90 per cent of the population of Japanese nationals residing in South-East Asia.[2]

Table 2

Japanese population, enterprises and assets
in former overseas territories

| Region | Population | Ratio (%) | Year | Enterprises | Assets (1000 yen) | Year |
|---|---|---|---|---|---|---|
| Kanto state | 238,624 | 7.63 | 1944 | – | – | – |
| Manchuria | 1,148,000 | 36.72 | 1943 | – | – | – |
| Korea | 712,583 | 2.80 | 1944 | – | – | – |
| Taiwan | 365,500 | 11.69 | 1941 | – | – | – |
| Mainland China | 488,883 | 15.64 | 1942 | – | – | – |
| North China | 330,771 | 67.70 | | – | – | – |
| Central China | 140,435 | 28.70 | | – | – | – |
| South China | 17,677 | 3.60 | | – | – | – |
| South Sea Islands | 51,723 | 1.66 | 1939 | 53 | 114,916 | 1939 |
| Philippines | 40,000 | 1.28 | | 82 | 505,458 | – |
| French-Indochina | 2500 | 0.08 | | 124 | 230,862 | – |
| Thailand | 2800 | 0.09 | | 222 | 301,386 | – |
| Burma | 2200 | 0.07 | | 90 | 567,099 | – |
| Indonesia | 60,000 | 1.92 | | 339 | 1,031,172 | – |
| Lesser-Sunda Ils. | 500 | 0.02 | | – | – | – |
| Malaya | 5761 | 0.18 | 1938 | 187 | 1,516,064 | – |
| New Guinea | 7000 | 0.22 | | – | – | – |
| Total | 3,126,074 | 100.00 | | – | – | – |

Source: Okurasho, *Nihonjin no Kaigai-katsudo ni Kansuru Rekishiteki Chosa* (Ministry of Finance, Historical Investigation Related to Japanese Activities Overseas, Regional Edition) (Tokyo, 1950).

To give some idea of the size of the Japanese overseas population at the end of the war, the Japanese population in Asia in October 1997 was 148,924. The majority were in Indonesia (25,355), next was Hong Kong (24,500), followed by Thailand (23,292), then China (19,379), Taiwan (13,664) and Korea (12,778).

[2] Okurasho, *Nihonjin no Kaigai-katsudo ni Kansuru Rekishiteki Chosa* (Ministry of Finance, Historical Investigation Related to Japanese Activities Overseas) (Tokyo, 1950).

Table 2 also gives the number of Japanese enterprises in Asia at the time of Japan's defeat. There were approximately 25,000 Japanese enterprises overseas. Most of these were concentrated in Manchuria, Korea and Taiwan. For instance, according to the *Manchurian Mine Yearbook* for 1944, there was a total of 538 companies in Manchuria, including sixty-three mining companies, fifty-one metalwork companies, seventy-eight machine tool manufacturing companies, eighty-six pharmaceutical companies, three electrical and gas companies, forty-one ceramic and civil engineering companies, thirty-six textile companies, thirty-seven lumber and wood product manufacturing companies, sixty-six food companies, fourteen printing and book binding companies, sixteen transportation and communication companies, six civil engineering and construction companies, and forty-one other companies in various sectors.

Japan's defeat in the war following its acceptance of the Potsdam Declaration in August 1945 brought with it the repatriation of Japanese nationals abroad, causing major changes in the South-East Asian region. Japanese repatriated from Manchuria, northern Korea and Sakhalin, regions occupied by the Soviet Union, were subjected to extremely harsh conditions. On the other hand, those repatriated from Nationalist Party controlled China and Taiwan, as well as from southern Korea and the South Sea Islands, areas controlled by United States forces, were returned under relatively benevolent conditions. Those returned from the Manchuria and Mongolia area had been in the front line of the war in Manchuria near the Soviet border and became war victims.

There were about 3,000,000 civilians repatriated, over one third of whom were from Manchuria and Daliang. At the same time there was close to an equal number repatriated from the Japanese army and navy who had been stationed in garrisons throughout Asia. Thus a total of almost 6,300,000 Japanese living overseas were returned to Japan

The total number of Japanese civilian and military overseas personnel is also listed in Table 3. It was believed that it would take almost three years to repatriate these people. However, by 1947 almost 90 per cent of these people had returned to their homeland. 1946–48 were the peak years for Japanese repatriation from the Soviet Union and Sakhalin, places located far from the Japanese capital. The repatriation of Japanese from nearer locations, such as Manchuria, Taiwan, China's Daliang and Korea, was accomplished relatively sooner. The peak year was 1945–46. Expressed in numbers, those repatriated from the Soviet Union reached only 5000 (almost 1 per cent) by 1946, but by 1947–48 as many as 370,393 (almost 80 per cent) had returned home. On the other hand, by 1946, 1,492,397 (99 per cent) of overseas Japanese had already been repatriated from China.

Table 3

Repatriation of Japanese from former Japanese
overseas territories

| | Until 1946 | Until 1947 | Until 1948 | Until 1949 | 1950–95 | Total |
|---|---|---|---|---|---|---|
| Soviet Union | 5000 | 200,774 | 169,619 | 87,416 | 10,136 | 472,945 |
| The Kuril Islands and Sakhalin | 5613 | 168,111 | 114,156 | 4710 | 906 | 293,496 |
| Manchuria | 1,010,837 | 29,714 | 4970 | 4 | 0 | 1,045,525 |
| Daliang | 6126 | 212,053 | 4914 | 2861 | 0 | 225,954 |
| China | 1,492,397 | 3758 | 4401 | 702 | 38,633 | 1,539,891 |
| Hong Kong | 19,050 | 147 | 14 | 11 | 125 | 19,347 |
| North Korea | 304,469 | 16,779 | 1295 | 3 | 39 | 322,585 |
| South Korea | 591,765 | 1425 | 1150 | 1041 | 1938 | 597,319 |
| Taiwan | 473,316 | 4958 | 775 | 255 | 240 | 479,544 |
| Islands around the Japanese mainland | 62,389 | 0 | 0 | 0 | 0 | 62,389 |
| Okinawa | 64,396 | 3484 | 996 | 490 | 50 | 69,416 |
| Dutch East Indies | 0 | 14,841 | 637 | 112 | 3 | 15,593 |
| French Indochina | 31,583 | 286 | 123 | 45 | 266 | 32,303 |
| Pacific Islands | 130,795 | 103 | 4 | 4 | 62 | 130,968 |
| Philippine Islands | 132,303 | 457 | 116 | 41 | 206 | 133,123 |
| South East Asia | 623,909 | 86,379 | 346 | 51 | 822 | 711,507 |
| Hawaii | 3411 | 1 | 100 | 80 | 67 | 3659 |
| Australia | 138,167 | 487 | 8 | 18 | 163 | 138,843 |
| New Zealand | 797 | 0 | 0 | 0 | 0 | 797 |
| Total | 5,096,323 | 743,757 | 303,624 | 97,844 | 53,656 | 6,295,204 |
| Ratio (%) | 80.96 | 11.82 | 4.82 | 1.55 | 0.85 | |

Source: Yasuo Wakatsuki, *Sengo Hikiage no Kiroku* (Documents on the Post-War Treatment of Japanese Overseas)(Tokyo, 1991).

While provisions were made in the Potsdam Declaration for the repatriation of military personnel ('General Injunction Related to the Capitulation and Disarmament of the Army and Navy'), no such concrete provision was

made for the repatriation of civilians. Consequently, many Japanese decided
to stay in Taiwan and Korea even after Japan's defeat.[3] The end of the war
was followed by confusion and growing public disorder that made living
conditions for such Japanese difficult.

Overseas employment surfaced as a problem in the former colonies after
Japan's defeat. On the one hand, it was important for the victors to continue
factory operations. The Japanese, on the other hand, needed to work in
these factories to sustain their livelihoods. Because of American air raids,
the Japanese islands lay in ruins and hunger had become a major problem.
Talk about 'going home to Japan and finding no food there' spread quickly.
People often had no choice but to remain where they were. Furthermore,
expatriates who had stayed a number of years in other countries, like Korea
and Taiwan, had no relatives who wanted them repatriated. For them, the
colonies they had lived in were home.

The use of Japanese overseas workers before their repatriation actually
began with the establishment of the Nisseki (Japanese Technologies and
Management Systems) in Manchuria in May 1946. Through these the number of Japanese engineers deployed in that area grew to about 10,000. If
family members are included, the number of Japanese reached around
33,000 This group planned the so-called North-Western Economic Revival
Plan and worked to preserve the operation of the factories and the coal
mines, occupying key positions in various enterprises. In due time, however,
as their technology and skills were transferred to the locals, the skilled
Japanese crew left and returned home to Japan.

A number of these personnel became involved in the whirlpool of Asian
independence movements as well as China's civil war. Amid the fires of
this war, they hesitated as to which army to follow — that of the National
Party or that of the Communist Party. Even the region of Manchuria was
not free from such tensions. By 1948 about 8000 Japanese veterans of the
Chinese civil war had been repatriated. However, in the case of the Fushuan
mines in Manchuria, for example, nineteen people stayed on under the
charge of Yuichiro Sibata, ex-director of the coal mining bureau. They were
finally discharged and sent home in May of 1953.[4]

Among the Japanese engineers, there were those who participated as
volunteers in the Chinese civil war. There were also those who cooperated

---

[3] Yoshio Morita, *Chosen Shusen no Kiroku* (Korean Chronicle at the End of War) (Tokyo,
1964).

[4] Association of South Manchuria Railway Company Staff, *Mantetsu Shokuin Shusen Kiroku*
(Post-War SMRC Staff Chronicles) (Tokyo, 1996).

in rebuilding the Chinese state after the war. For instance, Tsuneya Maru-sawa and nine other Japanese engineers acted as directors of the Manchurian Mines Experiment Centre until 1953. Some engineers, being Japanese, felt responsible for the Pacific War and thought seriously about the needs of the new China. There were also people whose purpose in volunteering their services was more than simply to eke out a living.[5] They included film engineers, such as Tomu Uchida, Tai Kato and Osamu Kuroda, who put themselves under the Chinese Communist Army and cooperated in the making of films. Returning to Japan, Uchida became a director and made *Strait of Starvation,* a very famous Japanese film.

In Sakhalin, Japanese also worked in the coal mines and pulp factories. Koichiro Kinoshita, who was managing director of the Sakhalin factory, and later the President of the Honshu Paper Company, became the agent of all the officers involved in factory operations. Under Soviet rule he recalls, 'My monthly salary is given to me in rubles but the value was about the same as it was when I worked before the Second World War'. Though the Soviets had occupied the region of northern Korea, there was no change in their treatment of Japanese prisoners there from that in Manchuria and Sakhalin.

The biggest factory in northern Korea was the Korean Nitrogen Factory located in Hungnam. The number of full-time employees reached 45,000 in 1945. The factory specialised in nitrogen-related products whose basic compound was ammonium sulphate ($NH_3 SO_4$), and was the largest indus-trial complex in northern Korea at the time. When the Soviet army took it over after the war, operations came to a halt, because the factory's key personnel were mostly Japanese labourers who were driven out. This policy was reversed from October 1945 and the labourers were brought back. By 1946 there was a complement of 2496 Japanese composed of 450 engineers, ninety administrative employees and 1956 technicians.[6] Ken Tanabe, who worked in the Korea Nitrogen Factory and later became the president of Sekisui House, related later, 'among the Japanese crew, the factory used 2500 members. Upon their return to their respective company houses, they had to line up and accept hand-outs of polished rice. There were those, however, who tried hard to eke out a living through engaging in day labour'.[7]

Japanese workers in Taiwan experienced the same conditions. In the spring of 1946 the first group were repatriated, numbering 7139 persons,

[5] Masanori Sato, *Ichi Kagakusha no Kaiso* (Scientists' Recollections) (Tokyo, 1971).

[6] Shoji Kamata, *Hokusen no Nihonjin Kunan-ki* (Record of Japanese Suffering in Northern Korea) (Tokyo, 1970).

[7] *My Autobiography,* Nippon Keizai Shinbun, 13 October 1985.

many of whom were engineers. The second set repatriated, numbering 1025, was returned home in December 1946. The final group sent home in spring 1947 numbered 260 people. Of the first group of 7000 repatriates, most were employed in the industries of mining technology, agriculture and forestry, and transport. Each of these industries accounted for 24 per cent of the repatriates; thus 72 per cent of the first 7000 repatriates were employed in these industries. As for the remainder, 10 per cent were in civil administration, another 10 per cent were in financial administration, 4.5 per cent in education, 2 per cent in security, and the remaining 1.5 per cent in other fields.[8] The largest employer of Japanese workers was the biggest provider of electricity in Taiwan, the Taiwan Electric Corporation. In April 1946, among 3153 Japanese repatriates, 422 were employed by the Taiwan Electric Corporation. These were employees responsible for the maintenance, control, transportation and power generation at the electric power plants, as well as for the electric substations, the transformers and the distribution of electricity.[9] A large number of Japanese workers were also employed in mainland China. There most of these employees were in charge of the maintenance of textile machines as well as production. Japanese personnel were even employed in the Hainan Islands.

Within the short period after it entered the war against Japan, in August 1945, the Soviet Union occupied the northern parts of China and the northern parts of the Korean peninsula. The Japanese army in those regions surrendered to the Soviet army, who transported their Japanese prisoners to Siberia. The number of prisoners taken by the Soviet army was about 600,000. The Japanese prisoners were subjected to harsh labour conditions from which 50,000 died. The Soviets did not apologise for their inhumane treatment of Japanese prisoners until 1990; no reparations have been made for Japanese losses during this time. Of these POWs, 969 captured in Manchuria were handed over to the China in 1950 as suspected war criminals and were taken to the Fushuan War Crimes Control Centre.

The difference between the treatment these prisoners received from the Chinese and Soviet governments was extreme. The Chinese treated the prisoners very humanely. Many Chinese citizens therefore complained about such treatment of Japanese war criminals, especially if they had been injured by the Japanese soldiers or had had relatives killed. But the Chinese government did not alter its fundamental policy. The prisoners were subjected

---

[8] *Survey of Japanese Reparation in Taiwan* (Record Office in Taipei, 1946).
[9] Taiwan Electric Power Company, 'The Development of Taiwan Electric Industry' (Taipei, 1989).

to education not hard labour.[10] For example, the daily routine of these Japanese prisoners was as follows: 5.00 a.m. wake up call; 8.00 a.m. breakfast; study time until 11.00 a.m.; 12.00 to 2.00 p.m. afternoon rest; 2.00 to 5.00 p.m. prison work detail; 6.00 p.m. evening meal; 8.00 p.m. night's rest.[11] It was like being in a hospital. Of course they were bullied by Chinese prisoners but were protected by prison security. In addition, the government of China acted to protect the safety of these Japanese prisoners. The treatment by the Soviets, in contrast to China, consisted hard labour under freezing conditions of -50 degrees to -60 degrees fahrenheit in winter.

In 1956 a High Tribunal on Special Military Affairs was established in Sen Yang. Here, in addition to the 969 prisoners handed to the Chinese government by the Soviets, there were 130 more suspected war criminals arrested in China. Forty-five out of the 1099 prisoners were convicted by the court. The sentences were death or imprisonment of not less than thirteen and not more than twenty years, without parole. However, for prisoners who had served time in Chinese and Soviet prisons, the number of years they had already spent in jail was deducted from the prison terms. In fact, the prison terms were reduced to a range of two years to nine years. All death sentences were also commuted to sentences of life imprisonment. The majority were acquitted and sent home before the trials. Ironic as it may seem, the Japanese war prisoners were sent on a tour around China before being sent home.

Why did China give favourable treatment to Japanese prisoners of war? Why did China and the Soviet Union treat prisoners so differently? Zhou En Lai, one of the most powerful leaders of the Chinese Communist Party, sat as one of the judges of the War Crime Tribunal. It is said that he ordered the humane treatment of the prisoners of war. But it was not only the Communist Party who adopted a benevolent policy on the treatment of prisoners. The Nationalist Party also adopted similar measures. The Party Leader, Chiang Kai Shek, himself ordered the humane treatment of Japanese prisoners of war.

Humane treatment of prisoners, however, was not confined to China. The United States and the European colonial governments in South-East Asia also showed humanity in their treatment of prisoners. But the humanitarian conditions the Chinese bestowed upon prisoners of war seemed overgenerous on their part. Japanese today still wonder why the Chinese

---

[10] The Organisation of POWs from China, *Watashi-tachi ha Chugoku de Nani wo Shita ka* (What did we do in China?) (Tokyo, 1987).

[11] The Organisation of POWs from China, *Kaettekita Senpan-tachi no Kohansei* (Returned War Prisoners' Half a Life) (Tokyo, 1996)

government treated the prisoners of war in this humane and generous way. Some pointers can be found.

By August 1945 the Japanese Forces had been defeated. In the parts of Asia where they were extended, their military strength amounted to 3,000,000 personnel. At that time their weapons became a major factor in Asian politics and decisively influenced South-East Asian military and political trends. The Japanese armed forces there influenced the independence movements This scenario was replayed in China as well. In the throes of the Chinese civil war, Japanese soldiers were faced with the problem of whether they should surrender their weapons to the Communist forces or to the Nationalist forces. Their decisions decisively influenced the combatants' military power because the defeated Japanese soldiers were not only in possession of arms but of technology as well. For the non-industrialised nations at that time, the Japanese military forces were a technically skilled group and this increased their significance. In planning for their rehabilitation, this matter was given serious consideration. They had high technology and discipline; how to make best use of these assets was a significant question in the post-war rehabilitation period.

In the case of the Soviet Union, the conditions when the Japanese prisoners were taken was different from China. Because it did not consider them internal political opponents, Moscow only wanted to use them as a work force and not for other purposes. China had a use for some of these Japanese prisoners until 1950, and did not send all of them home until 1956. The reason lay in the East Asian economic and political trends in the 1950s. 1950 was marked by the beginning of the Korea War and by the divergence in relations between China and Japan. Economic and political ties were cut. Men repatriated from China were sent home to establish a Sino-Japanese Friendship movement. It was for this purpose that the Chinese gave them such favourable treatment. As a result, the Japanese prisoners were made to recognise their war crimes as well as forming groups to strengthen Chinese-Japanese friendship.

# 11

# Towards Reconciliation: Japanese Reactions to Ernest Gordon

## Kazuaki Saito

> Father, to see thy face, wherein no cloud
> Of anger shall remain, but peace assured,
> And reconcilement; wrath shall be no more
> Thenceforth, but in thy presence joy entire.
>
> John Milton, *Paradise Lost*, iii, lines 262–65 [1]

What is peculiar to Milton's Satan is that the Prince of Hell is described, unlike Dante's, as one who has humane emotions. Dante's Lucifero is an abstract figure of evil, a giant figure, though with three human faces, something resembling a gigantic windmill in the distance with little show of humanity. Satan, however, becomes overcome with remorse because, when he was Lucifer in Heaven, he had seduced the celestial spirits against the Almighty, that he seems to entertain the notion that he might repent and be pardoned: 'is there no place/Left for repentance, none for pardon left?' [2] Unlike Dante's Lucifero, Milton's Lucifer can voice a pang of conscience: 'Under what torments inwardly I groan'.[3] Yet the psychology of the Prince of Darkness soon lets us become aware that temporary remorse only strengthens his pride, contempt, indignation and hatred against the Supreme Good. His arrogance as the chief of the angels does not allow him to come out of his own hell wherever he flies: that internal hell of detesting the enemy. For him and for many of us to overcome anger and hatred is hopelessly difficult.

The hardest obstacles to reconciliation are often found in matters related to war. On 14 August 1995, the Japanese Prime Minister Tomiichi Murayama, expressed remorse and apologised for past Japanese aggression and colonialism. This was received as courageous but disappointing, for it was the first

---

[1] John T. Shawcross, editor, *The Complete Poetry of John Milton* (New York, 1963), p. 275: *Paradise Lost*, iii, lines 262–65.

[2] Ibid., p. 289, iv, lines 79–80.

[3] Ibid., p. 290, iv, line 88.

apology coming from a Japanese Prime Minister, yet it did not deal with compensating either those Asians who had suffered from Japan's military expansion or those Allied and Asian POWs who had undergone appalling hardships and were the victims of atrocities inflicted by the Japanese. Such victims included Koreans, Chinese, Filipinos, Indonesians, Thais, British and Australians.[4] For a great number of people the war has not ended even today. Those who suffered in agony and hardship in a prison camp cannot easily forget the past. As C. S. Lewis believed, forgiveness is the most un-popular of the Christian virtues: 'Every one says forgiveness is a lovely idea, until they have something to forgive, as we had during the war. And then, to mention the subject at all is to be greeted with howls of anger'.[5]

When rivals are running a smear campaign against us or when we have to forgive the enemies after the war, how can we overcome our anger and hatred? Timon of Athens, deceived by the apparent candour of fair-weather friends, could only shake the dust of Athens off his feet with unbridled anger and bitter curses against all mankind. How can one not become misanthropic like Timon but achieve a peaceful and reconciled state of mind, not hatred and anger? One way is to look at classic examples of the 'unconquerable mind' of human beings in history.

In Japan the example of an unconquerable mind found in Ernest Gordon's account, *Through the Valley of the Kwai*, has captured the minds of many readers. Gordon was prompted to write as factual an account as possible in response to the widely-publicised misunderstanding of the POWs' situ-ation in Pierre Boulle's book *The Bridge over the River Kwai* and the film based on it. The story is an entertaining fiction, relating how British officers built the bridge in record time and demonstrated their technological supe-riority. Yet Gordon could not let 'such an impression go unchallenged' as it would 'do an injustice to the officers and men – living and dead – who worked on that bridge'.[6] However factual and objective an author tries to

---

[4] When I heard the news I was at Kanchanburi, participating with colleagues and students from Japan in the reconciliation ceremony commemorating the fiftieth anniversary of the Second World War. This was held at the war cemetery near the River Kwai site of the notorious Death railway. I sensed the expressions of dissatisfaction coming from the Allied war veterans and their families.

[5] C. S. Lewis, *Mere Christianity* (London, 1955), pp. 101ff.

[6] Ernest Gordon, *Miracle on the River Kwai* (London, 1981), p. 62. All quotations from Gordon's book are from the Fount Paperbacks edition. The original edition was published in 1962, New York. The Japanese translation by Kazuaki Saito was published in 1976, reprinted in 1981 and reprinted again in 1995, Tokyo.

On 21 October 1997 the BBC's *Timewatch* programme featured the story behind the film, *The Bridge on the River Kwai*, which won six Oscars. Lieutenant-Colonel Philip Toosey, who

be, and however touching his account proves to be, no book is altogether immune from criticism.

Ivan Morris, writing brilliantly on the tragic heroes made noble by their failure in the history of Japan, admitted that our information is scanty about the ancient heroes such as Masashige Kusunoki, the greatest hero of Emperor Godaigo's turbulent age, who is more a creature of legend than of history. 'Much that is known about Masashige is invention – that unconscious process of creating fiction which informs the psychology of hero worship more than any historical facts'.[7] For Morris, it was more important to recognise the image of a hero in the 'psychology' of the Japanese people, so he pursued the figures of the tragic heroes who appear vividly in the documents even if the accounts cannot be historically substantiated. Those heroes were not practical or efficient, not successful in actual history. (It was, incidentally, this very image of a failed hero, Satan in *Paradise Lost*, that attracted the readers to the epic in Japan, rather than the image of Satan as a solitary, strong champion of the underdog that English Romantic poets admired).

Although some of the factual details of his account may be questioned, Ernest Gordon gave direct, convincing testimony in person on various occasions when he visited Japan in 1996. His story of the Kwai camps revealed the historical, not fictional, presence of heroes. The author depicts, more dramatically than the novel, a vivid picture of 'hell on earth' and the 'moment of grace' that came to him and his fellows through a simple act of self-sacrifice. To most Japanese, including some of those who were actually engaged in the River Kwai operation, Gordon's book gave, in translation in 1976, an initial awareness of the issues raised by Japanese treatment of POWs in camps along the River Kwai in Thailand.

When in Japan, Ernest Gordon made a tremendous impact on the younger generation and on university students. That impact was twofold: a realisation of the war crimes of the Japanese army in Thailand, and also a consciousness of the needs of others. The effect was so great in Japan that we ought to

was portrayed by Alec Guiness in David Lean's film, was remembered by fellow prisoners, not as a crazed, vacillating collaborator with the Japanese over the bridge, but as a man who tried to slow down the construction. Toosey himself said, 'We did our absolute damnedest to sabotage the thing in every way … For instance we collected huge numbers of white ants and stationed them in various parts of the wooden bridge and they really did their job', *Observer*, 26 October 1997. What Toosey endeavoured to do is well summarised in the following words of a former POW who knew him: 'He was always there to stand between us and the brutality of the Japanese'. That particular POW was none other than Ernest Gordon.

[7] Ivan Morris, *The Nobility of Failure: Tragic Heroes in the History of Japan* (London, 1974), p. 113.

review what the author wrote and what he said directly to many Japanese when they heard him in the United States and in Japan. We should ascertain as far as possible what is true, not illusory.

In order to build that bridge over the Kwai the prisoners of war had to work at bayonet point and in scorching heat. By building the 415-kilometre Thai-Burma Railway, the Japanese planned to invade India through Burma. The initial calculations of the Japanese engineers suggested that it would take five to six years to complete the railway. It was done in less than twelve months, mainly by the use of cheap human flesh as tools: the cheap flesh of 60,000 or 65,000 prisoners of war, among whom 12,000 to 16,000 died. As for the flesh of the Asian labourers, their estimated number is 350,000. Statistics vary. According to SEATIC, 'South-East Asia Translation and Investigation Centre', in 1946, the total number of the dead from the Allied Forces was as many as 12,399 out of 61,806 sent to the Thai-Burma Railway prison camps. Lin Yone Thit Lwin estimates that 177,000 Burmese were drafted as labourers and 80,000 died.[8]

The POWs were tortured, diseased and starved. Ernest Gordon, too, had to lay his feeble body in a prison hospital at Chungkai along the River Kwai. The hospital was called the Death House – though officially it was a hospital – from which few came out alive. What frustrated and tormented him more than anything else, however, was not so much his own physical conditions, or the hated Japanese guards or the thought of approaching death, as the spiritual death that reigned over the whole prison camp. Captain Gordon's fellow prisoners were lying in a spiritual dungeon – hating each other, distrusting each other, stealing from each other. All that mattered for them was to survive, to live by the law of the jungle. They even stole from the dead.

Gordon was in agony over the fact that in this dehumanised situation human beings could so easily lose dignity and degenerate into human jackals. This young graduate from the University of St Andrews had originally wished to become a military or political adviser to a government in the East Asia. However the value of education, the value of cultural heritage, west or east, was seriously questioned in Gordon's book. In fact, Gordon found every branch of cultural inheritance, religion and philosophy, of which the western tradition was proud, powerless as a prop to support men

---

[8] Lin Yone Thit Lwin, *Shi no Tetsuro* (The Railway of Death) , translated from the Burmese original published in 1968 by Hisao Tanabe and published in Tokyo in 1981. See also Sibylla Jane Flower, 'Captors and Captives on the Burma-Thailand Railway', in *Prisoners of War and their Captors in World War II*, edited by Bob Moore and Kent Fedorowich (Oxford, 1996, and Tokyo, 1997), p. 228.

who were living in a hellish prison. At the same time Gordon's book lets the readers see that in the very depth of the bottomless abyss there is something more than despair at the extreme of life, for an unexpected thing happened.

A young fellow prisoner, Dusty Miller, posted to Gordon's company, began to visit and help Gordon, who was suffering from all sorts of diseases: diphtheria, malaria, amoebic dysentery, tropical skin ulcers, beriberi, blood infection. Every night and after his heavy labour, Miller came to wash him and massage his paralysed legs. Through his help Gordon began miraculously to regain his physical and spiritual strength, and came out of the Death House alive. Miller's persevering efforts were marvellous. Amidst the egoism and defeatism of that dehumanised state, his self-sacrifice moved Gordon, and his fellow prisoners to begin to recover and uphold human dignity in the prison camp.

Dusty Miller had the 'fresh complexion of a countryman' and 'fair, thick and curly hair.' He was a Methodist, who had worked with his father, a landscape-gardener, just outside Newcastle. While on 'Civvy Street' he had helped with the youth work in his local church. He was literally a Christ figure who was later 'crucified' by the Japanese, probably because of his meekness. He had indeed the role of an apostle in Gordon's life. When I interviewed Ernest Gordon at Amagansett in 1983, he said he was still searching for Miller's bereaved family, but in vain. In vain, he told me, even in 1996, too. One of the most moving passages shows how the author himself was deeply touched by an unforgettable incident related to 'a darned good soldier', an Argyll, in Gordon's company, called Angus McGillivray. Dusty with 'a soft North of England voice', told the moving story of Angus's heroic death from starvation and exhaustion for the sake of his friend.

There followed a similar story of self-sacrifice, reflecting the universal image of a true hero.

> Yet, noble as Angus's sacrifice was it was not the only one. Other incidents were now spoken of that showed that death no longer had the last word at Chungkai. One that went the rounds soon after concerned another Argyll, who was in a work detail on the railway. The day's work had ended; the tools were being counted, as usual. As the party was about to be dismissed, the Japanese guard shouted that a shovel was missing. He insisted that someone had stolen it to sell to the Thais. Striding up and down before the men, he ranted and denounced them for their wickedness, and most unforgiveable of all their ingratitude to the Emperor. As he raved, he worked himself up into a paranoid fury. Screaming in broken English, he demanded that the guilty one step forward to take his punishment. No one moved; the guard's rage reached new heights of violence.

'All die! All die!' he shrieked.

To show that he meant what he said, he cocked his rifle, put it to his shoulder and looked down the sights, ready to fire at the first man at the end of the them. At that moment the Argyll stepped forward, stood stiffly to attention, and said calmly, 'I did it'.

The guard unleashed all his whipped-up hate; he kicked the helpless prisoner and beat him with his fists. Still the Argyll stood rigidly to attention, with the blood streaming down his face. His silence goaded the guard to an excess of rage. Seizing his rifle by the barrel he lifted high over his head and, with a final howl brought it down on the skull of the Argyll who sank limply to the ground and did not move. Although it was perfectly clear that he was dead, the guard continued to beat him and stopped only when he was exhausted.

The men of the work detail picked up their comrade's body, shouldered their tools and marched back to camp. When the tools were counted again at the guard-house no shovel was missing.

As this story was told, remarkably enough, admiration for the Argyll transcended hatred for the Japanese guard.[9]

'It is difficult,' writes the author, 'to keep these atrocities in perspective. They were the result of behaviour codes fostered by the military for their own ends, codes such as *hakko ichiu, kodo* and *bushido*'.[10] *Hakko,* meant 'eight sides and corners of the world' and *ichiu,* 'under one roof', together with *kodo,* which meant 'the way of the Emperor' based upon the old code of the warriors, like the medieval knighthood, all these principles drove the soldiers to try to establish the *dai toa kyoei ken,* 'Greater East Asia Co-Prosperity Sphere.'

What impressed Japanese readers was that Gordon sees the difficulty of keeping the atrocities of the war in proper historical perspective. His viewpoint is indeed impartial:

> Many of the tormentors among the Japanese military delighted in carrying out the cruel mandate of their perverted codes. It is also plain that millions in the Western world still see no connection between their own consciences and mass slaughter and refuse to accept any responsibility for these manifestations.[11]

After their defeat in the war, the Japanese could not, of course, ignore or cease to remember the accusations the world laid against Japan and the Japanese: we remember the invasion of Manchuria, we remember Pearl Harbor, and we remember the death march at Bataan and we remember

---

[9] Gordon, *Miracle on the River Kwai,* pp. 88–89.
[10] Ibid., p. 47.
[11] Ibid.

the atrocities in expanding the sphere of 'Greater East Asia Co-Prosperity' and along the River Kwai.

'In rebuttal,' Gordon continues, 'the Japanese can point to the thousands of innocent non-combatants killed or horribly burned and maimed by the dropping of the atomic bomb on Hiroshima and Nagasaki.' In Hiroshima there were estimated to be 350,000 people in the city on 6 August 1945, of whom about 140,000 died within the year. According to the 1991 Hiroshima City Fourth Survey, the total number of the dead caused by the atomic bomb was now 221,407.

How important the education of the young can be is illustrated by the incidents at Featherston in New Zealand and Cowra in Australia where the young prisoners of war attempted to commit mass suicide by breaking out of the camp. They were inspired by the *Senjinkun* (Battle Field Code) in which it is forbidden to be taken prisoner and remain alive. In Featherston and Cowra, the prisoners were convinced that they would be regarded as criminals by their comrades and families at home for being captured. Ashamed to be alive as prisoners and unable to fight at the front, their only reason for being alive was to wait for a most appropriate chance to kill themselves in order to harass the enemy's rear. They did so one cold early morning in August 1944.[12]

With the amazing examples of self-sacrifice the Chungkai camp gradually changed. The author himself was transformed from being a sceptical man of the world, indifferent to anything more than ease and security, to one who became concerned for others and was able to help others.

Gordon was asked by an Australian sergeant to lead a discussion group to discover whether the Christian faith that had sustained western thought and civilisation was true or false, meaningful or meaningless. At first he was reluctant to come and meet with the group.

> I said, 'what good do you think it will do?' …
> 'Perhaps we haven't understood Christianity rightly in the past. Now we have to find out if it's absolute "dingo" or not'.
> 'What if it turns out that Christianity isn't "dingo"?' He scratched his chin and looked me in the eye.
> 'Then we'll bloomin'-well know it ain't. That could be important, too … We feel we've seen the absolute worst there is-right? Now we believe there's got to be something better'.[13]

---

[12] D. C. S. Sissons, 'The Break-Out: A Look from the Australian Side', in *The Cowra Japanese Prison Camp*, edited by Takashi Nagase and Akira Yoshida (Tokyo, 1990), pp. 18–26.
[13] Gordon, *Miracle on the River Kwai*, pp, 97–98.

This persistent quest for the justification of the truth in religion surprised many readers, including Shichihei Yamamoto, a severe critic of the irrational in the Japanese society, as well as of the Japanese army in the Second World War. Many saw it as something fundamentally lacking in the Japanese.[14] In the history of Japan the abhorrence of theological debate is so deeply ingrained that few would have thought of contributing to their own culture by assessing the truth of an established religion through theological discussion.

With meaning now restored to life, these POWs regained a thirst for knowledge and liberal arts education. Gordon's group grew larger and eventually founded a jungle university. Almost all branches of learning seem to have been taught there, including mathematics, natural sciences, economics and history, with seminars on Plato's *Republic* and Aristotle's *Nicomachean Ethics* as well as at least nine language courses including Greek, Sanskrit and Russian. Men regained their will to live and their appreciation of the talents of others. An orchestra was formed. Art exhibitions were held. A library was opened. All these were, of course, without the benefit of a building. We can observe the rebirth of, or evolution of, civilisation as epitomised in this jungle prison.

The POWs were taught the beauty, instead of the ugliness, of being human. It was the renaissance of man. One of the most moving occasions was the performance of the 'Dance of the Scarecrow', which impressed all the spectators who thought how wonderful it was to be alive, and to keep fighting against any enemy of life. The prisoners told each other, 'he keeps getting knocked down, and then bobbing back like that ... He says to you that life is a knock-about ... Whenever he stops a bit, he is just a scarecrow'.[15]

Many prison camps during the war had entertainments in various forms. Here the show was something that encouraged living, and the fight against the temptation to despair. The important thing is to keep fighting against the enemies of peace through peaceful means, however difficult. Problems were soon encountered by the awakened group when they were confronted with newly arrived prisoners more dejected than they themselves had once been. The original prisoners were also separated and moved to new camps where they had to begin their work again, encouraging the discouraged.

Shichihei Yamamoto's contribution to the promotion of rational analysis of the war crimes of the Japanese Army cannot be overemphasised. He found in Ernest Gordon's description of the POWs in the River Kwai camps something very different from Japanese war writings. One feature was the

---

[14] Shichihei Yamamoto, *The Japanese Imperial Army as Seen by a Junior Officer* (Tokyo, 1976).
[15] Gordon, *Miracle on the River Kwai*, p. 123.

intellectual search for spiritual answers which I have already discussed; a second was the willingness to sacrifice oneself to do good for others seen in Gordon's account. There was another aspect that caught Yamamoto's attention.[16] That is another scene described by Gordon. When the POWs were travelling to Bangkok and they were shunted to a siding, they saw carloads of Japanese wounded soldiers. The soldiers were on their own and without medical care.

> They were in a shocking state; I have never seen men filthier. Their uniforms were encrusted with mud, blood and excrement. Their wounds, sorely inflamed and full of pus, crawled with maggots ... We could understand now why the Japanese were so cruel to their prisoners. If they didn't care a tinker's damn for their own, why should they care for us? [17]

The wounded looked miserable. Although they were the enemy they were 'more cowed and defeated than we had ever been'. Most of the men in Gordon's section went over to the Japanese train to help them with part of their ration, a rag or two, water canteen in their hands. Guards of course tried to prevent them, but 'they ignored them and knelt by the side of the enemy to give them food and water, to clean and bind up their wounds, to smile and to say a kind word'.[18]

This act of spontaneous help for those in need is exactly what Takashi Nagase viewed as a challenge to him, as it drove him to search for the path of reconciliation, and his own self-sacrificial activities in South-East Asia. Nagase was a graduate of Aoyama Gakuin University, who served in the Japanese army as an interpreter for the notorious Kempeitai at the Kanchanaburi prison camp. Later he became an active campaigner for changes in nationalist attitudes in Japan to achieve reconciliation between the Japanese and their former enemies.[19]

Nagase was impressed by Ernest Gordon and his balanced view of the war crimes committed both by the Allied Forces and the Japanese. Inspired by Gordon's book on the River Kwai, Nagase published accounts of his own experiences in the war, including *The Tiger and the Cross*. He has made more than a hundred trips to Thailand to 'atone', in his own way, for the war crimes of Japan, with the aim of achieving reconciliation and peace with the peoples of South-East Asia who were forced to labour on the railway.[20]

---

[16] Yamamoto, *The Japanese Imperial Army*, p. 162.
[17] Ibid.
[18] Ibid., p. 163.
[19] Eric Lomax, *The Railway Man* (London, 1995), which describes how he and Nagase, former enemies, were reconciled at last.
[20] Ibid.

One effort Nagase made was to help a former Indonesian soldier, Boontum Wandee, to return home. He was brought to Thailand by the Japanese Army in 1943 and did not see his relatives for fifty-three years. Inspired by Nagase's books and pamphlets on the River Kwai, many study groups have been formed in schools, colleges and universities to seek ways to grasp what happened in South-East and East Asia during the war, and also to discuss the moral responsibility of the Japanese as individuals and as a nation. People have come to realise and to admit that the River Kwai camps were as bad as the Siberian concentration camps where 600,000 Japanese prisoners were transported and 60,000 died.

The reviews of the Japanese version of *Through the Valley of the Kwai* provide a range of attitudes and responses towards Japanese offences against the POWs in South-East Asia. There were negative comments, reflecting the average person's silent reaction. Many Japanese were moved by the forced labour of the Japanese soldiers in Siberian camps, but negative towards the atrocities of the Japanese army in South-East Asia. This is reflected in the output of popular publishers in Japan who print stories of the Japanese soldiers who went through physical and mental hardship. That is why Yuji Aida's account of his life as a prisoner of war in Burma, *The Alon Concentration Camp* (Tokyo, 1962), in which English and Japanese culture is compared, became a bestseller. Apart from such negative responses, the majority of comments were on the crimes of militarism and totalitarianism described in Gordon's book. Military totalitarianism regarded individual human beings as cogs in the machinery called the nation. We need to destroy that totalitarianism to achieve peace.

The year 1995 was the fiftieth anniversary of the end of the Second World War. Nagase organised a ceremony with the *Bangkok Post* to commemorate the anniversary with the expressed hope of attaining reconciliation between former enemies at the River Kwai. Before leaving for the River Kwai, Nagase told Professor Tsuyoshi Amemiya and myself that no memorial service in Japan had been held on the initiative of the Japanese for those POWs who died in Japan.

An excellent book, entitled *Return from the River Kwai*, depicts the further ill-treatment of the POWs after the completion of the Railway of Death.[21] Some of the prisoners were moved to Japan and again forced to labour. More than a thousand POWs were killed on the way to Japan, as several transport ships to Japan were sunk by American submarines. Those who survived the attacks were transferred to POW camps in Japan to work

---

[21] Joan and Clay Blair Jr, *Return from the River Kwai* (New York, 1962).

as forced labourers. Many never returned to their homelands. The remains of 1873 who died in Japan are buried in the Hodogaya British Commonwealth War Cemetery in Yokohama. On 5 August 1995 the first memorial service sponsored by the Japanese was held at the British War Cemetery in Yokohama. The organisers include Mr and Mrs Nagase and Professor Amemiya of Aoyama Gakuin University, who is also an admirer of Gordon's book and an inspiring leader of students who study peace. It has become an annual event in August with the participation of former POWs with their family and representatives from the British, Australian, Canadian, New Zealand and Netherlands embassies. Discussion regularly follows the service, with guests such as Dudley Cave from England and David Barrett from Australia, who gave stimulating messages to the younger generation at the meeting.

All the members who have helped the organisers have had one united wish, that is, to pay their respects to the dead buried in Yokohoma and to confirm our wish never to repeat the mistakes of the past. We all have learned that we should make any act of commemoration an occasion for strengthening the foundation of world peace. To refresh our memory about the war is meaningful, but meaningful only when we are not to be roused to anger and hatred and the urge to be revenged on former enemies. The occasion is bound to pose the question of whether a reconciliation can be brought about between the Allies and Japan, and peace between those peoples in Asia who suffered under Japanese occupation, and the people of Japan.

Another admirer of Gordon's book is Keiko McNicoll, a graduate of Aoyama Gakuin University and a member of Agape-Tokyo, a committee supported by the Fujimigaoka Church in Setagaya. With the Rev. Yoshinobu Togo, the committee promotes annual visits to Japan by former POWs and their families, and extends a welcome to those who come to Japan via Agape-UK. The organisers and participants of the Yokohama memorial service and the activities of the Agape-Tokyo are familiar with Ernest Gordon's work and many of them are influenced by his book.

Immanuel Kant's famous treatise, *For Attaining Perpetual Peace* (1795), written when he was in his seventies, is full of suggestions for achieving peace. He states that to enjoy peace is 'a right belonging to all human beings that allows one to form a friendship with each other on the basis of our right to possess mutually the surface of the earth'. We tend, in contrast, to admire the heroic elements in war. Kant said that even philosophers are prone to forget that famous maxim of the Greeks, 'War should be detested for it produces numberless evil men, rather than eliminating evil men' ('First Supplement'). Without recognising each other's common 'right to possess the surface of the earth', we tend to drive away those who look disagreeable.

The task of bringing about reconciliation between the hostile groups, and individuals, is enormously demanding. But human beings are also social beings, and called *Homo Sapiens*. We know, therefore, that we ought to continue to be concerned with reconciliation with others, and to make an effort to be the peacemakers within a community, an institution or in the world at large. Without this determination to try to be a reconciliatory element in society, much of what we do in a university would be meaningless.

At the recent discussion meeting with former POWs in Yokohama, Dudley Cave suggested that there are three types of POWs:

> There is a hard-core of POWs who hate everthing Japanese, there are moderates who want compensation, and then there are those like me who have decided to try to forget the past and live for the future.[22]

---

[22] See also the article by Micool Brooke, *Bangkok Post*, 14 August 1995.

# Bibliography

Adams, G. Pharaoh, *No Time for Geishas* (London, 1973).

Aida, Yuji, *Alon Shuyojo* (The Alon Concentration Camp) (Tokyo, 1962). Published also as *Prisoner of the British* (London, 1966).

Allbury, Alfred, *Bamboo and Bushido* (London, 1955).

Allen, Louis, *Burma: The Longest War, 1941–1945* (London, 1984).

Andrew, Christopher and Noakes Jeremy, *Intelligence and International Relations, 1900–1945* (Exeter, 1987).

Ariga, Nagao, *La guerre sino-Japanaise au point de vue du droit international* (Paris, 1896).

—, *La guerre russo-japonaise au point de vue continental et le droit international d'après les documents officiels du grand état-major japonais* (Paris, 1908).

Arnei, Stan, *One Man's War* (Sydney, 1989).

Association of South Manchuria Railway Company Staff, *Mantetsu Shokuin Shusen Kiroku* (Post-war SMRC Staff Chronicles), Tokyo, 1996.

Ba Maw, *Breakthrough in Burma: Memoirs of a Revolution, 1939–1946* (New Haven and London, 1968).

Baynes, L. L., *Kept: The Other Side of Tenko* (Lewes, 1984).

Beak, G. B., *Aftermath of War* (London, 1906).

Bevege, Margaret, *Behind Barbed Wire: Internment in Australia during World War II* (St Lucia, Queensland, 1993).

Blair Jr, Joan and Clay, *Return from the River Kwai* (New York, 1962).

Bland J. O. P., trans., *Germany's Violations of the Laws of War, 1914–1915: Compiled under the Auspices of the French Ministry of Foreign Affairs* (London, 1915).

Boissier, Pierre, *Histoire du Comité International de la Croix-Rouge: de Solferino à Tsoushima* (Paris, 1963).

Braddon, Russell, *The Naked Island* (London, 1951).

Brawley, Sean, *The White Peril: Foreign Relations and Asian Immigration to Australasia and North America 1919–78* (Sydney, 1995).

Burton, Reginald, *Road to the Three Pagodas* (London, 1963).

Busch, M. *Bismarck: Some Secret Pages of his History* (London, 1899).

Byas, Hugh, *The Japanese Enemy* ( London, 1942).

Cary Otis, editor, *Eyewitness to History: The First Americans in Postwar Asia* (Tokyo, 1975).

Chaen, Yoshio, *Dainihon Teikoku Naichi Furyo Shuyojo* (Tokyo, 1986).

Chapman, F. Spencer, *The Jungle is Neutral* (London, 1950).

Checkland, Olive, *Humanitarianism and the Emperor's Japan, 1877–1977* (London, 1994).

Churchill, Winston, *History of the Second World War* (London, 1951).

Clavell, James, *King Rat* (London, 1962).

Collier, Price, *The West in the East* (London, 1911).

Cosford, Jack, *Line of Lost Lives* (Northampton, 1988).

Crew, F. A. E., *History of the Second World War: The Army Medical Services Campaigns* (London, 1966).

Cross, John, *Red Jungle* (London, 1957).

Cruickshank, Charles, *The Fourth Arm: Psychological Warfare, 1938–1945* (London, 1977).

Dennis, Peter, *Troubled Days of Peace: Mountbatten and the South-East Asia Command, 1945–46* (Manchester, 1978).

Dockrill, Saki, editor, *From Pearl Harbor to Hiroshima* (London, 1994).

Dower, John W., *War Without Mercy: Race and Power in the Pacific War* (London, 1986).

—, *Japan in War and Peace* (New York, 1993).

Draper, G. I. A. D., *The Red Cross Conventions* (London, 1958).

Drea, Edward J., *MacArthur's Ultra: Codebreaking and the War against Japan, 1942–1945* (Lawrence, Kansas, 1992).

Dunlop, E. E., *The War Diaries of Weary Dunlop* (London, 1990).

Duus, Peter, Myers Ramon H. and Peattie Mark R., editors, *The Japanese Wartime Empire, 1931–1945* (Princeton, 1996).

Eastlake, F. Warrington and Yoshiaki Yamada, *Heroic Japan: A History of the War between China and Japan* (Yokohama, Shanghai, Hong Kong and Singapore, 1896).

Edwards, Jack and Walter Jimmy, *Banzai You Bastards!* (London, 1990).

Elphick, Peter, *Singapore: The Pregnable Fortress* (London, 1995).

Favre, Jules, *The Government of National Defence* (London, 1873).

Fletcher-Cooke, John, *The Emperor's Guest* (London, 1971).

Fox, John P., *Germany and the Far Eastern Crisis, 1931–1938* (Oxford, 1982).

Fraser, Mary and Cortazzi, Hugh, editors, *A Diplomat's Wife in Japan: Sketches at the Turn of the Century* (New York; Tokyo, 1982); trans. Toshio Yokoyama, *Eikokukoshi-fujin no mita Meiji Nihon* (1988, Tokyo).

Frei, Henry P, *Japan's Southward Advance and Australia* (Honolulu, 1991).

Friedman, Leon, Editor, *The Law of War: A Documentary History* (New York, 1972).

Friend, Theodore, *The Blue-Eyed Enemy: Japan against the West in Java and Luzon, 1942–1945* (Princeton, 1988).

Fujiwara, Akira, *Shiryo Nihongendai-shi* (Documents of Japanese Modern History), i, Tokyo, 1980.

Fukiura, Tadamasa, *Sekijuji to Henry Dunant* (The Red Cross and Henry Dunant) (Tokyo, 1991).

Furedi, Frank, *The Silent War: Imperialism and the Changing Perception of Race* (London, 1998).

Garner, James Wilford, *International Law and the World War* (London, 1920).

Gascoyne-Cecil, Lord William, *Changing China* (London, 1910).

*Gendai-rekishigaku to Senso-sekinin* (Modern Historiography and War Responsibility) (Tokyo, 1997).

Gilmore, Allison B., *You Can't Fight Tanks with Bayonets: Psychological Warfare against the Japanese Army in the Southwest Pacific* (Lincoln, 1998).

Goebbels, Joseph, *Goebbels' Diaries*, trans. and edited by Louis P. Lochner (Garden City, New York, 1948).

Gong, Gerrit W., *The Standard of 'Civilization' in International Society* (Oxford, 1984).

Goodman, David and Miyazawa Masanori, *Jews in the German Mind* (New York, 1995).

Goodman, Grant K., editor, *Japanese Cultural Policies in South-East Asia during World War*, ii (Basingstoke, 1991).

Gordon, Ernest, *Miracle of the River Kwai* (New York, 1962 and London, 1981); trans. by Kazuaki Saito, *Kwai-gawa Shuyojo* (Tokyo, 1976).

Hamilton, Angus, *Korea* (London, 1904).

Hardie, R., *The Burma-Siam Railway* (London, 1983).

Harries, Meirion and Susie, *Soldiers of the Sun: The Rise and Fall of the Imperial Japanese Army* (New York, 1991).

Harrison, Kenneth, *The Brave Japanese* (London, 1967).

Hartley, Peter, *Escape to Captivity* (London, 1952).

Hasegawa, Shin, Nihon Horyo Shi (*History of POWs in Japan*), in *Collected Works of Hasewawa Shin*, 9 (Tokyo, 1971).

Haug, Hans, *Humanity for All: The International Red Cross and Red Crescent Movement* (Geneva, 1993).

Hayashi, Hirofumi, *Sabakareta Senso Hanzai. Igirisu no Tai-nichi Senpan Saiban* (War Crimes That Were Tried: British Trials of Japanese War Criminals) (Tokyo, 1998).

Heisig, James W. and Maralso John C., editors, *Rude Awakenings: Zen, the Kyoto School, and the Question of Nationalism* (Honolulu, 1995).

Henny, Sue and Lehman, John-Pierre, editors, *Themes and Theories in Modern Japanese History: Essays in Memory of Richard Storry* (London and Atlantic Highlands, New Jersey, 1988).

Hino, Ashihei, *War and the Soldier* (London, 1940).

Honma, Hiroyoshi and Niwa, Toshiaki, editors, *Ryoshu no Uta* (Poems of the Captured) (private publication, 1997).

Horner, David, *Blamey: The Commander in Chief* (Sydney, 1998).

Howes, John F., editor, *Nitobe Inazo: Japan's Bridge across the Pacific* (Boulder, Colorado, 1995).

Hull, Cordell, *The Memoirs of Cordell Hull* (London, 1948).

Humphrey, Leonard A., *The Way of the Heavenly Sword: The Japanese Army in the 1920s* (Stanford, California, 1995).

Hutchinson, John F., *Champions of Charity: War and the Rise of the Red Cross* (Oxford, 1996)

Huttenback, Robert A., *Racism and Empire: White Settlers and Coloured Immigrants in the British Self-Governing Colonies, 1830–1910* (Ithaca, 1976).

Ikegame, Eiko, *The Taming of the Samurai: Honorific Individualism and the Making of Modern Japan* (Cambridge, Massachusetts, 1995).

Ikle, F., *German-Japanese Relations, 1936–1940* (Berkeley, California, 1953).

International Committee of the Red Cross, *Report on Activities of the Second World War* (Geneva, 1948).

Iriye, Akira, *Cultural Internationalism and World Order* (Baltimore and London, 1997).

Ishimaru, Tota, *Japan Must Fight Britain* (London, 1936).

Izumi, Kyoka, 'Kaijo Hatsu-den' (A Telegram from Haicheng), in *Gekashitsu; Kaijo Hatsu-den* (Tokyo, 1991).

JRCS, *Nihonsekijujisha Shashiko* (History of the Japanese Red Cross Society), 5 (Tokyo, 1969).

Kamata, Shoji, *Hokusen no Nihonjin Kunan-ki* (Record of Japanese Suffering in Northern Korea) (Tokyo, 1970).

Kameyama, Michiko, *Kindainihon Kango-shi*, i, *Nihonsekijujisha to Kangofu* (History of Nursing in Modern Japan, i, The Japanese Red Cross Society and Nurses) (Tokyo, 1983).

Kawamata, Seiichi, *Nihonsekijujisha Hattatsu-shi* (History of the Japanese Red Cross Society in Development) (Tokyo, 1916).

Keen, M. H., *The Law of War in the Late Middle Ages* (London, 1965).

Kennedy, M. D., *The Problem of Japan* (London, 1935).

Kibata, Yoichi, editor, *Daiei-Teikoku to Teikoku Ishiki* (The British Empire and Imperial Mentality) (Tokyo, 1998).

Kinvig, Clifford, *River Kwai Railway* (London, 1992).

Kirby, S. W. Woodburn, *The War Against Japan*, i, *The Loss of Singapore* (London, 1957).

Kosuge, N. Margaret and Nagai, Hitoshi, trans., *GHQ Senryo-shi*, v, *BC kyu-senso-hanzai-saiban* (GHQ/SCAP, History of the Non-Military Activities of the Occupation of Japan 1945–1951, v, Trials of Class 'B' and Class 'C' War Criminals) (Tokyo, 1996).

Kreissler, Françoise, 'Antisemitische Propaganda in Japan und die japanische Politik gegenüber den Juden in China', *Symposium: die deutsch-japanischen Beziehungen in den 30er und 40er Jahren 22.–24.6.1992* (Berlin, 1993).

Lane, Arthur, *One God Too Many Devils* (Stockport, 1989).

Lebra, Joyce, *Japan's Greater East Asia Co-Prosperity Sphere in World War II: Selected Readings and Documents* (Kuala Lumpur, 1975).

Lee, Ki-baik, *A New History of Korea* (Seoul, 1984)

Levie, Howard S., editor, *Documents on Prisoners of War* (Newport, Rhode Island, 1979).

Lewis, C. S., *Mere Christianity* (London, 1955).

Lin, Yone Thit Lwin, *Shi no Tetsudo* (The Railway of Death), translated by Hisao Tanabe (Tokyo, 1981).

Lomax, E., *The Railway Man* (London, 1995).

MacCarthy, Aiden, *A Doctor's War* (London, 1979).

Mao Tse-Tung, *Selected Works* (Peking, 1967).

Martens, M. de, *Recueil des principaux traités d'alliance, de paix, de trêve, de neutralité, de commerce, des limites, d'échange etc., 1791–1795* (Göttingen, 1826).

Matsumoto, Shigeharu, *Shanhai Jidai* (My Days in Shanghai), ii (Tokyo, 1974).

Matsushima, Eiichi and Shiromaru, Fumio, editors, *'Jiyushugi Shikan' no Byori* (Maladies of the 'Liberal View of History Group') (Tokyo, 1997).

McCormick, G. and Nelson H., editors, *The Burma-Thailand Railway* (St Leonards, New South Wales, 1993).

McKenzie, F. A., *The Tragedy of Korea* (London, 1908).

Meaney, Neville, *Fears and Phobias: E. L. Piesse and the Problem of Japan, 1909–39* (Canberra, 1996).

Mélignhac, A. and Lémonon, E., *Le droit des gens et la guerre de 1914–1918*, i (Paris, 1921).

Mendelssohn, Peter de, *Japan's Political Warfare* (London, 1944).

Michel, David, *A Boy's War* (Singapore 1973).

Mitchell, R. Keith, *Forty-Two Months in Durance Vile* (London, 1997).

Miyabe, Ichizo, editors, *Hakui no Tenshi* (Angels in White) (Tokyo, 1972).

Moore, Bob and Fedrorovich Kent, editors, *Prisoners of War and their Captors during World War II* (Oxford, 1996).

Morita, Yoshio, *Chosen Shusen no Kiroku* (Korean Chronicle at the End of War) (Tokyo, 1964).

Morley, James, Editor, *Dilemmas of Growth in Prewar Japan* (Princeton, 1971).

—, *Japan's Foreign Policy, 1868–1941: A Research Guide* (New York, 1974).

Morris, Ivan, *The Nobility of Failure: Tragic Heroes in the History of Japan* (London, 1974).

Morris, John, *Traveller from Tokyo* (Harmondsworth, 1946).

Moynahan, Brian, *The British Century: A Photographic History of the Last Hundred Years* (London, 1997).

Murakami, Shigeyoshi, *Yasukunijinja, 1869–1945–1985* (The Yasukuni Shrine, 1869–1945–1985) (Tokyo, 1986).

Mutsu, Munemitsu, *Kenkenroku* (A Diplomatic Record of the Sino-Japanese War) (Tokyo, 1941).

Nagao, Goichi, *Senso to Eiyo* (The War and Nutrition) (Tokyo, 1994).

Nagase, Takashi and and Yoshida Akira, editors, *The Cowra Japanese Prison Camp* (Tokyo, 1990)

Nagata, Yuriko, *Unwanted Aliens: Japanese Internment in Australia* (St Lucia, Queensland, 1996).

Nakamura, Kennosuke, *Senkyoshi Nikolai to Meijinihon* (Nikolai the Missionary and Meiji Japan) (Tokyo, 1996).

Nakatsuka, Akira, *Rekishi no Gizo wo Tadasu: Senshi kara Kesareta Nihon-gun no 'Chosen Okyu Senryo* (Rectifying a Falsification of History: Japanese Occupation of the Royal Palace in Korea Which Was Not Written in the Official War History) (Tokyo, 1997).

Nakauchi, Toshio, *Gunkokubidan to Kyokasho* (War Stories and School-Textbooks) (Tokyo, 1988).

Nelson, David, *The Story of Changi* (Perth, 1973).

Nish, Ian, editor, *Britain and Japan: Biographical Portraits* (Folkestone, Kent, 1994).

Nussbaum, Arthur, *A Concise History of the Law of Nations* (New York, 1954).

Nys, E., *Etudes de droit international et de droit politique* (Brussels, 1896).

Offer, Avner, *The First World War: An Agrarian Interpretation* (Oxford 1989).

Onoda, Hiroo, *No Surrender: My Thirty-Year War* (London, 1975).

Onuma, Yasuaki, editor, *Kokusai-ho, Kokusai Rengo to Nihon* (International Law, the United Nations and Japan) (Tokyo, 1987).

Parry, Clive, *The Consolidated Treaty Series* (Dobbs Ferry, New York, 1969).

Pavillard, Stanley, *Bamboo Doctor* (London, 1960).

Percival, A. E., *The War in Malaya* (London, 1949).

Piers, W. R., *The My Lai Inquiry* (New York, 1979).

Piggot, F. S. G., *Broken Thread* (Aldershot, 1950).

Pounder, Thomas, *Death Camps of the River Kwai* (Cornwall, 1977).

Powell, Alan, *War by Stealth: Australians and the Allied Intelligence Bureau, 1942–1945,* (Melbourne, 1996).

Pritchard, John R. and Zaide Sonia M., editors, *The Tokyo War Crimes Trial: The Complete Transcripts of the Proceedings of the International Tribunal for the Far East in Twenty-Two Volumes* (New York and London, 1981).

Probert, H. A., *The History of Changi* (Singapore, 1965).

Rivett, Rohan D., *Behind Bamboo* (Ringwood, Victoria, Australia, 1946).

Rosas, Allan, *The Legal Status of Prisoners of War* (Helsinki, 1976).

Rousseau, J.-J., *Contrat social: ou principes du droit politique* (Paris, n.d.).

Saikami, Tokio, *Matsuyama Shuyojo* (The Matsuyama POW Camp) (Tokyo, 1969).

Sastri, C. S. R., *To Malaya* (Tenali, 1947).

Sato, *Masanori, Ichi Kagakusha no Kaiso* (Scientists' Recollections) (Tokyo, 1971).

Schindler, Dietrich and Toman Jiri, editors, *The Law of Armed Conflicts: A Collection of Conventions, Resolutions and Other Documents* (Leiden, 1973).

Shi, Gang, *Shokuminchi Shihai to Nihongo* (Colonial Rule and the Japanese Language) (Tokyo, 1993).

Sleeman, Colin and Silkin S. C., *Trial of Sumida Haruzo and Twenty Others* (London, 1951).

Slim, Sir William, *Defeat into Victory* (London, 1954).

Smedley, Agnes, *China Fights Back: An American Woman with the Eighth Route Army* (London, 1938).

Smith, Arthur L., *The War for the German Mind: Re-Educating Hitler's Soldiers* (Oxford, 1996).

Smith, Donald, *And All the Trumpets* (London, 1954).

Stouffer, Samuel et al., editors, *The American Soldier: Combat and its Aftermath* (Princeton, 1949).

Sullivan, M. B., *Thresholds of Peace: Four Hundred Thousand German Prisoners and the People of Britain, 1944–48* (London, 1979).

Summons, Walter Irvine, *Twice their Prisoner* (Melbourne, 1946).

Takahashi, Sakuei, *Cases on International Law during the Chino-Japanese War* (Cambridge 1899).

Tanaka, Stefan, *Japan's Orient: Rendering Pasts into History* (Berkeley, California, 1993).

*The Issue of War: States, Societies and the Far Eastern Conflict of 1941–1945* (London, 1985).

The Organisation of POWs from China, *Kaettekita Senpan-tachi no Kohansei* (Returned War Prisoners' Half a Life) (Tokyo, 1996).

The Organisation of POWs from China, *Watashi-tachi ha Chugoku de Nani wo Shita ka* (What Did We Do in China?) (Tokyo, 1987).

The United Nations War Crimes Commission, *Law Reports of Trials of War Criminals*, i (London 1947).

Thorne, Christopher, *Racial Aspects of the Far-Eastern War of 1941–1945* (London, 1980).

Tomita, Hiroshi, *Bando Furyo Shuyojo* (The Bando POW Camp) (Tokyo, 1991).

Tsuji, Masanobu, *Singapore: The Japanese Version* (London, 1966).

Utsumi, Aiko, *Chosen-jin BC-kyu Senpan no Kiroku* (Stories of Korean Minor War Criminals) (Tokyo, 1982).

Vattel, E. de, *The Law of Nations: or The Principles of Natural Law, Applied to the Conduct of the Affairs of Nations and of Sovereigns* (New York, 1964).

Vespa, Amleto, *Secret Agent of Japan: A Handbook of Japanese Imperialism* (London, 1938).

Wakatsuki, Yasuo, *Sengo Hikiage no Kiroku* (Documents on the Post-War Treatment of Japanese Overseas) (Tokyo, 1991).

Wet, Christian Rudolf de, *Three Years War* (London, 1902).

Whitecross, Roy H., *Slaves of the Sons of Heaven* (Sydney, 1951).

Wigmore, L., *The Japanese Thrust* (Canberra, 1957).

Winter, Jay, *Sites of Memory, Sites of Mourning: The Great War in European Cultural History* (Cambridge, 1995).

Yamamoto, Shichichei, *The Japanese Army as Seen by a Junior Officer* (Tokyo, 1976).

Yasumaru, Yoshio and Miyachi, Masato, editors, *Shukyo to Kokka: Nihonkindai-shiso-taikei*, 5 (Religion and the State, 5, The Compendium of Ideology of Modern Japan) (Tokyo, 1988).

Yoshida, Yutaka, *Tenno no Guntai to Nankin Jiken* (The Imperial Army and the Nanking Incident) (Tokyo, 1985).

# Index